LEONARD BERNSTEIN: *WEST SIDE STORY*

Frontispiece One of the earliest sketches for *West Side Story*, from the verso of a sketch-leaf headed 'Romeo', originally in a folder on which Bernstein wrote 'Romeo Sketches, 1 Oct, 1955'. This may well be the first time Bernstein wrote down the 'Tonight' theme. The lyrics at the top read: 'Tonight, Tonight / And every other night / Of my life.' Below is another idea used in the 'Tonight' Quintet: the music for 'We're gonna rock it tonight, We're gonna jazz it up and have us a ball!'. Leonard Bernstein Collection, Music Division, Library of Congress, Washington DC.

Leonard Bernstein:
West Side Story

NIGEL SIMEONE
University of Sheffield, UK

ASHGATE

Published by
Ashgate Publishing Limited
Wey Court East
Union Road
Farnham
Surrey, GU9 7PT
England

Ashgate Publishing Company
Suite 420
101 Cherry Street
Burlington
VT 05401-4405
USA

www.ashgate.com

British Library Cataloguing in Publication Data
Simeone, Nigel, 1956–
    Leonard Bernstein – West Side story. – (Landmarks in music since 1950)
    1. Bernstein, Leonard, 1918–1990. West Side story.
    I. Title II. Series
    782.1'4–dc22

Library of Congress Cataloging-in-Publication Data
Simeone, Nigel, 1956–
    Leonard Bernstein, West Side story / Nigel Simeone.
      p. cm. – (Landmarks in music since 1950)
    ISBN 978-0-7546-6484-0 (hardcover: alk. paper) 1. Bernstein, Leonard, 1918–1990. West Side story. I. Title. II. Title: West Side story.
    ML410.B566S56 2009
    782.1'4–dc22

                                                                2009017747

ISBN 9780754664840 (hbk)

Bach musicological font developed by © Yo Tomita.

Mixed Sources
Product group from well-managed
forests and other controlled sources
www.fsc.org Cert no. SA-COC-1565
© 1996 Forest Stewardship Council
FSC

Printed and bound in Great Britain by
MPG Books Group, UK

Contents

List of Figures and Tables

Figures

Tables

List of Music Examples

Acknowledgements

Many people have helped in the preparation of this book. My first debt of gratitude is to Mark Eden Horowitz, Senior Music Specialist at the Music Division of the Library of Congress in Washington. As curator of the Leonard Bernstein Collection, not only was Mark immensely helpful during my visits to work in the library, but he has also sent me a good deal of additional material and has always been willing to answer my questions. Mark's detailed comments on a draft of the text were invaluable. He is a prince among music librarians.

Other librarians have been unfailingly kind and hospitable. I owe particular thanks to Suzanne Eggleston Lovejoy at the Irving S. Gilmore Music Library, Yale University (Goddard Lieberson Papers), and to Michael Ryan, Jennifer B. Lee and all the staff in the Rare Books and Manuscripts Library at Columbia University (Sid Ramin Papers).

Marie Carter, Vice-President Licensing and Publishing for the Leonard Bernstein Office, Inc., gave me permission to make photocopies of the manuscripts in the Library of Congress and Columbia University Library, making my work on the sources immeasurably easier. She has been immensely helpful with the permissions for the musical examples reproduced in this book, as has Andy Chan at Boosey & Hawkes. All music examples and excerpts from the published score are reproduced by kind permission of Boosey & Hawkes Ltd and are © 1955, 1956, 1957 Amberson Holdings LLC and Stephen Sondheim, Leonard Bernstein Music Publishing Company LLC. Extracts from unpublished music and lyrics are reproduced by kind permission of the Leonard Bernstein Office, Inc., Stephen Sondheim, and the Music Division, Library of Congress, Washington DC. I am most grateful to them all.

Three of the creators of *West Side Story* assisted me in various ways. Stephen Sondheim generously granted permission for me to quote from his letter to Bernstein about the original cast recording of *West Side Story*, as well as from unused lyrics for the show. He also gave me an interview that included some fascinating insights, and patiently answered e-mails. I am immensely grateful to him for reading the proofs of this book, and for subsequent comments that included invaluable new information and welcome corrections. Arthur Laurents was helpful and gracious in giving permission to use long extracts from his unpublished 1956 outline, and from other letters and documents in the book. Sid Ramin kindly allowed me to copy items from his papers in Columbia University Library and brought the orchestration process to life in a wonderful way when I interviewed him. To all three, I offer my deepest thanks. Larry Blank generously sent me the relevant pages of the unpublished memoirs of his mentor, Irwin Kostal. Quotations from documents and letters by Jerome Robbins are used by kind permission of the Literary Executors of the Jerome Robbins Foundation, and thanks are due to Christopher Pennington, the Foundation's Executive Director.

I owe a particular debt to Stephen Banfield, whose contribution to the literature on Broadway musicals is of such enormous significance. He has been a constant support, and has offered help, encouragement and kindly advice at every stage. He was among the first people to ask me to present some of my research on *West Side Story*, and was instrumental in the commissioning of this book.

Friends and colleagues have provided opportunities for me to discuss the ideas in this book. They include Mervyn Cooke, Sarah Hibberd, Lucie Kayas, Gerald Levinson, Robert Pascall, Caroline Potter and Philip Weller. I am most grateful to all of them. In the Department of Music at the University of Sheffield, special thanks go to George Nicholson, Stephanie Pitts and Peter Hill. A number of my students at Sheffield were involved in workshop performances related to some of the research presented in this book. My thanks are due to all of them, especially Sarah Graves, Gina Walters, Emily Webb (now Emily Melland), Rosie Williamson, Sam Jones, Jonathan Kirwan, Gareth Lloyd, Oliver McCarthy, Tom Owen, Matthew Palmer and Daniel Townley.

For various acts of kindness, thanks are also due to William Crawford, the late James J. Fuld, Dominic McHugh, Bob and Alison Petrilla, Sophie Redfern, Thomas Z. Shepard, Penelope Stowe, Steven Suskin and Paul Ydstie. Above all, Jasmine Simeone has been a constant pillar of support during the writing of this book.

Wyndham Thomas has been a model of what an editor should be: shrewd, and always encouraging. Heidi Bishop and Lianne Sherlock at Ashgate have been immensely supportive from the outset. I extend warmest thanks to Tom Owen who set the music examples, and to Lauren Doughty who made the index. The text has been improved beyond recognition thanks to Polly Fallows's copy-editing and Michael Wood's proofreading. Its faults, however, are all mine.

Nigel Simeone
Sheffield, August 2009

General Editor's Preface

Since its inception (in 2002/3) Ashgate's 'Landmarks in Music' series has aimed to promote studies of compositions from a wide range of idioms, genres and countries. Although the choice of works has never been conditioned by popular taste alone, public esteem *has* been a guiding principle – as is the desire to draw on the very best research by younger as well as more established scholars. Indeed the volumes already published testify to these objectives, with individual books devoted to chamber music, song, opera and orchestral music (of varying types) by Russian, Hungarian, Dutch, French and British composers. In each case, the authors have refined appropriate analytical strategies and critical methods in order to reveal the cultural and technical significance of their chosen work. Notated examples are used in conjunction with recorded ones (CDs) so that commentaries are never distanced from the real sound-world being described. Interviews with performers and/or the composer serve to augment the discussions of reception, context and aesthetics within the main text.

West Side Story, of course, is both immensely popular and highly esteemed by musicologists and theatrical historians. Despite its overall attribution to Leonard Bernstein, however, Nigel Simeone is at pains to dispel the concept of single authorship by emphasizing the essentially collaborative nature of the work. For anyone who still holds dear the concept of a 'finished' score that somehow helps to define authenticity in performance, this book will have the effect of a lightning flash as it opens up the frenetic world of pre-Broadway tryouts in which radical changes are made in any sphere, from the ordering of numbers to their orchestration and choreography. The author's critical/narrative style is itself redolent of Broadway – punchy, colourful and sharply focused.

This volume extends the area covered by the 'Landmarks in Music' series beyond European confines for the first time – and there are plans to extend further still. *West Side Story* is quintessentially American – both as stage show and as musical film – and it is to the author's great credit that he has resisted the temptation to glamorize the show's theatrical success, as might be the case if the study were devoted solely to the film version. What Professor Simeone has created is a scholarly, yet vibrant, study that will appeal to all who have experienced the unique quality of the score that bears Bernstein's name.

Wyndham Thomas
University of Bristol

Introduction

Scope and Sources

'*West Side Story* is the best score ever written for musical theatre and still sounds ahead of its time.' So declared Stephen Schwartz in 2008.[1] This book sets out to explore a Broadway show that is often seen as a turning point in the history of musicals. In particular, it aims to consider aspects of the musical score in detail, but I should confess from the outset that this results in a title that is misleading: *West Side Story* is not 'by' Leonard Bernstein, but is the result of a collaboration by a remarkable creative quartet each of whom deserves equal credit for the work. My study cannot do them all justice, but the contribution of Jerome Robbins, Arthur Laurents and Stephen Sondheim is of the greatest significance: without Robbins the show would never have existed at all, nor would Bernstein have had the opportunity to compose so much instrumental music for the extended dances; Arthur Laurents devised one of the most concise and least dated books for any Broadway musical – one that also served as a direct inspiration for several of the songs; and Stephen Sondheim – on the point of becoming Broadway's most innovative and exciting musical voice, but already a lyric writer of genius – made his Broadway debut with lyrics that only he has ever found it necessary to criticize. Like almost every musical, *West Side Story* was very much a joint venture, and the combination of talents in this case was especially successful; other vital contributions included those of the design team: Oliver Smith's strikingly evocative sets, Jean Rosenthal's lighting and Irene Sharaff's costumes. Moreover, as can be seen in Chapters 2 and 3, the collaborative nature of the project made a direct mark on the score: Bernstein's music gained greatly in impact and focus thanks to the theatrical instincts of his three colleagues. I am all too conscious that their contribution may seem undervalued in this book, with its emphasis on just one aspect of the show.

After a brief survey of Bernstein's work in the theatre up to 1957 (Chapter 1), the collaborative creative process of *West Side Story* – spanning nearly a decade – is considered in detail in Chapter 2, drawing on archival evidence, while Chapter 3 is devoted to a detailed discussion of the musical manuscripts. Chapter 4 examines aspects of Bernstein's musical language, first in broad terms (genre, the role of the orchestra, stylistic fingerprints), and then with reference to individual musical numbers. The way in which the show was financed is examined alongside a

---

[1] Schwartz 2008. Schwartz (b. 1948) has written the music and lyrics for several shows, including *Godspell*, *Pippin* and *Wicked*. He worked with Bernstein on the libretto for *Mass* (1971).

consideration of the critical reception of *West Side Story* in Chapter 5, and the book concludes with an account of the original Broadway cast recording, a copy of which is also included on the accompanying compact disc.

I have laid particular emphasis on the genesis of *West Side Story*, especially its music, book and lyrics. A substantial part of this monograph is the result of a study of the magnificent collection of primary source material in the Leonard Bernstein Collection in the Music Division of the Library of Congress. The vast majority of the manuscripts, letters and drafts referred to in the book are to be found in this collection, which is by far the most important source for anyone researching Bernstein's music. Appendix I is a list of the musical manuscripts for *West Side Story* in the Leonard Bernstein Collection, referred to in the text by the abbreviation LBC. A heavily annotated copy of the earliest surviving full orchestral score for the complete show (1957 FS) is to be found in the Sid Ramin Papers in the Rare Books and Manuscripts Library at Columbia University. The Ramin full score, and the reminiscences of both the show's orchestrators (Sid Ramin and Irwin Kostal), make it possible to discuss the orchestration of *West Side Story* in some detail – an essential aspect of the musical character of a Broadway show that is often overlooked. The Ramin papers also include the full orchestral score of Ramin and Kostal's completely reorchestrated film version of *West Side Story*, but this lies outside the scope of the present study.

Since *West Side Story* was written for the commercial theatre, the wrangling over producers, the subsequent raising of the necessary finance to capitalize the show, and the economics of a Broadway run are also examined. This is possible thanks to another collection in the Music Division of the Library of Congress, the papers of the theatrical producer Roger L. Stevens.

The printed scores of *West Side Story* are noted in the Bibliography. The Sid Ramin papers include several of the separately printed piano-vocal scores used during rehearsals (1957 RS); these provide fascinating evidence for the state of the music and lyrics between Bernstein and Sondheim's manuscripts and the first public performances. Schirmer and Chappell published the first complete piano-vocal score in 1959 (1959 VS), but a definitive edition, revised and completely re-engraved, was issued by Boosey & Hawkes in 2000 (2000 VS). The 1994 Boosey & Hawkes edition of the full score (1994 FS) is a valuable source, and it has the unusual status of being one of the first orchestral scores of a Broadway show ever to be available for sale. For the libretto, references are to the first edition (Random House; 1958 LIB).

Anyone writing about Bernstein owes an enormous debt to Humphrey Burton's *Leonard Bernstein* (1994), a biography that is as scrupulous as it is entertaining and which contains a wealth of information not to be found elsewhere. Other sources that have been particularly valuable for my research include Craig Zadan's *Sondheim & Co.* (1974), Deborah Jowitt's *Jerome Robbins: His Life, his Theater, his Dance* (2004), Stephen Banfield's *Sondheim's Broadway Musicals* (1993), the memoirs of Arthur Laurents and Carol Lawrence, and the perceptive and provocative musical commentaries on the work by Joseph P. Swain and Geoffrey Block. All four creators of *West Side Story* participated in a Dramatists Guild Landmark Symposium in 1985, providing much valuable first-hand information about the show's origins and genesis.[2] Invaluable groundwork on primary sources was published in Paul R. Laird's *Leonard Bernstein: A Guide to Research* (2002). Other literature is listed in the Bibliography.

Particular attention has also been paid to more ephemeral writings on *West Side Story*, especially newspaper articles from the time when the show was new. These reveal much about reactions to the work during its tryouts in Washington and Philadelphia, as well as the opening on Broadway; they also include interviews and features that are helpful in plotting the show's genesis – the Broadway gossip-column of the *New York Times* was clearly given much of what it reported about the show by one member or another of the creative team.

West Side Story since 1960

There are some important aspects of *West Side Story* that I have chosen to place outside the scope of this book. Most conspicuous among these is the 1961 film version of *West Side Story*. Without doubt, this played a large part in the work's wider appreciation, as well as being showered in Oscars, including Best Picture. But my main concern has been to look at the processes involved in creating the stage show, as well as examining the score as it was composed for Broadway, rather than its later movie adaptation. In a 2007 radio broadcast on National Public Radio (NPR), Arthur Laurents voiced the opinion that the film was fundamentally flawed:

> The movie, I thought, and still think, was appalling. Film is either realistic or surreal. And a musical, to succeed, needs illusion. *West Side Story* begins, and you see all these boys, with dyed hair and color-coordinated sneakers, doing tour jetés down a New York street. Not in this life. And then, when the so-called Puerto Ricans came on, made up to look like day-glo characters for some caricature of what they think Hispanics are – it was really disgraceful.[3]

In the same broadcast, Frank Rich was not quite so critical, but clearly felt that some of the immediacy of the original had been softened, its impact blunted. He described the film as 'very clean, and it seems sort of a Disneyfied version of gang warfare, but that was also, to some extent, true of the show'.[4] According to John Mauceri, Bernstein, too, disliked the film, considering it 'too sentimental'.[5]

---

[2] Printed in Guernsey 1985, and in the *Dramatists Guild Quarterly*, 22 (3) (1985).

[3] NPR 2007.

[4] NPR 2007. Frank Rich, a senior journalist at the *New York Times*, was the paper's chief drama critic from 1980 to 1993.

[5] Mauceri 2007, p. 17.

Stage productions since 1960 have included two particularly significant revivals: the Jerome Robbins production in 1980 at the Minskoff Theatre on Broadway and, more recently, the production directed by Arthur Laurents that opened in December 2008 at the National Theatre in Washington – where *West Side Story* had its world premiere in August 1957 – before transferring to New York in 2009. But the show's success has been enduring. Freddie Gershon of Music Theatre International estimated that there had been a total of approximately forty thousand productions around the world in the half-century since *West Side Story* was first performed.[6] This extraordinary statistic demonstrates the impact the work has had far beyond the professional theatre (where there have been comparatively few full-scale revivals), with countless productions in schools, colleges, amateur and community groups, and even in Sing Sing maximum security prison (Ossining, NY). The show has also been used as the basis for social education programmes: in spring 2007, 'the Seattle police department hosted a youth-oriented anti-gang initiative based around the musical, featuring summits on gang violence and a performance of the musical by at-risk high school students'.[7]

'A social disease'? The Reality of New York Gangs

In 1954, a United States Senate Subcommittee held televised public hearings on juvenile delinquency. Gang violence had become a national concern, but not necessarily the stuff of a musical. Frank Rich believes that '*West Side Story* was one of the first pieces of mainstream popular culture to put its finger on what was going to be a huge movement of social change in America in a new generation'.[8]

During the 1950s, Puerto Rican immigration was an important issue in America's largest cities. It was an article in a Los Angeles paper that Laurents and Bernstein always claimed was the spur for setting the story among rival gangs of Puerto Ricans and native New Yorkers. Gang violence was a frightening reality at the time, and in 1950 a news report painted a grim picture of gang warfare in the Bronx:

> The increase in killings and other vicious acts by young gangsters has been the greatest in the few years during which families have been streaming from Harlem and East Harlem into the Bronx in one of the biggest population shifts in the city.
>
> Most of the influx of Negro and Puerto Rican families has been into East Bronx. The Irish and Italian street gangs of the Bronx, whose occasional rowdyism had rarely reached the murderous stage, made savage war on the newcomers.
>
> The Negro and Puerto Rican youths quickly formed separate gangs in which they had been members in Manhattan … and bloody war was on.

---

[6] NPR 2007.

[7] Wise 2007.

[8] NPR 2007.

The pitched battles in the streets and parks of the Bronx have taken about twenty lives. For every youth killed, there have been at least five seriously wounded by knives and guns. … Rivalry for the attentions of teenage girls has sparked some of the worst battles between some of the Puerto Rican and Italian gangs.[9]

Newspaper coverage ranged from a glossary of 'Gang slang'[10] to interviews and profiles of gang members. In 1958, while *West Side Story* was in the middle of its first Broadway run, the *New York Times* published the second of a series of articles on 'New York City's students and their backgrounds and delinquency problems'. The principal subject was Vincent, leader of the 'Silver Arrows', a young Puerto Rican man who seems in some ways to resemble a real-life Bernardo:

Vincent has been the leader of his gang, based in one of Brooklyn's older public housing projects, for about eighteen months. He is a slender Puerto Rican youngster of 17 years of age who looks a little like an African prince. He combs his black hair in a massive crest and carries his head high.

When Vincent came from Puerto Rico in 1949 his family first settled in Manhattan, near 110th Street and First Avenue. …

In some ways, Vincent is not a typical gang member. For one thing he is a leader. Gang leaders are above average intelligence and ability – they must be or the gang will not long survive. But the façade of normality that Vincent presents can vanish in a twinkling. For Vincent like the other gang members is 'shook up.' Beneath the veneer – and not far beneath it – lies a disturbed and unstable personality. …

Most gang members come from broken families. Not Vincent. He lives with his father and mother and eight brothers and sisters. The family is on relief. Vincent is the only member of his family who is involved with gangs. 'I'm the only bad one,' he says shyly.' …

Vincent learned street fighting in the Italian neighborhood into which his family first moved. He remembers being beaten up every day 'just because I was a Puerto Rican.'[11]

While the plot of *West Side Story* was motivated by contemporary social problems, the result is a piece of theatre, not a documentary; Robbins, Laurents, Bernstein and Sondheim aspired to move, to shock and to thrill, not to preach a sociological tract.

---

[9]   Grutzner 1950.

[10]   Benjamin 1957. This includes several words and phrases that also occur in Laurents's book and Sondheim's lyrics for *West Side Story*. For example: 'Cool it – to call off the rumble', 'Jump – a dance or other social event' and 'Turf – the neighborhood territory ruled by a gang. Rumbles frequently happen as a result of invasions of a gang's turf, or from disputes over whose turf it is.' Perhaps the quaintest definition in this article is 'Pot – marijuana'.

[11]   Salisbury 1958.

This is perhaps the reason for the show's continuing success today: half a century later, the precise circumstances that inspired it may have changed, but the value of human life – and the simple power of love – have not.

Chapter 1
Bernstein on Broadway before *West Side Story*

At the end of January 1945, a feature in the *New York Times* declared that:

> Probably the biggest stir in the musical world during the past year has been
> caused by the emergence from relative obscurity of a 26-year-old Boston boy
> named Leonard Bernstein. Others may have made a more lasting and important
> contribution, but for sheer éclat Mr. Bernstein has carried away all the honors.[1]

In September 1943, at the age of 25, Bernstein had been appointed Assistant
Conductor of the New York Philharmonic-Symphony Orchestra, and two months
later his last-minute substitution for an ailing Bruno Walter at the Philharmonic
became front-page news.[2] But while this was an auspicious start to his career as
a conductor, the origins of Leonard Bernstein's success as a Broadway composer
came, prophetically, from a ballet. On 18 April 1944, the first performance of *Fancy
Free* at the Metropolitan Opera marked the earliest collaboration between Bernstein
and Jerome Robbins. The press reaction was ecstatic:

> To come right to the point without any ifs, ands, and buts, Jerome Robbins' *Fancy
> Free*, which the Ballet Theatre presented in its world première last night at the
> Metropolitan Opera House, is a smash hit. This [is] young Robbins' first go at
> choreography, and the only thing he has to worry about in that direction is how in
> the world he is going to make his second one any better. ... The music by Leonard
> Bernstein utilizes jazz in about the same proportion that Robbins' choreography
> does. It is not in the least self-conscious about it, but takes it as it comes. It is a
> fine score, humorous, inventive and musically interesting. Indeed, the whole ballet,
> performance included, is just exactly ten degrees north of terrific.[3]

This rave review from John Martin in the *New York Times* (19 April 1944) was
echoed a few days later in an article by Edward Alden Jewell in the same paper,
concerned mainly with the impact of the war on (visual) artists. Jewell concluded his
piece with a comment on *Fancy Free*:

---

[1]   Schubart 1945.

[2]   For example: 'Young aide leads Philharmonic, steps in when Bruno Walter is ill', *New
York Times*, 15 November 1943.

[3]   Martin 1944.

Speaking of art that is truly 'native' – that grows from the soil and the environment that have nourished and helped form the artists responsible for it – the new ballet, 'Fancy Free,' which had its Ballet Theatre première Tuesday evening at the Metropolitan, is a most hastening document. All of our painters and sculptors should see it: that superbly danced tale of three sailors ashore, choreography by Jerome Robbins, music by Leonard Bernstein, setting by Oliver Smith. It is American art through and through.[4]

The 'tale of three sailors' told in *Fancy Free* led directly to the first big Broadway success for Robbins and Bernstein, again with sets by Oliver Smith: *On the Town* opened at the Adelphi Theatre, New York, on 28 December 1944.[5] Though the score is quite different, the story owes a great deal to the earlier ballet. The task of turning it into a Broadway book and libretto was taken on – at Bernstein's suggestion – by his friends Betty Comden and Adolph Green. It was their first Broadway show too, but, as Betty Comden put it, 'Lenny said that we were the ones to do the book. That was a good break!'[6]

Bernstein and Green met in 1937, and they became lifelong friends. The 19-year-old Bernstein had taken a summer job as a counsellor (tutor) in music at Camp Onota near Pittsfield, Massachusetts, in the Berkshires. Green, then aged 22, had been asked to sing the Pirate King in the camp's production of *The Pirates of Penzance*; it was directed by Bernstein, who also played the piano.[7] Gershwin's *Of Thee I Sing* was also performed at Onota that same summer. This was a show for which both Bernstein and Green had huge enthusiasm. Bernstein was to discuss it in his 1956 *Omnibus* broadcast about American musical theatre, and Green had seen the original production in 1932: 'I remember getting a tremendous thrill out of it – I was knocked out by it. I had a standing room ticket for a buck ten. … It was hysterically funny and so beautiful.'[8] The earliest surviving photograph of Bernstein conducting was also taken at the camp that summer, with the Onota Rhythm Band.[9] Bernstein and Green performed together again at Onota in 1938; as Seymour Wadler recalled in a letter to the *New York Times* in 1990, it was the turn of *The Mikado*:

In the summer of 1938 I was an athletic counselor at Camp Onota in Pittsfield, Mass., and a fellow from Harvard named Lenny (though he preferred to be called Leonard) was the dramatic and music counselor. Lenny impressed us greatly with

---

[4]   Jewell 1944.

[5]   The out-of-town tryout for *On the Town* opened at the Colonial Theatre, Boston, MA, on 13 December 1944.

[6]   Online interview with Comden and Green at www.broadway.com.

[7]   For more details of their earliest encounter, see Burton 1994, pp. 38–9.

[8]   Online interview with Comden and Green at www.broadway.com.

[9]   An online version of this photograph can be found at http://lcweb2.loc.gov/music/lbcoll/lbphotos/box199/42a026_u.tif.

his piano playing, and I knew that his interpretations of Beethoven sonatas were considerably better than my sister's, who was a fine pianist.

At the end of the summer the camp put on Gilbert and Sullivan's *Mikado*, with Lenny as producer, director and piano accompanist. The performance by these youngsters (with the help of an amateur musician named Adolph Green from the Bronx) was positively thrilling. The audience thought Leonard Bernstein was marvelous, without realizing how marvelous he was destined to be.[10]

In April 1939, during his senior year at Harvard, Bernstein composed and conducted his first theatre score: incidental music for a production by the Harvard Classical Club of *The Birds* by Aristophanes. According to the *Christian Science Monitor*, the score was an eclectic amalgam of Debussy and Stravinsky; Bernstein had just attended a concert of Indian music and incorporated elements of that too, as well as snatches of Verdi. This wasn't quite as haphazard as it sounds. According to Bernadette A. Meyler in her detailed account of this student work, 'Just as Aristophanes poked fun at the styles of Homer and Hesiod, Bernstein latched onto musical references that his audience would recognize, employing them as a type of auditory shorthand.'[11] After graduating from Harvard in 1939, Bernstein soon found himself working with Green again in New York: while studying conducting with Fritz Reiner at the Curtis Institute in Philadelphia, Bernstein was the pianist on a recording made by The Revuers, a group of comic actors who were successful in Greenwich Village nightclubs. They included Adolph Green, Betty Comden, Judy Holliday (then still known as Judy Tuvim), Alvin Hammer and John Frank. Made in March 1940 for Musicraft, *The Girl with the Two Left Feet (A Musical Satire)* is an amusing burlesque on Hollywood movie stars and directors (it's a spoof about what was described as an 'epic' $86 million intermission feature, produced by 19th-Century Wolf). This was Bernstein's first recording as an accompanist,[12] and, as Humphrey Burton puts it, 'Bernstein's fully-integrated sound track gives the best idea we have of his brilliance as a boogie and honky-tonk pianist.'[13]

On the Town was an instant hit: 'the freshest and most engaging musical show to come our way since the golden days of *Oklahoma!* Everything about it is right.' So wrote Lewis Nichols after the first night, in a review that makes some interesting observations about why *On the Town* was so successful, describing it as 'a perfect

---

[10]   Wadler 1990.

[11]   Meyler 1999, p. 76.

[12]   His first ever recording was made two months earlier in January 1940, as a solo pianist: David Diamond's Prelude and Fugue no. 3 in C sharp major, for New Music Recordings. The Musicraft set of *The Girl with the Two Left Feet* also included 'Joan Crawford Fan Club' as the sixth side, again with Bernstein at the piano. The whole set has been reissued on CD by Pearl in *Leonard Bernstein: Wunderkind* (GEMS 0005).

[13]   Burton 1994, p. 71.

example of what a well-knit fusion of the respectable arts can provide for the theatre'.[14] The 'fusion' Nichols mentions had some highly original features, including several extended dance numbers containing some of Bernstein's boldest music; the show's veteran producer George Abbott had 'teased him about "that Prokofieff stuff" in portions of the score but didn't cut a bar of it'[15] during rehearsals. Comden and Green were also singled out for praise by Nichols: '*On the Town* even has a literate book, which for once instead of stopping the action dead speeds it merrily on its way.'

The first tentative steps towards *West Side Story* were taken in January 1949 (see Chapter 2), but Bernstein's next Broadway assignment was to provide the incidental music for a 1950 revival of J.M. Barrie's *Peter Pan*, starring Jean Arthur as Peter, Marcia Henderson as Wendy and Boris Karloff as Captain Hook. Bernstein's contribution was a score that included not only some charming songs (with lyrics by the composer) but also instrumental numbers. Brooks Atkinson, in an enthusiastic review of the first night, wrote:

> Leonard Bernstein has taken time off from serious work to write a melodic, colorful and dramatic score that is not afraid to be simple in style. He has also written some amiable lyrics … Not all the music is vocal. Some of it underscores the mock melodramatic moments, and some of it is for the rather artless but agreeable ballet.[16]

A wider public was able to hear the results in July 1950 when Columbia released a long-playing record that included the five Bernstein songs: 'Here Am I', 'Build My House' and 'Peter, Peter' sung by Marcia Henderson, and 'The Pirate Song' and 'The Plank' sung by Karloff. The rest of the Columbia album used incidental music by Alec Wilder, and thus gave only a partial impression of what Bernstein's theatre score sounded like. The simplicity alluded to by Atkinson is certainly an important feature of the music – a fresh and attractively idiosyncratic melodic style that Bernstein was to develop in some of his later vocal music and stage works (memorably so in parts of *Mass*, for example). The gentle charm of the *Peter Pan* songs results in music that serves its purpose extraordinarily well, even though the songs were apparently composed at great speed (Daniel Felsenfeld writes that 'most of [them] were dashed off on the train between engagements').[17] Bernstein, an inveterate recycler, used some music from *On the Town* during the 'Tinkerbell Sick / Tink Lives!' sequence – when Tinkerbell finds herself revived in Times Square.[18] At least one song intended for *Peter Pan*, cut before the first night, may later have

---

[14]   Nichols 1944.

[15]   Jowitt 2004, p. 94.

[16]   Atkinson 1950.

[17]   Felsenfeld 2005.

[18]   The original version of this passage is part of the 'Times Square Ballet'. See *On the Town*, piano-vocal score (Boosey & Hawkes, 1997), p. 128, from letter L onwards.

been a candidate for inclusion in *West Side Story*: in a handwritten list by Bernstein headed 'Romeo Numbers', dating from around October 1955, 'Dream With Me', or at least its title, is listed by Bernstein as a possible song for use in the Balcony Scene, no less.

For *Wonderful Town*, which opened at the Winter Garden Theatre on 26 February 1953 after a tryout in New Haven, Bernstein was reunited with his old friends Comden and Green. This brilliant comic confection was hailed by Brooks Atkinson as:

> the most uproarious and original musical carnival we have had since *Guys and Dolls* appeared in this neighborhood. ... Sometimes gifted people never quite get attuned to each other in the composition of a musical circus. But in *Wonderful Town* everyone seems to have settled down joyfully to the creation of a beautifully organized fandango – the book, the score and the ballets helping each other enthusiastically.[19]

It's the purest fun and games, and it shares with both *On the Town* and *West Side Story* a New York setting. Musically, it includes what is perhaps Bernstein's zaniest pastiche of Latin American music in the gloriously silly 'Conga', and in 'The Wrong Note Rag' the composer anticipates the use of comic dissonance that crops up in 'Gee, Officer Krupke'. Although *Wonderful Town* is a very different kind of show from *West Side Story*, these aren't the only musical features that seem to look forward to the later work: the instrumental climax of 'Swing' is almost like a witty foretaste of the 'Cool' Fugue. The whole score was written at great speed, between early November and mid-December 1952.[20] It was a joyous collaboration, and the result was a triumph, winning the 1953 Tony Award for Best Musical (book by Joseph Fields and Jerome Chodorov, lyrics by Comden and Green and music by Bernstein), as well as awards for Rosalind Russell (Best Actress in a Musical), Donald Saddler (Choreography), Lehman Engel (Musical Director) and Raoul Pène Du Bois (Scenic Design). Three years later, Comden and Green were approached to write the lyrics for *West Side Story*, but they were busy with other projects and so the job went to Stephen Sondheim.

The name of Jerome Robbins is missing from the credits for *Wonderful Town*, but he did have a part to play in the show. The choreographer Donald Saddler – whose first Broadway production this was – did an outstanding job by all accounts, but as the opening night approached he became so nervous that he lost his voice.[21] Robbins was called in to do some necessary show-doctoring during the Boston tryout. It was his idea to change the opening: 'Christopher Street' was added in Boston (Bernstein, Comden and Green came up with the song and Robbins choreographed it)[22] as a way

---

[19]   Atkinson 1953.
[20]   Burton 1994, p. 224.
[21]   Jowitt 2004, p. 219.
[22]   Jowitt 2004, pp. 219–20.

of introducing the members of the Greenwich Village community – a touch that has elegant parallels with the similar stroke of inspiration he came up with a decade later for the opening of *Fiddler on the Roof*.[23] Betty Comden summarized the result of Robbins's work on the show: 'Everything was very good; it was just taken several notches above where it had been and made really great.'[24]

The last word on *Wonderful Town* should go to Olin Downes, the distinguished music critic of the *New York Times*. Writing on 10 May 1953, three months after the show's opening, Downes was lost in admiration for a musical and, in particular, a score that he considered to be altogether exceptional, much more sophisticated than *On the Town* and an indicator for what a great American opera might be:

> Leonard Bernstein's *Wonderful Town* is a wonderful pleasure to hear and behold. The youthfulness and exhilaration of the music are companioned and fully matched by every artistic element of the production. ... It has the reckless mastery of means and the sure cooperation of artists, each expert in his or her part, and all in accord in the joyous achievement of the common task. ... Mr. Bernstein, long before this, had written adroit and expert dance music for his ballet *Fancy Free* and other works. *Wonderful Town* is basically different from his earlier show, *On the Town*, which presaged this one. The new score is not only richer in its invention and warmer in its feeling, but it is vibrant throughout with the spirit of the dance. For this is no musical show with interpolated dance 'numbers' to afford surcease from its ditties. This is an opera of which dance is warp and woof, an opera made of dance, prattle and song; and speed. Its unflagging pulse is characteristic of its restless time and nervous environment. In days to come, it may well be looked upon in some museum exhibit as the archetype of a kind of piece which existed peculiarly in America of the neon lights and the whiz and zip of the mid-twentieth century. Very well! So it is, a reflection, with all its carefreeness and exuberance and irreverence, of this place and epoch, and the dynamic forces that are flashing dangerously about us. ... The show stands for so much that is spontaneous and unfettered and fertile within us! Indeed we are coming to believe that when the American opera created by a composer of the stature of the Wagners and Verdis of yore does materialize, it will owe much more to the robust spirit and the raciness of accent of our popular theatre than to the efforts of our prideful emulators, in the upper esthetic brackets, of the tonal art of Bartók, Hindemith and Stravinsky.[25]

---

[23]   The choreographer Robert LaFosse has noted this as a constant thread in Robbins's work: 'I really believe this is true about all of his ballets: they all have a community of people that are involved in every one of them. Even his musicals are about a community of people' (Robert LaFosse, interview, www.nycballet.com/company/viewing.html).

[24]   Jowitt 2004, p. 220.

[25]   Downes 1953.

The idea for *Candide* originally came from Lillian Hellman in 1953. She and Bernstein both saw the potential of Voltaire's play as a bitter satirical response to McCarthyism and other anti-communist witch-hunts. Both had been mentioned in the notorious *Red Channels: The Report of Communist Influence in Radio and Television* (1950), issued by the right-wing journal *Counterattack* and listing 151 people in the entertainment industry who were purportedly members of subversive and communist organizations. Richard Wilbur, who wrote most of the lyrics, is not on the *Red Channels* list, but both the writers credited with additional lyrics – John Latouche and Dorothy Parker – are named.[26] The period during which *Candide* was created coincided with a new series of hearings by the House Committee on Un-American Activities (usually known as HUAC), a Congressional committee that fostered a climate of fear among many in the performing arts. Lillian Hellman was one of those who refused to testify in the 1951 hearings (as did her fellow playwright Arthur Miller). The film director Elia Kazan chose to cooperate with the committee, and duly named those who he believed harboured communist sympathies. In the round of hearings held between 1953 and 1955, Jerome Robbins was among those who chose to appear as a friendly witness before the committee;[27] he didn't name Bernstein to the committee, but he did name Jerome Chodorov, whom he had almost certainly encountered while working on *Wonderful Town*.

The initial impetus for *Candide* was interrupted when Bernstein went out to Hollywood for four months (February–May 1954) for the filming of *On the Waterfront* (directed by Elia Kazan, one of HUAC's star canaries). In a long review for *The Score*, Hans Keller described Bernstein's music as 'about the best film score that has come out of America'.[28]

On his return to the East Coast, Bernstein spent the summer at a house in Martha's Vineyard hard at work on *Candide* and on the *Serenade* that he was writing for Isaac Stern. After the uncomplicated pleasures of the collaboration with Comden and Green on *Wonderful Town*, progress on *Candide* was painfully slow, in addition to being interrupted by a trip to Venice for the premiere of the *Serenade*. In New York that autumn, Bernstein got back to the new show, and had numerous meetings with Hellman and Latouche. Still only one act was finished and, as Humphrey Burton tells us, Bernstein and Hellman decided to break with Latouche in November

---

[26]   Several more of Bernstein's friends and collaborators were on the *Red Channels* list, among them Marc Blitzstein, Jerome Chodorov, Aaron Copland, Olin Downes, Judy Holliday and Arthur Laurents. Others listed included Abe Burrows, Jack Gilford, Morton Gould, E.Y. Harburg, Lena Horne, Langston Hughes, Gypsy Rose Lee, Ella Logan, Burgess Meredith, Arthur Miller, Zero Mostel, Edward G. Robinson, Harold Rome, Artie Shaw, Sam Wanamaker and Orson Welles.

[27]   See Schwartz 2000.

[28]   Keller 1955, p. 81.

1954.[29] This caused yet more delay: neither of the remaining collaborators could produce all the lyrics that were needed and the project ground to a halt.

Bernstein was in Italy during the spring of 1955, conducting Bellini's *La Sonnambula* at La Scala (with Callas), and he also tried to recruit Lucchino Visconti as a possible director for *Candide*. Back in America, Bernstein had other things on his mind, not least the birth of his son Alexander on 7 July, as well as meetings with Robbins and Laurents to get *West Side Story* back on track. Just as work on *Candide* might have been resumed, Bernstein agreed to write the incidental music for a play that Hellman had translated and adapted: Jean Anouilh's *The Lark* (*L'Alouette*). It opened at the Longacre Theatre on 17 November 1955 and enjoyed a respectable run, for a straight play, of 229 performances. The cast included Julie Harris as Joan, Christopher Plummer as Warwick and Boris Karloff as Cauchon. Brooks Atkinson commented in his enthusiastic review that 'Leonard Bernstein's musical recreation of Joan's medieval voices gives the play a new dimension'.[30] It was something of a new departure for Bernstein too: open fifths and octaves and the use of modes produce an interesting encounter between medieval music and twentieth-century America. The original scoring was for a vocal septet with percussion. The incidental music consists of three choruses based on Medieval French folk songs with hand drum, and five Latin choruses (on texts from the Mass) with tubular bells. The music was recorded for performance in the theatre by the pioneering early music group New York Pro Musica Antiqua, directed by Noah Greenberg.

Intriguing as *The Lark* was, *Candide* was stalled. In December 1955 Hellman and Bernstein decided to ask the poet Richard Wilbur to join the project, and during the summer of 1956 all three of them worked on the show in Martha's Vineyard, where the director Tyrone Guthrie was also on hand. '*Candide* was virtually completed in August 1956', according to Humphrey Burton.[31] Bernstein had written an enormous amount of music, and Burton tells us that Hellman's script went through 14 versions. The score is a dizzying homage to the music of Europe, full of clever pastiche of opera and operetta. Initially, at least, it was also far too expansive: during the Boston tryout cuts were made and new numbers written. By the time *Candide* got to the Martin Beck Theatre on Broadway on 1 December 1956, it was a much tighter show but still received a mixed press. Brooks Atkinson was a fan ('a brilliant musical satire'), Tom Donnelly in the *World-Telegram and Sun* even more so ('one of the most attractive scores anyone has ever written for the theatre'), but Walter Kerr in the *Herald Tribune* hated it:

> Three of the most talented people our theatre possesses – Lillian Hellman, Leonard Bernstein and Tyrone Guthrie – have joined hands to transform Voltaire's *Candide* into a really spectacular disaster. Who is mostly responsible for the great ghostly

---

[29]   Burton 1994, pp. 241–2.
[30]   Atkinson 1955.
[31]   Burton 1994, p. 258.

wreck that sails like a Flying Dutchman across the fogbound stage of the Martin Beck? That would be hard to say, the honors are so evenly distributed. ... Pessimism is the order of the evening.[32]

Candide contains some glorious music, but it was the subject of several later revisions, and remains a problematic work in the theatre.[33] The original production closed after a couple of months on 2 February 1957, but Goddard Lieberson and David Oppenheim produced the Columbia cast recording (made at Columbia's 30th Street Studio on 9 December 1956), which preserves the performances of Max Adrian (Doctor Pangloss), Barbara Cook (Cunegonde) and Robert Rounseville (Candide), conducted by the show's musical director Samuel Krachmalnick. Listening to this sparkling, well-sung and strongly conducted performance, it's hard to see where the problems lay. In fact, this cast recording did much to rescue the show's reputation. John S. Wilson reviewed the record on its first appearance in February 1957:

> In both the score by Leonard Bernstein and the lyrics provided by Richard Wilbur, Dorothy Parker and the late John Latouche, this adaptation of Voltaire's satire has much pungent wit and vitality, qualities that are brilliantly projected in the zestfully sardonic singing ... Yet the spark and spirit that light up the show in its earlier portions start to run low toward the end of the first act and, through the final half, the lyricists and composer stagger toward the ultimate curtain.[34]

Despite Wilson's reservations, the cast recording sold well – *Candide* came to be seen as a misunderstood gem, and by 1964 Richard F. Shepard was able to write that 'as a Columbia record, it became a hit album'.[35]

---

[32]   Walter Kerr, quoted in Suskin 1990, p. 132.

[33]   For comprehensive information about the production history and the different versions of *Candide*, see Michael H. Hutchins: 'A Guide to Leonard Bernstein's *Candide*', http://www.sondheimguide.com/Candide/contents.html.

[34]   Wilson 1957a.

[35]   Shepard 1964.

Chapter 2

Genesis

On 18 September 1957,[1] Bernstein wrote an invented journal outlining some key moments in the history of *West Side Story*. 'Excerpts from a West Side Log', written well after some of the events it describes, provides an account (sometimes embroidered) of meetings that took place between the collaborators on the show. It was published in the edition of *Playbill* that coincided with the Broadway opening, and begins eight years earlier, with an entry dated New York, 6 January 1949:

> Jerry R[obbins] called today with a noble idea: a modern version of *Romeo and Juliet*, set in slums at the coincidence of Easter–Passover celebrations. Feelings running high between Jews and Catholics. Former: Capulets, latter: Montagues. Juliet is Jewish. Friar Lawrence is a neighborhood druggist. Street brawls, double death – it all fits. But it's all much less important than the bigger idea of making a musical that tells a tragic story in musical comedy terms, using only musical comedy techniques, never falling into the 'operatic' trap. Can it succeed? It hasn't yet in our country. I'm excited. If it can work – it's a first. Jerry suggests Arthur Laurents for the book. I don't know him, but I do know *Home of the Brave* at which I cried like a baby. He sounds just right.[2]

The 'noble idea' was one that Robbins devised after talking to an actor friend who, on being offered the part of Romeo, said that he thought the role was rather passive: 'So I asked myself, "If I were to play this, how would I make it come to life?" I tried to imagine it in terms of today. That clicked in, and I said to myself, "There's a wonderful idea here." So I wrote a very brief outline.'[3] On 10 January 1949, four days after their initial meeting, the three future collaborators – Jerome Robbins, Arthur Laurents and Bernstein – met together for the first time, an event recorded in the log: 'Met Arthur L. at Jerry's tonight. Long talk about opera versus whatever this should be. Fascinating. We're going to have a stab at it.'[4]

News of the project travelled fast. Less than three weeks after this first meeting, the story was out and plans were announced in the press. On 27 January 1949, the *New York Times* printed an article by Louis Calta under the headline 'Romeo to receive musical styling'. Writing a month after the successful opening of *Kiss Me, Kate*

---

[1] Information from Bernstein's datebook, LBC.

[2] Bernstein 1957, entry for 6 January 1949.

[3] Guernsey 1985, p. 40.

[4] Bernstein 1957, entry for 10 January 1949.

(based on *The Taming of the Shrew*),[5] Calta began, not surprisingly, by speculating on whether Cole Porter's show had started a vogue for Shakespearean musicals. He then described the new project:

> The latest song and dance project drawing its inspiration from a work of the Bard's is a modern musical drama, as yet untitled, based on *Romeo and Juliet*. Involved in getting it on the local boards are none other than Leonard Bernstein, the well-known pianist-composer-conductor, Arthur Laurents, author of *Home of the Brave*, and Jerome Robbins, the choreographer. Mr. Bernstein will write the music, Mr. Laurents the book, which is still in the preliminary stages, and Mr. Robbins the choreography, which he will also stage. ... According to the present scheme of things, the musical will arrive in New York next season ... Indications are that Oliver Smith will design the show's scenery, in which case the occasion would reunite the team of Robbins, Bernstein and Smith, responsible for such noteworthy items as *Fancy Free* and *On the Town*. Howard Hoyt, representative of Messrs. Robbins and Bernstein, remarked yesterday that the idea of basing a musical on the famous Shakespearean love story has been with Mr. Robbins for some time.[6]

The Earliest Plans

Documents in LBC provide some clues about the initial scheme of the show. The earliest source may be a typed list of scenes on Jerome Robbins's headed writing paper, annotated by Bernstein (his notes are shown in square brackets). It certainly seems possible that this is the 'very brief outline' described by Robbins:

1. Hideout [Initiation: beat up Jews]
2. Street Carnival [Dance: meeting of R. & J.]
3. Balcony [Duet love scene]
4. Drugstore [R. works for druggist: Rendezvous is planned]
5. Bridal [Marriage (dummies)]
6. Playground [Big street fight – death of Tyb. and Merc.]

1. Chase Seder
   [1a – Small ballet / love]
2. Cellar [Love scene (poss. fuck): Druggist gives R. pills]
3. Ballet transition [(Large ballet) abstract]
4. Family argument [House closes in: J. fakes suicide]
5. Drugstore (message) [Juke-box – Prejudice of kids against T.]
6. Cellar [Death of Romeo]

---

[5]   *Kiss Me, Kate* opened at the New Century Theatre on 30 December 1948.
[6]   Calta 1949.

The 'T.' refers to 'Tante', the original name for Anita, who is mentioned in another very early source. Bernstein's annotated copy of Shakespeare's *Romeo and Juliet* includes a few more details, and a few differences. The updating was to involve rival factions of Christians and Jews, probably around the time of Easter and Passover:

Act I
I. Street scene – pushcarts – Enter R. – or Mulberry St. Festival – or Easter = Passover
II. Ball or Seder or motza'e shabbat [written in Hebrew][7]
III. Balcony Scene
IV. Drugstore (Rendezvous, Tante)
V. Bridal Scene
VI. Street Fight

Act II
I. Chase (Roofs?)
II. Sex – Plan to escape to Mexico
III. Scene chez Capulet
IV. Romeo's death with Tante
V. Juliet's death[8]

These schemes may be quite remote from the show's final shape, but even so there are key moments, especially in Act I, that were to remain in place: an opening street scene, a dance, the Balcony Scene, the Bridal Scene and the act ending with a fight.

Any prospect of the show arriving in New York 'next season' (1949–50), as Calta had suggested in his column, soon faded, although according to Bernstein's log some kind of start was made. On 15 April 1949, while conducting in Columbus, Ohio, Bernstein noted that he had 'just received the draft of first four scenes. Much good stuff'.[9] Whether he really thought it was 'good stuff' is called into question by Bernstein's later comments, quoted by Craig Zadan: 'I remember receiving about a dozen pages and saying to myself that this is never going to work. ... I had a strong feeling of staleness of the East Side situation and I didn't like the too-angry, too-bitchy, too-vulgar tone of it.'[10] Whatever Bernstein made of these 'dozen or so pages', the same 15 April 1949 log entry indicates that he faced up to the realities of the circumstances in which he and Laurents were trying to fashion a new show:

---

[7] 'Motza'e shabbat' is the Saturday evening following the end of the Sabbath. My thanks to Katherine Peveler for assistance with deciphering Bernstein's handwritten Hebrew.

[8] LBC.

[9] Bernstein 1957, entry for 15 April 1949.

[10] Zadan 1974, p. 15.

Table 2.1   Early plan for Act I music

I	II	III	IV	V	VI	VII
Initiation Ritual (Prologue)	Street Party	Transition (gang)	Balcony Scene	Drugstore	Bridal shop Ceremony	Playground
Dogged, intense, quiet, machine	1) General dance 2) Mercutio & gang 3) Rosalind & Rom. Duet follows 4) Juliet entrance w. Tante & Tybalt 5) Slow motion, interrupted by T. 6) Hostility, Schrank: Gang follows him off, jeering, back in high spirits (in one)		1) Juliet solo add Romeo add Tante 2) Farewell	1) Mercutio number with girls 2) R. & druggist 3) J. & Tante 4) Romeo shows off 5) Make rendezvous 6) Tybalt & gang & victim – kid 7) J. & Tyb. before Bridal shop	(rendezvous to elope that night)	1) Basketball 2) Romeo happy song? 3) Fight, double murder 4) Sound ending

Table 2.2   Early plan for Act II music

I	II	III	IV	V	VI	VII
Seder Chase	J. & Tante Duet	Transition:	Cellar: Post-lay	Transition ballet ?	Capulet house	Drugstore
Schrank enters seder, announces bad news	(crowds still moving) J. goes down fire escape to meet R.	Girls winding down after J.: to ballet with boys; sex	Song, duet He has sword Plan to run away		J. kicked out Letter scene	Cellar Duet ?

This is no way to work. Me on this long conducting tour, Arthur between New York and Hollywood. Maybe we'd better wait until I can find a continuous hunk of time to devote to the project. Obviously this show can't depend on stars, being about kids; and so it will have to live or die by the success of its collaborations; and this remote-control collaboration isn't right. Maybe they can find the right composer who isn't always skipping off to conduct somewhere. It's not fair to them or to the work.[11]

The scenes Bernstein received may have been those in a draft typescript of Act I, scenes 1 and 2.[12] It is unlikely that Bernstein composed any music at this stage, but he jotted down a plan of the musical numbers for the whole show in a document that probably dates from early 1949 (Tables 2.1 and 2.2). A few of the ideas proposed in this plan were to survive: in Act I, the dance music in scene 2, the Balcony Scene with its 'farewell', the 'marriage ceremony' in the bridal shop, and music for a fight and double murder; in Act II, the idea of a ballet sequence, and a taunting scene with a 'derisive dance'. But the project was to lie dormant for several years – as Bernstein put it, 'slowly the project fizzled out'.[13] When it was taken up again, there were to be far-reaching changes.

Romeo Revived and Rethought

Robbins, Laurents and Bernstein were all too busy with other projects to make any further progress until 1955. Six years after their initial meeting, the plan for a *Romeo and Juliet* musical was resuscitated, at Robbins's urging. He was convinced that the idea had potential, and his collaborators agreed. Bernstein's next log entry, dated New York, 7 June 1955, records that: 'Jerry hasn't given up. Six years of postponement are as nothing to him. I'm still excited too. So is Arthur. Maybe I can plan to give this year to *Romeo* – if *Candide* gets on in time.'

Candide had already become a problem child (see Chapter 1), but the intention to revive plans for the *Romeo* musical was evidently serious enough for the press to be told about them, and for the first time there was a working title too. Lewis Funke reported in his Broadway gossip column on 19 June 1955:

Last week Leonard Bernstein, Arthur Laurents and Jerome Robbins, as formidable an array of talent as any daydreaming producer would care to conceive of, took from their idea bank a notion they have been saving for some time, looked it over, and gleefully decided it was still as fetching as when it had been put away because of other commitments. Note, therefore, the trio's current high resolve to

---

[11] Bernstein 1957, entry for 15 April 1949.
[12] Copy in LBC.
[13] Zadan 1974, p. 15.

be represented in the neighborhood with a new musical and note too, that for the present the project is being labelled *East Side Story*. It will be modern in content, dealing with young people in New York, and Mr. Bernstein, to be sure, will be creating the tunes. Mr. Laurents is to be credited with the book and Mr. Robbins with the staging and the choreography. As for the lyrics, they will be essayed by Messrs. Bernstein and Laurents. Mark the venture as being in work with hopes for production set for a year or so hence.[14]

From mid-1955 onwards, the show's growing pains were regularly reported in the press. On 18 September 1955, Funke wrote of further progress on *East Side Story*: 'Anyone who made a record of the fact that Jerome Robbins, Arthur Laurents and Leonard Bernstein are going to do a musical together will wish to add that the early steps are being taken … for what is tentatively being called *East Side Story*.'[15]

The Puerto Rican Solution

One of the most crucial 'early steps' had been taken a few weeks earlier, beside a swimming pool in Beverly Hills. During the summer, Laurents and Bernstein were both in California. On 25 August, they had a meeting which produced a turning point in the genesis of the show, described by Bernstein in his log:

> Had a fine long session with Arthur today, by the pool. (He's here for a movie; I'm conducting at the Hollywood Bowl.) We're fired again by the *Romeo* notion; only now we have abandoned the whole Jewish–Catholic premise as not very fresh, and have come up with what I think is going to be it: two teen-age gangs as the warring factions, one of them newly-arrived Puerto Ricans, the other self-styled 'Americans.' Suddenly it all springs to life. I hear rhythms and pulses, and – most of all – I can sort of feel the form.[16]

Laurents recalled this meeting too:

> Legs dangling in the pool of the Beverly Hills Hotel across from the moguls and the beauties in their cabanas, we discussed the recent phenomenon: juvenile delinquent gangs. They were in the headlines of the morning's Los Angeles papers: 'More Mayhem From Chicano Gangs'.[17] Lenny began chattering away

---

[14]   Funke 1955a.

[15]   Funke 1955b.

[16]   Bernstein 1957, entry for 25 August 1955.

[17]   Laurents may have been using his imagination here. However, the *Los Angeles Times* did carry a story on 22 August with the headline 'Six Jailed in Fight Death' reporting that Robert C. Garcia, aged 20, 'leader of a local gang known as the "Junior Raiders", died at

in half-Spanish (he dropped foreign phrases like names), but no comic strip light bulb went off, no 'Olé' in a little cloud over his head. 'We could set it out here,' Lenny mused, hearing Latin music.

For Laurents, though, it had to be set in New York, but the new idea was certainly promising: 'it would have Latin passion, immigrant anger, shared resentment. The potential was there, this could well be a *Romeo* to excite us all. We called Jerry.'[18]

By mid-September Laurents was finishing his movie assignment, just as Robbins arrived to work on the choreography for the film version of *The King and I*. As with Bernstein a month earlier, Laurents took advantage of the spare time with Robbins on the West Coast to work on what was still provisionally called *East Side Story* (though in his notes from the time Bernstein usually refers to it simply as *Romeo*). Robbins remained in Hollywood while Bernstein and Laurents (now back in New York) pressed on in his absence. Funke was on hand to speculate on progress in the *New York Times*, evidently basing his report on information from Robbins:

> Hardly a day passes without [Robbins] being informed by his partners, Leonard Bernstein and Arthur Laurents, about their progress on *East Side Story*, the musical on which they are working here until Mr. Robbins can personally join them. *East Side Story* is coming along nicely, thank you, and it is likely to be a spring entrant, with Mr. Robbins overseeing both the choreography and the direction. With *The Bells Are Ringing*[19] carded as a fall possibility, Mr. R. probably will not be at home to new clients for a while.[20]

The result of Laurents and Bernstein's labours during September and October was a new six-page outline by Laurents (probably with help from Bernstein), entitled *Romeo*. This is a document of great significance in the genesis of the show, since several scenes are much as they were eventually to be set, but within a three-act structure. Tony and Maria are still called Romeo and Juliet, and both of them die at the end, but gone are the Catholics and Jews of the 1949 drafts; they are now replaced by rival gangs of Americans and Puerto Ricans.

San Bernadino County Hospital following a fist fight with Rudolf M. Sena, 19, outside the Johnson Community Hall'. My thanks to Mark Eden Horowitz for drawing my attention to this article.

[18]   Laurents 2000, pp. 337–8.

[19]   Starring Judy Holliday, *Bells Are Ringing* ('The' was dropped) opened on 29 November 1956, with book and lyrics by Betty Comden and Adolph Green, and music by Jule Styne; it was directed by Jerome Robbins, with choreography by Robbins and Bob Fosse.

[20]   Funke 1955c.

Act I

Scene 1: Back Alley – Nightfall. Against music, we see two or three shadowy figures beating up a boy. …

Scene 2: Crystal Cave – Later. A wild mambo is in progress with the kids doing all the violent improvisation of jitterbugging. … Romeo sees a lovely young girl, dressed more simply, more innocently than the others … Romeo goes to Juliet and, as they meet, the music goes into half-time. … Bernardo is Juliet's brother and Romeo's opponent. Thus, the two lovers learn, to their mutual dismay, that they belong to opposing factions. …

Scene 3: Gang Hangout – Later. A shack of some sort … War Chieftains from the two gangs (Mercutio and Bernardo and aides) are to meet in Doc's Drugstore at midnight. Mercutio, in song, proceeds to give Romeo some advice about love: the older bon vivante [!] (probably just old enough to vote if that) to the neophyte. The gang joins in a razzing, possibly they chase Romeo – who tries to duck them – in a number which overflows out of the set. And at the end, he does elude them.

Scene 4: Tenement – Later. This is in the Puerto Rican area and shows the scrabbly building Juliet lives in, with a fire escape. … she comes out on the fire escape and the 'balcony' scene begins. This should go from dialogue to song and back, ending in song. … It might end with 'Good night' and 'Buenas noches', the latter repeated lovingly by Romeo.

Scene 5: Street or outside Crystal Cave. Bernardo taking his girl, Anita, home, before he goes to the Rumble meeting. Various points can come up here: Bernardo's hatred of the 'American' gang and thus his hate for Romeo as beau for his sister (as opposed to Anita's feeling that love is love and it all ends anyway); note of future disaster, heightened by Anita's plea to B not to get into bloody rumble. …

Scene 6: Drugstore – Midnight. … There must be some sharp note to underline the prejudice that stands between Romeo and Juliet, then Doc goes (his closeness to Romeo must emerge here, too) leaving Romeo to close up, turn out the lights as he sings softly of his love.

Act II

Scene 1: The Neighbourhood. This is a musical quintet which covers various parts of the neighbourhood in space and the whole day in time. Its theme is 'Can't Wait for the Night'; its mood is impatience of different kinds, exemplified by five of the principals: Mercutio (with humor) and Bernardo (with anger) can't wait for the rumble; Romeo can't wait to see Juliet; Juliet, at her bridal shop sewing machine, can't wait to see Romeo. Only Anita strikes a different note: she is afraid of the night because of what the rumble may bring. It should end with Juliet and thus go directly into:

Scene 2: The Bridal Shop – Late Afternoon. Everyone has gone except Juliet … Romeo comes in and they arrange the mannequins as a bridal party, almost like children playing a game, and marry themselves. Here again, dialogue goes in and out of song. …

Scene 3: Outside the Park. Bernardo and his aides come from one side and, after a moment, Juliet and Romeo from the other. Bernardo is furious that his sister is with a member of the other gang. … Romeo is going to take her home and no one is going to stop that – and no one does. Alone with his aides, Bernardo says the hell with a fair fight: get ready for a real rumble.

Scene 4: Central Park – Sundown. Mercutio and his gang are waiting for Bernardo and his. They, too, are actually prepared in the event that the 'fair fight' should bust into a bloody rumble. … It does break out into a fracas when Bernardo, almost beaten, whips out a knife and stabs Mercutio. Romeo, horrified at what has been done to his protector, grabs a broken bottle from A-Rab and plunges it into Bernardo. There is a wild moment of mêlée – then everybody clears because of the two still bodies on the ground. Both Bernardo and Mercutio are dead. This is horrifying even to the kids. A clock begins to chime as they slowly leave the scene. Romeo stares at the bodies. A police whistle, a siren … music – the chase is on and Romeo runs as – CURTAIN.

Act III

Scene 1: Juliet's Apartment – Sundown. This is a very crowded place: room made into rooms for all purposes: a curtained corner for Juliet who is dressing up happily as her family sings a gay street song in Spanish. … Romeo appears on the fire escape … His one drive has been to find her and tell her it was a horrible mistake. But her first reaction is: you killed my brother. … As he goes, Anita comes into the flat and sees him. Anita's attitude has changed. Bitter, angry over the death of her lover, Bernardo, she tells Juliet to stick to 'your own kind'. This is a duet for both girls. But Juliet's confusion resolves itself during the duet: Romeo *is* her own kind, for she loves him. …

Scene 2: Love Ballet. As Juliet shins down the fire escape, other girls wind down the other fire escapes, all going to meet lovers representing

Romeo. The dance goes from forgiveness to love to passion to actual sex. It ends with –

Scene 3:   The Hangout. Romeo and Juliet are in the positions the dancers were at the end. Romeo sings a happy song to Juliet about what their world will be and, in dialogue, they agree to run away together and be safe with each other. ...

Scene 4:   Streets. Romeo running from the police who fire at him and wound him. He escapes.

Scene 5:   The Drugstore. The same jitterbugging tune is being played in a muted way and the gang is going through the motions of dancing to avert suspicion from the police. Doc comes up from the cellar to get more bandages and medicine. Romeo is down there: he has been hit badly. Doc goes down again and the gang vents its bitterness against Puerto Ricans ... Juliet comes in, seeking Doc, and all the hatred is turned against her. The kids tell her Romeo is dead and jeer at her extreme reaction. She almost faints and instead of offering her water etc., they hideously offer her all kinds of poison so she can kill herself for love and pay for the evil she has done. This is done with macabre humor. All their prejudice and hate and violence comes out in the taunting until, able to bear no more, she grabs the bottle Benny holds and runs out of the store. ...

Scene 6:   The Bridal Shop. This scene is almost completely in song. Juliet has put on the wedding veil ... her strangeness is explained by the empty bottle of poison which she addresses for a moment. She is becoming more and more delirious when Romeo comes in. He is very weak but so happy to see her. ... He doesn't realize at first that she has taken poison. But when he does discover the truth, it is too late. She sinks to the floor, he cradles her in his arms, they both start a reprise of their balcony song but they never quite finish. The lights change, the walls disappear, the music soars upward and the audience swoons.[21]

This scenario was sent to Robbins, who replied to Laurents and Bernstein on 15 October 1955: 'I want you to know that I think it's a hell of a good job, and very much on the right track', but he had several significant objections. First, there was the division into three acts: 'there's not sufficient material in Acts II and III to stand up by themselves. And it's a serious mistake to let the audience out of our grip for 2 intermissions.' Robbins then goes through scene by scene: 'Act I, Scene 2. Would like to suggest that the meeting between Romeo and Juliet be more abrupt rather than an observing of each other from a distance at first. In general, suddenness of

---

21   Carbon copy in LBC.

action is something we should strive for.' Robbins was particularly concerned about the depiction of Anita:

> Act I, Scene 5. You are away off the track with the whole character of Anita. She is the typical downbeat blues torch-bearing second character (Julie of *Showboat*, etc.) and falls into a terrible cliché. The audience will know that somewhere a 'my man done left me' blues is coming up for her.

When it came to the question of a ballet, Robbins, not surprisingly, took a critical look at his collaborators' proposal and found it wanting: 'Act III, Scene 2. I am starting to feel we're in serious trouble with the so-called love ballet.' He also made some shrewd observations on the outline for the final scene, which left him confused and unconvinced:

> Act III, Scene 6. From the outline I'm inclined to feel that it's all a little too goofy. Juliet becomes Ophelia with the reeds and flowers and is playing a 'crazy' scene. I had to read the whole thing a couple of times to find out why Romeo died and I also think it's too right on the head placing it back in the bridal shop.

Robbins ends this robust and perceptive critique with some general comments, emphasizing that there could be no room for any self-pity among the characters:

> As for the overall picture, we're dead unless the audience feels that all the tragedy can and could be averted, that there's *hope* and a wish for escape from that tragedy, and a tension built on that desire. … It's another reason why I dislike qvetchy Anita so much. Let's not have anyone in the show feel sorry for themselves.

Finally, he turned to potential difficulties with the effective integration of dance. The solution he proposed was for some of the principals to be primarily singers, and for others to be dancers:

> About the dancing. It will never be well incorporated into the show unless some of the principals are dancers. I can see, easily, why Romeo and Juliet must be singers, but Mercutio has to be a dancer, maybe Anita, and for sure some of the prominent gang members … with all the experience I've had it's by far easier to have the principals do everything. It's a sorry sight and a back-breaking effort, and usually an unsuccessful one, to build the numbers around some half-assed movements of a principal who can't move. Think it over.[22]

---

[22]   LBC.

Bernstein jotted down a music list, presumably dating from the same time as the new outline, for a three-act version of the show:[23]

Romeo Numbers:

[Act] I
1.   Opening & Rumble Song (canon?)
2.   Mambo (& meeting routine) [ends with orch. 'Maria']
2A. Maria
3.   Mercutio's Song (Cool?)
4.   Balcony Scene ('Maria'? ~~Dream with me?~~ Goodnight 1000 times)
5.   Anita's Song (~~Dance?~~) (Girl number) (PR singing chorus)
6.   Jitterbug number (mambo reprise?) (Perc. for war council?)

[Act] II
1.   Quintet
2.   Marriage Scene (E major tune)
3.   Fight music (canon?)

[Act] III
1.   Puerto Rican nostalgic music
2.   Anita–Juliet duet
3.   Love Ballet
4.   Shack Song (Duet?)
5.   Taunting Scene
6.   Ophelia Scene

This is an intriguing document, suggesting that some musical ideas had been sketched: the 'E major tune' for the marriage scene is a reference to the sketch of a 'Love Duet' originally planned for *Candide*[24] but soon to become 'One Hand, One Heart', although its first appearance was initially intended to be in the Balcony Scene. Were the Quintet and 'Cool' already sketched by this point? Mention of them by name suggests that possibility, and the music for 'Cool' certainly came before the lyrics;[25] but we also have Bernstein's word for it that 'Maria' was only a sketch at this stage:

---

[23]   LBC.

[24]   LBC.

[25]   Zadan 1974, p. 22, quoting Bernstein: 'Steve [Sondheim] and I worked together in every conceivable way – together, apart, sometimes with the tune first ("Cool" and "Officer Krupke"), sometimes with the words first ("A Boy Like That").'

I had a song called 'Maria,' for which I had the title and some kind of lyric that I had written which was there when Steve came in. I think it took longer to write that song than any other. It's difficult to make a strong love song and avoid corn.[26]

In conversation with Mel Gussow, Bernstein elaborated on this:

I had already jotted down a sketch for a song called 'Maria,' which was operable in Italian or Spanish. It's still rather Italian in character. I had a dummy lyric, a terrible lyric. 'Lips like wine... divine.' Very bad. Like a translation of a Neapolitan street song. ... We sat for weeks trying to get the right lyrics for 'Maria.' And when the idea occurred – and I'm sure it came from Steve – of the sound of the name, then we were headed for home.[27]

It is also possible that the fight canon – which became the (abandoned) 'Mix!' – existed in some form. The potential music for the Balcony Scene in the list includes 'Dream With Me', a song that had been cut from the 1950 *Peter Pan* score,[28] and the mention of 'Goodnight 1000 times' is indicative of the lyrics that eventually ended the 'Tonight' duet, but the idea for that was a long way off. Though it is likely that some of the music mentioned in the '*Romeo* Numbers' had been sketched, a more pressing concern now presented itself: Bernstein needed someone to help him write the lyrics.

Stephen Sondheim Joins the Team

Robbins was unsparing in his criticism of the three-act outline, but the result was that all three members of the creative team now set their minds to starting work on the show in earnest. At the same time, there was another important development: in October 1955, Stephen Sondheim joined the project. Bernstein's invented log first mentions him on 14 November: 'A young lyricist named Stephen Sondheim came and sang us some of his songs today. What a talent! I think he's ideal for this project, as do we all. The collaboration grows.'[29]

Bernstein doesn't mention that, in the few weeks before this, Betty Comden and Adolph Green – the lyricists of *On the Town* and *Wonderful Town* – had also been approached. *West Side Story* seems an improbable prospect for the brilliant wit of

---

[26]   Zadan 1974, p. 22.

[27]   Gussow 1990.

[28]   This rather beautiful song is included in the 2005 recording of the complete *Peter Pan* music issued by Koch International Classics.

[29]   Bernstein 1957, entry for 14 November 1955.

these two old friends of Bernstein's who also knew Robbins from *On the Town*. As it turned out, they were unable to get out of existing commitments.[30]

According to Bernstein's datebook, Laurents and Sondheim had their first meeting with him on 18 October, a month earlier than the log entry. Sondheim adds some interesting details: he heard about the project from Arthur Laurents at the opening-night party for Ugo Betti's *Island of Goats* on 4 October, and played for Bernstein the following day, on 5 October:

> I auditioned for him without Arthur, and it was the day after the *Isle of Goats* opening.[31] Remember, Lenny and Arthur had to wait for a week till Betty and Adolph knew whether they could get out of *Winter Wonderland* (I think that was the title). I was put on hold for that week, which is when I went to consult Oscar [Hammerstein]. My first official meeting after accepting the job was with Arthur alone, the next with both of them.[32]

For the next few months there were numerous working sessions, either with Bernstein and Sondheim or with other collaborators. Bernstein's datebook is littered with meetings: 17 in November, 13 in December, seven in January (1956), another seven in February, and so on until 14 May 1956, when there was evidently enough of the score written for some of it to be tried out: 'Romeo singers here. Cheryl [Crawford], Dr. S[irmay]'. Crawford was the show's co-producer at the time, and Sirmay was a leading light at Chappell's, which was to co-publish the score.[33] According to Crawford (in a letter to Arthur Laurents of 11 April 1957), a demo recording was made at this time: 'By May 30th we had recorded the songs.' In other words, during the spring of 1956, a substantial part of the score was composed. Though very little of it had been written by the start of the year, it is likely that much of Act I was complete by May 1956. Bernstein described his collaboration with Sondheim in the warmest terms:

---

[30]   There is confusion about a 'Romeo' story plan that has been attributed to Comden and Green (see, for example, Garebian 1995, p. 35). This is a document that was sent *to* them rather than written *by* them – it is the six-page plan devised by Laurents (with Bernstein) to which Robbins responded. Laurents's plan for the book was progressing, so there was no reason for Comden and Green to produce another one. However, when they were asked to help with writing the lyrics, they were sent a copy of the latest plot outline so that they could see what the project was about. Owing to their obligations elsewhere, Comden and Green wrote nothing for *West Side Story*.

[31]   Originally written in 1946, Betti's *Delitto all'isola delle capre* was produced in an English adaptation by Henry Reed (published by Samuel French in 1960 as *Crime On Goat Island*), with incidental music by Norman Dello Joio. It opened at the Fulton Theatre on 4 October 1955.

[32]   Stephen Sondheim, e-mail to Mark Eden Horowitz, 4 September 2007.

[33]   Sirmay evidently liked the show, and not just as a publishing prospect: he was one of the original backers, investing $500.

When Steve came into the picture and we began working together, he became part of the team and the contribution he made was enormous. It far exceeded even *my* expectations. What made him so valuable was that he was also a composer and I could explain musical problems to him and he'd understand immediately, which made the collaboration a joy. It was like writing with an alter ego.[34]

Funke's gossip column in January 1956 – before this flurry of creative activity – gave an impossibly optimistic progress report, but Sondheim was now mentioned:

Postponed: That Leonard Bernstein–Arthur Laurents–Steve Sondheim musical *West Side Story* is finished. But, says our man, you no longer are to count it among this season's entrants. The creators of this modernized treatment of the Romeo and Juliet legend have the notion that they want unknowns for the leading parts. Consequently they figure they're going to need all the time they can get for searching. Look for it, therefore, early next season under the direction of Jerome Robbins.[35]

The score was very far from finished in January 1956: there was little or no music for Act II until well over a year later. One reason for the further delay in both composing the score and producing the show was Bernstein's concurrent work on *Candide* – a fraught and ambitious project that had been in progress since 1953, eventually opening on 1 December 1956. Bernstein himself saw some value in allowing *West Side Story* to lie for a while, or at least he did by the time he compiled his log:

Candide is on again; we plunge in next month. So again *Romeo* is postponed for a year. Maybe it's all for the best: by the time it emerges it ought to be deeply seasoned, cured, hung, aged in the wood. It's such a problematical work anyway that it should benefit by as much sitting-time as it can get. Chief problem: to tread the fine line between opera and Broadway, between realism and poetry, ballet and 'just dancing', abstract and representational. Avoid being 'messagy.' The line is there, but it's very fine, and sometimes takes a lot of peering around to discern it.[36]

---

34 Zadan 1974, p. 16.
35 Funke 1956.
36 Bernstein 1957, entry for 17 March 1956.

The Book and Lyrics Take Shape

As the plot, character and settings began to take on a surer sense of direction, Arthur Laurents set to work on redrafting the book for the show, and produced a number of different versions. At least eight drafts of the script survive.[37] One of the three typed scripts in LBC – undated, but probably from early 1957 – has a list of numbers written in pencil by Bernstein on the verso of the last page:

> [Act I]
> Opening
> Mix
> Mambo
> Maria
> One
> America
> Cool
> Quintet
> Marriage
> Rumble
>
> [Act II]
> Pretty
> Ballet
> Duet (A Boy Like That)

This presents a version of the book that has significant differences from the published libretto, including a quite different ending from that proposed in the outline of autumn 1955 (see above) and in the final version.[38] Table 2.3 summarizes the most significant differences between this early script and the published libretto.

---

[37] There are eight versions in the Stephen Sondheim Papers 1946–1965 at the Wisconsin Center for Film and Theater Research, Wisconsin Historical Society Archives, Madison, Wisconsin. I must record warmest thanks to Stephen Banfield for giving me copies of his detailed notes on these scripts. See also Block 1997, p. 382, note 13. Block records the dates of all eight drafts: January 1956, spring 1956, 15 March 1956, winter 1956, 14 April 1957, 1 May 1957, 1 June 1957 and 19 July 1957.

[38] 1958 LIB.

Table 2.3 Summary of differences between an early typescript and the published version

West Side Story. **Typescript, 56 and 28pp.,** **[undated, ?early 1957], LBC.**	*West Side Story* **[libretto] (New York: Random House, 1958), 143pp.**
ACT I	*ACT I*
Scene 1: An Alleyway – Late afternoon A shallow brick or cement alley; trashcans in front of a high wall. **No music.** A-RAB … sings or whistles a few bars of **My greatest day.** Suddenly, two dark-skinned boys plummet down from the wall, crashing him to the ground. His cries are smothered in **sudden, percussive music.** A third boy – dressed like the others in the gang garb of the Sharks – appears on the wall and perches there as a lookout. The pummeling is stopped by his whistled signal: **the music cuts.** One of the assailants takes out a knife, bends over the still figure of A-RAB and makes a sharp, quick movement. **A shriek from the orchestra** which continues as the three attackers run off. **A comment from the orchestra, silence**, and then several boys – dressed like A-Rab – run on from the opposite side. …	Scene 1: 5:00 p.m. The Street A suggestion of city streets and alleyways. A brick wall. **The opening is musical**: half-danced, half mimed, with occasional phrases of dialogue.
End of scene: DIESEL: You're due for the khaki, Riff. If we're ever gonna rumble – RIFF: Yeah, but you gotta dig what you're doin'. (This leads into a number about rumbles based on the **Moon music**, formerly used for the opening of the scene. Its mood is bright and energetic; its tone shows that the kids really don't know what they may be letting themselves in for.)	End of scene: ACTION: Tony ain't been with us for over a month. SNOWBOY: What about the day we clobbered the Emeralds? A-RAB: Which we couldn't have done without Tony. BABY JOHN: He saved me ever lovin' neck. RIFF: Right. He's always coming through for us and he will now. (sings) **Jet song**.
Scene 2: Drugstore Fountain – Late afternoon A piece of a set. RIFF sitting on the one stool in front of the section of the fountain seen; a good looking young blond boy drying glasses and whistling **Greatest day** behind it: TONY. Note: **The song itself can be introduced during this scene.**	Scene 2: 5:30 p.m. A back yard On a small ladder, a good-looking sandy-haired boy is painting a vertical sign that will say: Doc's. …
End of scene: RIFF: It'll be a great night, you'll see! TONY: Maybe. Could be. Why not? (**Starts to whistle again** as the light goes quickly.)	End of scene: RIFF: Who knows? Maybe what you're waitin' for will be twitchin' at the dance! TONY (sings): **Something's coming**.
Scene 2(A): Bridal Shop – Late afternoon MARIA: Please, Anita. Make the neck lower.	Scene 3: 6:00 p.m. A bridal shop MARIA: Por favor, Anita. Make the neck lower!
End of scene: MARIA: Because it is the real beginning of my life as an American lady.	End of scene: MARIA: Because tonight is the real beginning of my life as a young lady of America!

West Side Story. **Typescript, 56 and 28pp., [undated, ?early 1957], LBC.**	*West Side Story* **[libretto] (New York: Random House, 1958), 143pp.**
Scene 3: The Crystal Cave – Night Stage directions mention that 'the tune the kids are dancing to is called **The Atom Bomb Mambo**'. TONY (worried): You're not thinking I'm someone else? MARIA: No.	Scene 4: 10:00 p.m. The gym GLAD HAND: All right, boys and girls. Attention please!
End of scene: DIESEL: Hey lover boy! Aw. I'll see you at Doc's. TONY (sings): **Maria.**	End of scene: RIFF: Tony! DIESEL: Ah, we'll see him at Doc's. TONY: (Speaking dreamily over the music – he is now standing alone in the light) Maria … (sings) **Maria**.
Scene 4: Back of the Tenements – Night TONY (**sings**): Maria, Maria MARIA: Ssh! Duet: **One hand, one heart** End of scene: **America**	Scene 5: 11:00 p.m. A back alley TONY (**sings**): Maria, Maria MARIA: Ssh! Duet: **Tonight** End of scene: **America**
Scene 5: Drugstore – Night ACTION: 39 – 40 – where the devil 're they – 41 **Cool** End of scene: DOC: So soon, boychik, so soon?	Scene 6: Midnight. The drugstore ACTION: Where the devil are they? Are we havin' a war council tonight or ain't we? **Cool** End of scene: DOC: Why? I'm frightened enough for both of you.
	Scene 7: 5:30 p.m. The next day. The bridal shop ANITA: She's gone! The old bag of a bruja has gone! End of scene: MARIA: Now you see, Anita, I told you there was nothing to worry about (**Music starts** as she leaves the dummy and walks up to TONY) … TONY: With this ring I thee wed. (Sings): **One hand, one heart**
Scene 6: The Neighbourhood A musical **quintet** for the five principals … we pick up one after another of them as they are introduced musically. The time is from morning to late afternoon of the next day and each person expresses his reason for looking forward eagerly to the night's events.	Scene 8: 6:00 to 9:00 p.m. The neighbourhood Spotlights pick out RIFF and the Jets, BERNARDO and the Sharks, ANITA, MARIA and TONY against small sets representing different places in the neighbourhood. All are waiting expectantly for the coming of night, but for very different reasons. **Quintet** [Ensemble].
Scene 7: Bridal Shop – Late afternoon ANITA: Finish that tomorrow. Ampara has gone. End of scene: reprise of **One hand, one heart**	

West Side Story. **Typescript, 56 and 28pp., [undated, ?early 1957], LBC.**	*West Side Story* **[libretto] (New York: Random House, 1958), 143pp.**
Scene 8: A Street – Sundown The Jets march on as the curtains close on the previous scene, singing the **Rumble song: Mix!** As they sing, the song becomes a canon. The Sharks are singing against them, from behind a curtain. This becomes a scrim and we can see BERNARDO and his gang singing and marching in a direction opposite to that of RIFF and his gang. Both gangs march off, the voices fading away as **the orchestra takes over as a prelude for the next scene.**	
Scene 9: The Park – Sundown There is **an orchestral prelude before the curtain. The music continues** for a moment or two under the beginning of the scene. RIFF: Your boy ready? CHINO: Any time yours is. BERNARDO: Come on, you yellow-bellied Polak bas– (He never finishes, for RIFF hauls around him and socks him. Immediately, DIESEL yells 'Jets!' – which becomes the first word of the **Rumble song [Mix!]**; and CHINO yells 'Sharks!' which becomes the first word of his gang's part of the song, now done entirely in canon with orchestra. The singing and music are tense, hushed, as RIFF and BERNARDO fight in a stylized balletic fashion.	Scene 9: 9:00 p.m. Under the highway BERNARDO: Ready? CHINO: Ready! BERNARDO: Come on, you yellow-bellied Polack bas– (He never finishes, for RIFF hauls him off and hits him. Immediately, the two gangs alert and the following action takes on the form of a dance.) **Rumble**
End of scene: TONY: Maria! (Curtain)	End of scene: TONY: Maria! (Curtain)
ACT II	*ACT II*
Scene 1: An Apartment – Early evening **I feel pretty**	Scene 1: 9:15 p.m. A bedroom **I feel pretty**
[Scene includes Maria's mother and father, and a detective named Magill, all cut. Tony does not appear in this scene and there is no mention of a ballet]	End of scene: MARIA: But it's not us! It's everything around us **Ballet sequence – Somewhere**
Scene 2: A Street – Night KRUPKE: Yeah: *you.* A-RAB: It *is* Officer Krupke, Baby John.	Scene 2: 10:00 p.m. Another alley A-RAB: They get you yet? BABY JOHN: No. You? **Gee, Officer Krupke**
End of scene: BABY JOHN and A-RAB: Bug You, Jack!	End of scene: ANYBODYS: Thanks, Daddy-o.

West Side Story. **Typescript, 56 and 28pp., [undated, ?early 1957], LBC.**	*West Side Story* **[libretto] (New York: Random House, 1958), 143pp.**
Scene 3: Police Station – Night A police interrogation for boys and girls from both gangs. Two dancers representing Tony and Maria come forth from the haze at the back as there is **music based on the Mambo theme** … In dance she is drawn away from [Tony] by her brother … The dancing lovers are together for a moment …	
Scene 4: Street – Night [End of scene:] **A boy like that – Once in your life**	Scene 3: 11:30 p.m. The bedroom **A boy like that – I have a love** End of scene: SCHRANK: And his name? MARIA: José.
Scene 5: Drugstore – Night TONY **sings a reprise of Once in your life**. The music from the previous scene has never really stopped: thus the number ends with Tony's affirmation of love. DOC: Who wants advice when what he needs is money. [later:] MARIA runs in breathless End of scene: TONY: What have you done now???	Scene 4: 11:40 p.m. The drugstore A-RAB and some of the Jets are there as ANYBODYS and other Jets run in. … The shop doorbell tinkles as ANITA enters. Cold silence, then slowly she comes down to the counter. They all stare at her. A long moment. Someone turns on the juke-box. A **mambo** comes on softly. The **Taunting** breaks out into a wild, savage dance. End of scene: DOC: Get out of here!
	Scene 5: 11:50 p.m. The cellar End of scene: (TONY backs away, then suddenly turns and runs out the door. As he does, the set flies away and the stage goes dark. In the darkness we hear TONY's voice.) TONY: Chino? Chino? Come and get me, too, Chino.
Scene 6: The Docks – Night The actual locale of this scene depends on the designer. The writing and form of this scene depends on how much it will be underscored and how much will be sung. The rough line is that MARIA comes in wild, angry, raging. She **sings** of her hatred for everything that has destroyed her love. … TONY enters, however, and her hate and anger are swept away by joy that he is alive and by her love for him. … DIESEL, BABY JOHN and ANITA hurry on: the BOYS with a few dollars they have scrounged from the gang for Tony and Maria: ANITA with a little bundle of clothes. The lovers are happy even though TONY is too weak to rise and take the money. HE and MARIA **reprise one of their love songs** and are singing happily, unaware – as they all are – of the COP who has followed Diesel, Baby John and Anita, and is standing there, waiting.	Scene 6: Midnight. The street **Somewhere** (Maria begins to sing – without **orchestra**) MARIA: Hold my hand and we're halfway there. Hold my hand and I'll take you there. Someday, Somehow… (Tony has started to join in on the second line. She sings harder, as though to urge him back to life, but his voice falters and he barely finishes the line. She sings on, a phrase or two more, then stops, his body quiet in her arms. A moment, and then, as she gently rests TONY on the floor, the orchestra finishes the last bars of the song.) End of scene: MARIA: Te adoro, Anton. **Epilogue**

Act I, scene 1 of the typed script is set in 'An Alleyway – Late afternoon' and a song, 'My Greatest Day', is mentioned in the stage directions, though there are no lyrics given for it. The directions at the end of the scene refer to another song that did not survive as a vocal number: 'This leads into a number about rumbles based on the "Moon music", formerly used for the opening of the scene. Its mood is bright and energetic; its tone shows that the kids really don't know what they may be letting themselves in for.' The 'Moon music' was so called because the opening lyrics of the sung version of the opening began: 'How long does it take to reach the moon-a-rooney?'.

Scene 2 opens with Tony whistling the song 'Greatest Day', and there is a note that: 'The song itself can be introduced during this scene.' A typescript in the Sondheim papers[39] includes the lyrics of this song, which began:

> My greatest day was the day I was born
> And the day I was eight
> And the day I was five –
> Also the day when I first blew a horn,
> When I first stayed out late,
> When I first learned to drive.

This was later revised to become the 'Jet Song'. Some lines spoken by Tony later in the scene were to prove a useful source, very late in the show's evolution, for the lyrics of 'Something's Coming':

Tony:	It's right outside that door, around the corner: maybe buried under a tree in the park, maybe being stamped in a letter, maybe whistling down the river, maybe –
Riff:	*What* is?
Tony (*shrugs*):	I don't know. But it's coming, and it's the greatest.

Scene 2(A) in this script is the first appearance of Anita and Maria in the bridal shop. Scene 3 is set in 'The Crystal Cave – Night' and the music is specified as 'The Atom Bomb Mambo'. At the end of the scene, the lyrics of 'Maria' are in place, although they were to be revised (the third line – later 'All the beautiful sounds of the world in a single word' – is here 'The most beautiful, wonderful, marvelous magic word').

Scene 4 is the Balcony Scene. In the final show, this is where the 'Tonight' duet was to appear, but in this early script the song is specified as 'One Hand, One Heart'. This early version of lyrics for the Tony–Maria duet is by Bernstein himself. The song opens with Tony's lines:

---

[39] This script is marked as 'Revised March 15, 1956'.

What can they do?
I'm part of you,
And we are one.

One hand, one heart,
Your hand, my heart,
Your eyes make me see:
You're the breath and life of me.

The scene ends with 'America', the lyrics only slightly different from those in the final version.

Scene 5, the drugstore at night, includes all the lyrics of 'Cool'. The Bridal Shop Scene that follows this in the final version is placed one scene later, after the Quintet. Scene 6 here is the same as the eventual scene 8: 'The Neighbourhood. A musical quintet for the five principals'. Then comes the scene in the bridal shop with a 'reprise of One Hand, One Heart' at the end, including the lyrics:

Tony: One life, one love.
Maria: Your life, my love.
Both: One now, one to be – !

Scene 8 in the typescript was later deleted. The stage directions specify 'A Street – Sundown' and a song: 'The Jets march on as the curtains close on the previous scene, singing the Rumble Song, Mix!' The directions at the start of scene 9, set in 'The Park – Sundown', mention an 'orchestral prelude before the curtain'. The setting was eventually to become '9:00 p.m. Under the highway'. As in the final version, the curtain falls after Tony has cried out 'Maria!'

Act II opens in 'An Apartment – Early evening', and 'I Feel Pretty' is mentioned as the song. It also includes Maria and Bernardo's parents, who are visited by a detective named Magill; he has come to break the news about Bernardo being 'in the Catholic hospital'. The most interesting aspect about this cut passage of dialogue is the language barrier: the parents speak in Spanish, and Magill has to use Maria as an English-speaking intermediary. There is no mention of a ballet, and Tony/Romeo does not arrive to see Maria.

Scene 2 is set in a street at night, as it is in the final version. The directions for scene 3 are 'Police Station – Night'. Its purpose is an interrogation of members of both gangs, but this is intercut with an early version of the ballet sequence. Scene 4 is where 'A Boy Like That' appears, in a version that matches the autograph manuscript described in Chapter 3, including Tony's reprise of 'Once In Your Life' (an earlier lyric set to the music of 'I Have a Love') to cover the scene change. Scene 5 is very different here, since it is not Anita who visits the drugstore but Maria, and it is Tony who interrupts the taunting of her by the gang. The final scene is an outline rather than a script. While, in some early versions, both Tony and Maria die, in this version they are both alive as the curtain falls: Tony is weak and badly wounded, but here they receive gifts of money and clothes for their escape from members of both gangs, all watched by an unseen 'Cop'.

Another draft in the Sondheim papers is of what appears to be a slightly later version of the script, 'revised on 15 April 1957'. It has no lyrics, but mentions the position of songs in the score. The most interesting are some of those in Act II. For the first time, the placing of 'Somewhere' is described – but it is given as a number sung by Tony to Maria, prefaced by the lines:

> We'll go someplace where there are no streets. We'll go tonight. I can get money from Doc. We'll go down the river, way down where it curves away and widens and the buildings turn into fields, and there is only you and me and all the time we've always wanted. (And tenderly, he sings to her…)

The place for a humorous song to be sung by the Jets is also clear, but at this point it appears as the 'comedy number: "I Agree With You, Judge" wherein the kids play at being hauled into court and themselves reel off all the endless reasons for their "delinquency" before the judge can say anything'. The end of the show, from Anita's arrival at the drugstore, is as in the final version. Though the music had not all been written by mid-April, the script of *West Side Story* was starting to take on something like its eventual shape.

Auditions and Producers

With *Candide* over and done with at the start of February 1957, a major problem emerged for *West Side Story*: casting the 'unknowns' was proving to be something of a nightmare for Robbins, Laurents, Bernstein, Sondheim and Cheryl Crawford (who was still the show's producer at this stage). Funke's gossip column again reveals the difficulties of finding the right kind of actors:

> Quest: Considering the advertised tantrums and noises made by temperamental tenors, you would think there are plenty of them in the woods, and out. But, lament Cheryl Crawford and Jerome Robbins, such does not appear to be the case, at least when you are looking for good young tenors. Miss Crawford who, with Roger L. Stevens, is supposed to produce the musical *West Side Story* (Mr. Robbins directing), has been listening to hundreds of young American tenors and so far has not turned up a prospect for what is one of the leading roles in the Arthur Laurents–Leonard Bernstein creation. Specifically, what is needed is a tenor who can sing, act, and look as though he is 18. Colleges, singing societies and 'all agents known to man' have been alerted. Help![40]

---

[40] Funke 1957a.

It is surprising to find that Bernstein's invented log has no entries between February and July 1957, since his datebook tells a quite different story. During February there are 12 meetings with one or more of the collaborators noted in the datebook, including Sondheim and Bernstein playing through what existed of the score to William Paley on 26 February (a ghastly occasion: the show was met with incomprehension and hostility; see Chapter 6). March meetings noted in Bernstein's datebooks included the first auditions (on 26 and 28 March), and these continued on 5, 11 and 15 April.

Just as the team was starting to cast the show, there was suddenly serious doubt about whether it would happen at all when the vastly experienced Cheryl Crawford quit as producer.[41] Laurents recalled that 'Cheryl Crawford and Roger Stevens were going to produce the show, after it was turned down by everyone else'.[42] She was no stranger to 'serious' musicals: her Broadway credits already included three shows by Kurt Weill, and Marc Blitzstein's *Regina*. But she could not see how *West Side Story* was going to work, and she was also struggling to find the financial backing.[43] On 11 April she wrote to Arthur Laurents voicing alarm about the shape the show was in. Her letter began starkly: 'This is for your eyes alone. I think we are in trouble. Although I want so much to be constructive and not destructive, it does no good to shut my mind and trust to blind luck.' She had misgivings about Laurents's book ('you, the author, have not had a chance to really get at the material as an artist but almost like a carpenter') and was alarmed by the lack of new music: 'On April 5th last year I saw you and Steve. By May 30th we had recorded the songs. Since that date I have heard *one* new song. That's damn near a year.'[44] In Crawford's opinion, 'the story at present has no real depth or urgency', and she felt that the main characters were severely underdeveloped. After giving examples of ways in which she thought Tony, Riff, Chino and others could be given greater depth, Crawford makes a more general point about the characters in the show as representative of the needs and wants of a whole generation:

---

[41] Cheryl Crawford (1902–1986) co-founded the Group Theatre in 1931 and was Executive Producer of the Actors Studio. She served as producer for Weill's *Johnny Johnson* (1936), the 1942 revival of Gershwin's *Porgy and Bess*, Weill's *One Touch of Venus* (1943), Lerner and Loewe's *Brigadoon* (1947), Weill's *Love Life* (1948), Blitzstein's *Regina* (1949) and Lerner and Loewe's *Paint Your Wagon* (1951).

[42] Zadan 1974, p. 16.

[43] Hal Prince recalled that Sondheim told him, '"We have no show." I said, "What happened?" He said, "Cheryl Crawford walked out – she can't find the backers for it"' (NPR 2007).

[44] The May 1956 demo recording of *West Side Story* mentioned by Crawford remains something of a mystery. Sondheim has 'no recollection of any demo' (e-mail to the present author, 13 November 2008).

I know that other individualities and backgrounds can be given beside those I throw out and I don't care as long as they are richer, giving more fabric and conflict. Besides I think we want to say this is 'youth' today, not just juvenile delinquents and young psychos. Their yearnings are strong and shared by youths all over the world and in other sections of society. What is happening to kids seems to be one of our most urgent problems today and although we've picked these special kids their desires and conflicts should be representative of more. One of the typical things about them is that they *can't wait*. Can't wait to be men, to have money, to have everything they find desirable and attractive. If the characters are more developed (and I have ideas about Maria too) then the story will get more exciting. For instance, I now can't accept Tony's killing as inevitable.

I didn't mean to write so much but I wanted to try to get some of my thoughts down on paper since at the conference I could only voice my objection. So glad I'm not an author![45]

Laurents's reply is dated 'Thursday night'.[46] He was caught in an invidious position, since Crawford's request for secrecy made it difficult for him to discuss her criticisms with the rest of the creative team. But Laurents did not disguise that there were pressing problems, above all the lack of music: 'We do not have and have never had anything near a complete score. In point of fact, we are without a second act score. It would seem to me that this is a big problem which should be attacked at once – and hard.' He also felt unduly hemmed in: 'I cannot go on rewriting to please different people. I am so beleaguered by all this that it is difficult to have firm convictions of my own: to write for myself. I begin to think Lenny has a point: if you don't write, you can't be asked to rewrite.' Worryingly, Laurents added that 'the whole atmosphere around the show is depressing and discouraging, the last thing to stimulate creativity'. But he then went on to defend the essentials of the show against Crawford's criticisms, and in doing so provided an eloquent explanation of his creative vision for *West Side Story*:

I think it is or should be a strong love story against a heightened, theatricalized, romanticized background based on juvenile delinquency. I think the reality should be an emotional, not a factual one. It is here, it seems, that we sharply diverge. I feel that, in general, your suggestions tend toward a social opera about today's youth, with the minor story of two lovers. This is not the show we intended to do and it is not the show that I, at any rate, want to do. Furthermore, I think it would be a sure flop. Tension, anger, hate, etc. all the dark emotions may not be customary in a musical, but I do not feel they will depress or repel an audience when they are

---

[45]   Carbon copy in the Roger L. Stevens Collection, Library of Congress.

[46]   11 April 1957, the date of Crawford's letter, was a Thursday. Laurents's letter must either date from the same night, or from a week later, 18 April.

done in a theatrical, romantic style. When they are done in a social, documentary style, I feel they will.

Laurents then responded to the specific points in Crawford's critique, starting with reservations she had expressed about the opening scene, and revealing in the process that it was Laurents himself who was largely responsible for making initial suggestions about musical numbers:

> Your criticism that the story has no real urgency. I agree and am trying to fix that. I also agree that the rumble might well be initiated in the Crystal Cave scene and suggested that to the group at our last meeting. Jerry vetoed it. Furthermore, this left a void for a musical number to end the [first] scene. All the ideas, every idea for every musical number has come from me; I cannot think of one for the scene without the rumble beginning; no one has an idea.

To Crawford's charge that Tony's killing was not inevitable, Laurents responded robustly:

> Neither is Romeo's or Juliet's. And I don't think it matters. What does matter to me is that the audience is convinced of his desire to be killed. That is character and that is more important than all the sociological, crotch-scratching facts in the naturalistic world. I apologize for my vehemence on this subject of naturalism but it is something I am sick to death of in the theatre and is one reason why I wanted to do a musical.
>
> So there we are. I'm off to rewrite. I can only say I hope you feel better when you read the latest revision. But I wish there were a score to go with it.[47]

Despite the compelling arguments presented by Laurents in his letter, it seems that Crawford did not feel any better about the show. Nor did Laurents, when recalling this unhappy episode almost twenty years later:

> Cheryl was known as a lady of great morality, but not the way she behaved on this show. For one thing she would say to me 'You can't listen to Jerry, he doesn't know anything about writing.' And she would go to Jerry and say 'You've got to do something about Arthur!' Then after the show was written, Roger [Stevens] came to me and said, 'Listen, I think Cheryl's gone cold on the show but I'll stick.' And Cheryl called a meeting – we were six weeks away from rehearsal and since everyone had other commitments, if we didn't go on time, the show would never be done. Cheryl announced that she thought the book was terrible and that it would be insane to proceed. And I asked her how Roger felt, and she said, 'Oh exactly the

---

[47] Carbon copy in the Roger L. Stevens Collection, Library of Congress.

same way.' And I said, 'Cheryl, you're an immoral woman', and we all got up and walked out and went to the Algonquin to have a drink.[48]

Bernstein's datebook includes a meeting with Crawford at 5 p.m. on 22 April (which was Easter Monday). It was on this occasion that she announced her withdrawal from the project. Carol Lawrence, who was being considered for the part of Maria at the time, recalled Crawford's reasons for giving up the project:

> How could the show miss? In any number of ways – at least, that's what some pros thought. As Cheryl Crawford said when she backed out, 'It's got an operatic score, four ballets … It's about a bunch of teenagers in blue jeans, and people are reading enough about them in their daily papers without paying good money to see a show about them. It's got a cast of total unknowns, and it ends tragically. Sorry fellas, it will never work.'[49]

Cheryl Crawford's place was taken within a couple of weeks by Robert E. Griffith[50] and the young Harold S. Prince.[51] Griffith and Prince had been stage managers for *Wonderful Town* in 1953,[52] and their recent production successes had included *The Pajama Game* (1954) and *Damn Yankees* (1955). Prince and Sondheim were already friends, and they discussed the situation on the phone. When Crawford withdrew, Prince was in Boston with Griffith for the tryout of *New Girl In Town*. Prince spoke to Griffith and called back within 15 minutes to say that they could come to New York the next Sunday. In fact, Prince was already familiar with the score: 'I knew the show backwards and forward, though Bobby [Griffith] had not heard it, for Steve had played all the music for me, unbeknownst to Lenny, since he didn't want anybody to hear it.'[53] *New Girl In Town* opened on 14 May 1957, and the next day Griffith and Prince got to work raising the capital for *West Side Story* ($300,000 'within the week'[54]), and the show was able to go into rehearsal only a few weeks later than originally planned.

At the time of Crawford's departure the casting of the principals was not finalized. Carol Lawrence was near the start of her career when she was eventually cast as Maria. Her Broadway debut had been in *Leonard Sillman's New Faces of 1952*, since when she had appeared as a replacement dancer in the Albert Hague musical *Plain*

---

48 Zadan 1974, p. 16.
49 Lawrence 1990, p. 38.
50 Robert E. Griffith (1907–1961) began his Broadway career as an actor in 1929 and later turned to stage management and production.
51 Hal Prince [Harold S. Prince] (b. 1928) first worked on Broadway in 1950 as Assistant Stage Manager for the revue *Tickets, Please!* and the hit musical *Call Me Madam*.
52 Griffith was credited as Production Stage Manager, Prince as Stage Manager.
53 Zadan 1974, p. 17.
54 Zadan 1974, p. 17.

and Fancy in 1955,[55] then in the flop *Shangri-La* (which ran for just 21 performances in June 1956). In March 1957 she joined the *Ziegfeld Follies of 1957* (starring Bea Lillie) at the Winter Garden Theatre. The role of Maria offered her the chance of a major break, but it was certainly not easy for Lawrence to get the part:

> Over quite a long period, I auditioned thirteen times for the role of Maria in what they finally called *West Side Story*. Even then thirteen auditions was a lot, and today Actors Equity would not permit it.[56] But I was working in other shows and I could be patient. Besides, maybe people were right – maybe *West Side Story* would never happen.
>
> When I was called back for the thirteenth time, Larry Kert was there to audition for the role of Tony. We had read for the roles together before, but this time I had asked if we could take the scenes home and memorize them. Jerry Robbins had agreed. But instead of asking us to sing a few songs, Jerry told Larry to go backstage and wait there. Then he said 'You,' pointing to me but calling me 'Maria.'
>
> 'See that scaffolding up there over the stage?' he said. 'Look around, find out how to get up there. Then stay there out of sight.'
>
> It was an unusual request, but … I found a narrow metal ladder leading up to who knows where, and up I went. Jerry called Larry onstage and told him to find me and take it from there. Up where I was, I began to feel as if I really were Maria, watching Tony search for me, but afraid to call out for fear of alerting my family. And Larry/Tony was genuinely desperate to find me. By the time he saw me and climbed up to where I was, the two of us were almost breathless. We did the Balcony Scene from there.
>
> When we came down, Jerry said 'You've both got the parts,' and then went onto other things. He was like that. I burst into tears of relief. The producer, Hal Prince, said 'No, really – you're Maria!' Then I cried for pure joy.[57]

It had apparently been a close-run thing. As the *New York Times* revealed a few days before the Broadway opening, 'almost to the end Miss Lawrence ran even with a Lebanese girl whose voice was greatly admired'.[58] By 3 June 1957, the *New York Times* was able to report that the principal roles had been cast: 'The cast is to include

---

[55]   Hague's biggest Broadway success was *Redhead* (1959), starring Gwen Verdon, directed and choreographed by Bob Fosse. Hague (1920–2001) achieved celebrity in later life as the music teacher Benjamin Shorofsky in Alan Parker's film *Fame!* and in the subsequent television spin-off series.

[56]   Actors' Equity would not permit someone to audition that many times today without being paid.

[57]   Lawrence 1990, pp. 38–9. In an e-mail to the present author (28 September 2009), Stephen Sondheim wrote: 'The reason that Carol got the part was that after many auditions in which she seemed no more than a possible Maria understudy, Arthur suggested she read with a Puerto Rican accent. We hired her immediately.'

[58]   Schumach 1957.

Carol Lawrence, Larry Kert, Chita Rivera and perhaps David Winters.'[59] All four were to be in the show, but there are some intriguing names (and comments) to be found in the audition lists annotated by Bernstein. On 7 May 1957, those auditioning included Chita Rivera as Anita (no comment from Bernstein, but a tick next to her name), Lee Becker as Anybodys (Bernstein thought she was 'terrific'), Larry Kert trying for the part of Bernardo ('Great songs & performer. But looks? Read Riff better') and Carol Lawrence as Maria ('Lovely soprano. Not quite Maria. Much realer with accent'); all of them were eventually cast (though with Larry Kert as Tony rather than either of the parts he read that day). Mickey Calin – the original Riff – obviously came a long way during rehearsals: at his audition, Bernstein had noted 'Wrong for R[iff]. No actor. Tappish dance, clean, good looking'. Also auditioned that day were three others who were to make it into the original cast: Tony Mordente (A-Rab), Arch Johnson (Schrank), Art Smith (Doc) and David Winters (Baby John).

Just over a week later, on 16 May, Lawrence was back again and Kert now auditioned for Tony. But we also find Warren Beatty – later to achieve renown in Hollywood – up for the part of Riff ('Good voice. Can't open jaw. Charming as hell') and Jerry Orbach – the future star of *Promises, Promises* (Chuck Baxter) and *Chicago* (Billy Flynn) – trying for the part of Chino ('Good read. Good loud bar[itone]'). Suzanne Pleshette – who played Annie Hayworth in Alfred Hitchcock's *The Birds* (1963) and was Bob Newhart's wife in the television sitcom *The Bob Newhart Show* – auditioning for the part of Maria, was obviously having a bad day: Bernstein notes simply that she was 'hoarse'. Laurents recalled that 'In casting *West Side*, we had to make compromises, and I think most of them were made by Lenny and Steve. People didn't expect much acting in musicals then. We had to find people who could move, who could dance.'[60] True enough, although in terms of singing the young cast made a good job of the music in the end. This was Larry Kert's first Broadway show, but Sondheim encouraged him to audition for Tony (after he had been rejected as Bernardo, Riff and even as a chorus member). Chita Rivera had taken a few small roles on Broadway since 1955, most recently as the standby for Mehitabel in *Shinbone Alley*, a show in which Reri Grist and David Winters – both to be cast in *West Side Story* – were also performing. The assistant conductor was Frederick Vogelgesang, who was to perform the same function in *West Side Story*.[61]

As well as revealing some of the cast, Sam Zolotow's article on 3 June in the *Times* also reported that the show's title had changed again: '*Gangway!* is the new title for the Arthur Laurents–Leonard Bernstein–Steve Sondheim musical formerly

---

[59] Zolotow 1957.

[60] Zadan 1974, p. 17.

[61] *Shinbone Alley*, with music by George Kleinsinger, lyrics by Joe Dalton, and a book by Joe Dalton and Mel Brooks, was based on the *Archie and Mehitabel* stories by Don Marquis. It opened on 13 April 1957 and closed on 25 May after 49 performances. Among the show's other credits are additional orchestrations by Irwin Kostal.

titled *West Side Story*.'[62] On the same day the *Herald Tribune* gave a slightly different version of the new title: it would 'henceforth be known as *Gang Way!*'. This idea did not last long, as Lewis Funke reported three weeks later:

> Not the least of the thousand and one crises that afflict the preparation of shows is the quest for a title. … For instance, take the musical that has been fashioned by Arthur Laurents, Leonard Bernstein and Steve Sondheim. For a year or more it was known as *West Side Story*. Not so long ago the news went forth that henceforth the show would be called *Gangway!* Now reports indicate that *Gangway!* is in decline.[63]

However, the title still appeared as *Gang Way!* in next morning's *New York Times*, which announced that rehearsals were starting that day, Wednesday, 24 June 1957.

At the very end of June, Bernstein was interviewed in the *Washington Star* and talked, among other things, about his uneasiness with the show's titles:

> What Mr. Bernstein came to Washington with was a title problem. The new musical … has been variously known as *West Side Story* and *Gang Way!*
>
> 'I'm not happy about either of those,' said Mr. Bernstein. 'I don't like that "Story." It sounds like a documentary or a class B movie. And the action doesn't necessarily take place on the West Side. *Gang Way!* is worse. It makes me think of *Sailor Beware* or *Anchors Aweigh*. In fact, we're having a meeting tomorrow to make a final decision on this.'[64] …
>
> 'This isn't *Romeo and Juliet* in modern dress,' he explains. 'But we do have a Romeo and Juliet situation in that the boy and girl are kept apart by the feud between rival gangs, one of Puerto Rican immigrants. The Puerto Rican influx in New York figures in the story and has tremendous excitement, even violence.' …
>
> 'This has tremendous potential,' he said. 'If it comes off Broadway musicals will never be the same again.' He paused to reflect, then added, 'If it doesn't, they will be.'[65]

By the time this article appeared on 30 June the meeting had already taken place, as the *Daily News* revealed a day earlier: 'The title of the new Leonard Bernstein musical play, due at the National for three weeks starting August 19, has been finally nailed down. It's *West Side Story*.'[66] A week later, Arthur Gelb in the *New York Times* gave a reason for the change – and added details of the Musical Director: 'A

---

[62]   Zolotow 1957.

[63]   Funke 1957b.

[64]   According to Sondheim (e-mail to the present author, 28 September 2009), Bernstein suggested the title 'Tony 'n' Maria'.

[65]   *Washington Star*, 30 June 1957.

[66]   *Washington Daily News*, 29 June 1957.

spokesman for the musical explained that *Gangway* was "felt to be a misleading title." … Max Goberman was signed last week as musical conductor.'[67]

A Conductor for *West Side Story*

Max Goberman was hired to conduct *West Side Story* seven weeks before the first night of tryouts in Washington, and a week after Robbins, Bernstein and Sondheim had started to rehearse the cast. He was to prove a good choice for dealing with such a complex new Broadway score. Born in 1911, Goberman had studied the violin with Leopold Auer and conducting with Fritz Reiner; he played in the Philadelphia Orchestra before embarking on a successful conducting career. As well as *West Side Story*, Goberman's Broadway conducting credits included Bernstein's *On the Town* (1944), Morton Gould's *Billion Dollar Baby* (1946), Frank Loesser's *Where's Charley?* (1948), Arthur Schwartz's *A Tree Grows In Brooklyn* (1951) and Jerry Herman's *Milk and Honey* (1961). But there was more to Goberman. Something of his energy – and his wide range of enthusiasms – comes across in a review by Ross Parmenter in the *New York Times* describing a Goberman concert of Baroque music:

> Max Goberman, the wiry little conductor with the pointed beard who leads *West Side Story* with such dynamic intensity, is what some of the rough-talking youngsters in the Broadway show might call a baroque buff.
>
> Earlier this season, in breaks between Saturday matinee and evening performances of the Leonard Bernstein musical, Mr. Goberman led the New York Sinfonietta in two all-Vivaldi programs. Yesterday, a Sunday when he had the whole day free, he turned to Handel, an even greater baroque master. And this time the conductor did something he has not done in more than twenty years. He appeared in public as a violinist.[68]

Goberman was the first conductor to embark on recording a complete series of the Haydn symphonies (before his death, 45 symphonies were set down for his own label, Library of Recorded Masterpieces, using H.C. Robbins Landon's new edition of the scores, which were also included in the original issues of the records) and on an even more ambitious project to record all of Vivaldi's concertos (which included copies of the Ricordi editions) – a project that was even pursued in the orchestra pit during performances of *West Side Story*.[69]

---

[67]   Gelb 1957.

[68]   Parmenter 1959.

[69]   Goberman studied the scores of Vivaldi concertos in the pit at the Winter Garden during stretches of dialogue and wrote an amusing article on the subject. 'The question naturally arises in the minds of some people, "How does a theatre conductor (especially a ten-time offender) get involved in this baroque music?" The answer to this is perhaps another

During rehearsals, conductor, composer and orchestrators did not always see eye to eye. Irwin Kostal recalled that

> the orchestra rehearsals were terrific, and also very difficult. The conductor was Max Goberman ... Max had a special clause in his contract forbidding Lenny from conducting, even at rehearsals. One day we were rehearsing in the theatre second floor lobby, under very crowded conditions, and Lenny, Sid [Ramin] and I were sitting very close to Max as he was conducting. At the end of a never-before played orchestration, Max turned around and facing the three of us said, 'That's without doubt the worst arrangement I have ever heard,' to which Lenny answered 'Give me the baton and I'll show you how it should be done.' Max answered, 'No, no, it says in my contract ...' Lenny interrupted him saying, 'Now you do it in the right tempo, and you'll find it's perfectly all right.'[70]

Goberman's death in Vienna, on 31 December 1962, was barely reported at the time: there was a newspaper strike in New York. Later tributes included one from the musicologist Paul Henry Lang, who described him as a 'devoted musician of sterling integrity',[71] while Bernstein himself, at a New York Philharmonic concert in May 1963, dedicated a performance of Vivaldi's 'Spring' from *The Four Seasons* to the memory of his friend, describing Goberman's work as 'witty and lyrical',[72] epithets that can well be applied to his conducting of *West Side Story*, to judge from the cast recording.

West Side Story in Rehearsal

As noted in the *New York Times*, rehearsals started on 24 June. Two weeks later, the *Herald Tribune* described the unusually long rehearsal period for *West Side Story* – almost twice as long as the norm for Broadway musicals – and interviewed the show's new producers:

---

question, which goes this way. "How does an admirer of baroque music get trapped in the theatre, especially ten times?" Part of the answer lies in those periods of a musical show that do not call for music. It is amazing to discover the speed with which one can signal the last note of a Ballet Sequence and resume studying the sequence and harmonies of a Vivaldi score, while the characters on stage continue with dialogue or mayhem. Of course, one develops another set of reflexes aimed at being aware of the next place where music must start. You must be able to tear yourself away from a long basso ostinato in Vivaldi (even before it has given in) to face a sometime obstinate bass player in real life and warn him to be ready to start on time. This was standard operating procedure in the "Cool" number in Leonard Bernstein's excellent score for *West Side Story*' (Goberman 1959).

[70]   Kostal, unpublished memoirs.
[71]   *Musical Quarterly*, 51 (3) (1965), 586.
[72]   Reported in the *New York Times*, 10 May 1963.

The show will have eight instead of the traditional (for musicals) five weeks of rehearsal, to give Mr. Robbins time for direction and choreography. It will open in Washington 'because everything there is air-conditioned, the people are used to going to theater in the heat and you do good business there in the summer.' Beyond the 'kind of fascinating' Oliver Smith sets, which Mr. Griffith considers 'the most exciting scenery Smith has done,' the big offering in this 'love story between young people of conflicting racial backgrounds' is, Mr. Griffith said, that 'it introduces forty kids, between the ages of sixteen and twenty-two, who are loaded with talent.'

'We'll have every movie scout in town knocking on our door,' Mr. Prince said contentedly.[73]

Jerome Robbins ran notoriously arduous and demanding rehearsals, driving his young cast beyond exhaustion. He 'pushed everyone past the comfort level, sometimes blind to everything but the task in hand'.[74] Larry Kert called the rehearsals with Robbins 'a very painful experience',[75] and Carol Lawrence described Robbins's punishing methods in some detail:

Never have I worked with anyone more tyrannical than Jerome Robbins. When he is working, it is the work that matters and not any of the people involved in it … We learned very quickly that he demanded more of us than we ever thought we could give – and that if we didn't meet those expectations, we were out.

We rehearsed and lived by strict rules. We had to literally become our roles. We were not allowed to call ourselves or each other by our real names. We had to use the names of the characters we played. I was Maria, never Carol. The actor playing my brother was Bernardo, not Kenny [Le Roy]. To keep us from slipping out of character, Jerry would suddenly ask us questions about our parents – not our real parents, but the parents of the characters we were playing, even if those parents weren't mentioned in the show. He trained us to imagine what it would be like to *be* the characters we played, and to discover why we were the way we were … We humane, civilized actors became the hate-filled, violent street gangs we were portraying. If you think onstage was exciting, it didn't compare to backstage! The Sharks and the Jets lived! Violence and sexual intimidation, fights and injuries, you name it – it was going on and getting worse … In rehearsal, Jerry was unmerciful in his pursuit of perfection. The slightest mistake in a dance step, gesture or word met a fate worse than death.[76]

Brutal they may have been, but Robbins's methods certainly got results – even when the cast was outside the theatre. The *Washington Post* reported:

---

[73] *Herald Tribune*, 7 July 1957.
[74] Jowitt 2004, p. 276.
[75] Zadan 1974, p. 19.
[76] Lawrence 1990, pp. 42–3.

Policemen along the 52nd St. beat are having a spot of trouble trying to decide which passing youths are juvenile delinquents and which are merely singers and dancers on their way to rehearsals for *The West Side Story* at the ANTA Theatre. Tough youths are the theme of the show, and the members of the cast look and dress the part.[77]

By contrast, working with Bernstein and Sondheim was a much less gruelling experience. Photographs show their smiling faces with the cast gathered around the piano, and these suggest a very different atmosphere from the harsh method-acting regime that was the norm in Robbins's rehearsals.[78] Bernstein seems to have been at his most encouraging and supportive during these music calls, and Carol Lawrence remembers that rehearsals with him were an oasis of calm after the stormy sessions with Robbins:

The opposite style, and in this show the balance to Jerry's, was Leonard Bernstein's. Here, too, was a genius, but one who was sensitive to the feelings, needs and anxieties of human beings. Very often after Jerry took us apart, Lenny would put us back together again. None of us was an opera singer, and we knew it,[79] yet we were singing opera. If Lenny saw that we were having difficulty with a passage in a song, he would say: 'Tell me, how does that note feel in your mouth? If it doesn't feel comfortable, I'll change it.' He would work with each of us on an individual basis for hours, and we couldn't take our eyes off his face, because so many emotions were written there ... He didn't drive us: he led us by believing in us. He is one of the gentlest, most thoughtful men I have ever known, and we knocked ourselves out for him because we loved him.[80]

Chita Rivera, who auditioned six times before she was given the role of Anita, remembered learning 'A Boy Like That' with Bernstein. It was a song she initially found very difficult to pitch; Bernstein was patient but determined:

I remember sitting next to Lenny and his starting with 'A Boy Like That,' teaching it to me, and me saying, 'I'll never do this, I can't hit those notes, I don't know how to hit those notes.' And he made me do it, and he taught me *how* to hit those

[77] Kilgallen 1957.

[78] These rehearsal photographs include a series by Friedman-Abeles printed in the souvenir programme book for the original production, and earlier used for a photo story in *New York Times* 1957.

[79] The exception was Reri Grist, the original Consuelo, who went on to a highly successful operatic career in Europe (including regular appearances with Karl Böhm at the Salzburg Festival and the Vienna State Opera) and in New York at the Metropolitan Opera.

[80] Lawrence 1990, p. 46.

notes, and once I got past the fact that I was sitting on a piano stool next to Leonard Bernstein, I was okay![81]

Bernstein himself clearly played for a few rehearsals, and there are rehearsal photographs of Sondheim sitting at the piano. But according to Sondheim, 'I played almost nothing for the rehearsals; most of them were played by Betty Walberg.'[82] Walberg (1921–1990) was a pianist, composer and arranger who often worked with Jerome Robbins (her later credits included *Gypsy* and *Fiddler on the Roof*). Her name is also to be found in one of the manuscripts of the 'Cool' Fugue in LBC, which includes a note written to 'Betty' by Bernstein.[83]

What were the cast singing at the start of the rehearsal process? A handwritten music list by Bernstein, probably dating from May 1957, just before rehearsals started, gives a running order, complete with the forces required for some of the numbers.[84]

[Act I]
Opening: Dancers
Jet Song: Riff – Snowboy, Action, Jets
Crystal Cave: Dancers (Gangs – Atom Bomb Mambo)
Maria
Balcony
America: Shark girls (Shark boys?)
Cool: Riff, Jets
Quintet: Gangs too?
One
Mix (Rumble): Gangs

[Act II]
Pretty: Shark girls (2 or 4)
Somewhere: Dancers
Krupke: Snowboy, Action, (Baby John), Anybodys, A-Rab, (Baby John as Krupke?), (Diesel as Krupke)
Boy Like That
Taunting: Jets
Finale: Maria, Tutti?

---

[81]   NPR 2007.

[82]   Stephen Sondheim, e-mail to the present author, 13 November 2008.

[83]   'Cool – Extra Variation, Insert A'. The note at the top of the first page of music reads: 'Betty – don't try to play the canon. Play the bass only.'

[84]   LBC.

In this list, 'Mix!' (discussed in detail in Chapter 3) has been moved from the first scene to the end of Act I. The final form of the Quintet as a large ensemble is hinted at here with Bernstein's suggestion that 'Gangs too' could be added. The Act II Finale was to prove intractable, but at this point Bernstein was clearly envisaging either a solo for Maria or something to be sung by the whole company. In the end, neither of these things happened. But of the other songs, the 'Jet Song', 'Maria', 'America', 'Cool', 'One Hand, One Heart', 'I Feel Pretty' and 'Somewhere' existed in some form, as did some of the instrumental numbers, and the 'Opening' (almost certainly still in its vocal version). But many changes were made before the show moved to Washington in the second week of August. The most revealing evidence for this is to be found in Bernstein's manuscripts, the subject of the next chapter.

Chapter 3
The Musical Manuscripts

There are comprehensive holdings of sketches and musical manuscripts for *West Side Story* in LBC (see Appendix I). This material reveals a great deal about the show's musical genesis, although only a few of the manuscripts are dated. Given the way a Broadway show is composed, it is not surprising that there is no single autograph manuscript of the complete work. Nor is there any autograph material in orchestral score, but the manuscripts do include a number of earlier versions of familiar songs, some that were cut, some that were borrowed from earlier works, and some that reveal a complex revision process. This summary highlights the music that was either cut or extensively revised. First, the surviving cut numbers are described, then follows an overview of the musical revisions of the whole show, scene by scene.

Cut Numbers

There are manuscripts in LBC of several numbers that were unused in the final version of the show. These include 'Mix!' and 'This Turf Is Ours!', both originally written for the end of the opening scene; the First Mambo and Huapango, both intended for the Dance at the Gym; and 'Like Everybody Else', a trio for Anybodys, A-Rab and Baby John in Act I, scene 6. The instrumental Prologue as eventually performed was an extensively revised version of an earlier vocal setting, using much the same musical material. Arthur Laurents originally wrote the final scene as a dummy lyric, and Bernstein, according to his own testimony, made several abortive attempts at setting it: 'I can't tell you how many tries I made on that aria. I tried once to make it cynical and swift. Another time like a Puccini aria. In every case, after five or six bars, I gave up. It was phony.'[1] It is possible that Bernstein sketched some ideas, although no manuscript material is known to survive for any setting of Maria's final speech in the Finale.[2]

This is a very low casualty rate for a Broadway show, compared with Bernstein's own *Candide* or a famous hit like *Fiddler on the Roof* (whose second act was almost

---

[1] Bernstein quoted in Stearns 1985.

[2] However, as John Mauceri has recalled, 'On a number of occasions [Bernstein] played for me a parody of what he had attempted in 1957. Hearing him sing "How do you fire this gun, Chino?" as a recitative, remains a vivid memory' (Mauceri 2007, p. 16).

completely rewritten during out-of-town tryouts).[3] Relatively few songs in *West Side Story* were cut, and they are of high quality.

'Mix!' (Act I, Scene 1)

'Mix!' was originally intended as the second number in Act I, scene 1 – where the 'Jet Song' now comes. There was to be a rumble at this early point in the show (and when the fight was moved to the end of the act, so was 'Mix!' before being cut completely). The uncompromising lyrics of 'Mix!' leave us in no doubt of the Jets' intentions:

> Mix! Make a mess of 'em.
> Pay the Puerto Ricans back,
> Make a mess of 'em.
> If you let us take a crack,
> There'll be less of 'em,
> There'll be less of 'em.
>
> Mix! We can cut 'em up.
> If you only say the word,
> We can cut 'em up.
> Go ahead and say the word,
> And we'll shut 'em up,
> We can shut 'em up.

There was apparently a problem with hearing these splendidly nasty lyrics in performance, especially when Bernstein makes a canon of the theme. As he later put it, 'That was a very exciting song, but you couldn't understand anything the players were saying because it was too fast, too complicated, too canonical, too contrapuntal. So we wrote another one, called the "Jet Song."'[4] But 'Mix!' was also too aggressive for the opening of the show, pre-empting as it did the eruption of violence at the close of the act, and even when it was moved to the end of the act, it was felt not to work there either (Ex. 3.1).

Never one to waste a good idea, Bernstein used almost all of this number in the second movement of the *Chichester Psalms* (1965). His eventual recycling of the 'Mix!' music had uncanny parallels with the idea of conflict in the original song: 'Lamah rag'shu goyim' ('Why do the nations rage'), a passage from Psalm 2 about the futility of nation fighting nation. When Walter Hussey first wrote to Bernstein to commission the *Chichester Psalms*, he asked particularly that Bernstein 'might

---

[3]   Of the musical numbers listed for Act II in the programme for the Detroit tryout of *Fiddler on the Roof*, just one song ('Far From the Home I Love') remained by the time it reached Broadway; one of the casualties was a long Act II ballet devised by Jerome Robbins.

[4]   Kasha and Hirschhorn 1985, p. 15.

consider a setting of Psalm 2', adding 'we should not mind if it had a touch of the idiom of *West Side Story*'.[5] Little did Hussey realize that Bernstein gave him rather more than a 'touch' of *West Side Story* for this psalm setting.[6]

Example 3.1 'Mix!', opening

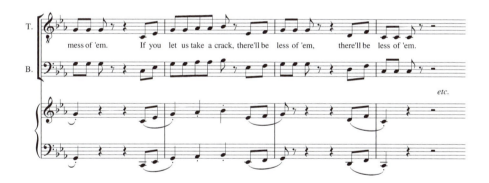

'This Turf Is Ours!' (Act I, Scene 1)

This was written in Washington as a possible replacement for the 'Jet Song' and on one sketch the start of the number is described as 'Prologue variant', and so it is: the tune starts with the familiar rising figure C–F–F–B (Ex. 3.2).

---

5   Hussey 1985, p. 112.

6   The *Chichester Psalms* drew heavily on earlier works. As well as rescuing 'Mix!', it also used music that Bernstein had originally composed for a production of Thornton Wilder's *The Skin of Our Teeth* (the whole of the first movement and the slow parts of the second are both reworkings of this incidental music).

Example 3.2 'This Turf Is Ours!', opening

A little later in the song, the music used in the 'Jet Song' for 'You're never alone, / You're never disconnected' is set to the words 'We're stakin' a claim / The boundaries are set out'. Sondheim told Craig Zadan about the reasons for writing the song, and for its subsequent rejection: 'We wrote a new opening because everyone felt the opening wasn't violent enough. The new opening, "This Turf is Ours!", was *really* violent and everyone thought it was *too* violent, so we went back to the "Jet Song".'[7] Sondheim is not exaggerating about the forcefulness of the lyrics:

> This turf is ours!
> Drew a big white line
> With a keep out sign
> And they crossed it!
>
> This turf is ours!
> Got ta hold our ground
> Or we'll turn around
> And we've lost it!
>
> We're stakin' a claim
> The boundaries are set out.
> The foreigners came,
> Well now they're gonna get out!

The music for this number was recycled a few years later for an altogether more celebratory purpose: the main tune formed the basis of Bernstein's *Fanfare for the Inauguration of John F. Kennedy*, scored for wind, brass and percussion (by Sid Ramin) and first performed at Kennedy's Inaugural Gala at the National Armory, Washington DC, on 19 January 1961.

First Mambo and Huapango (Act I, Scene 3)

The dance scene (eventually called the 'Dance at the Gym') was originally set at the Crystal Cave, a nightclub, and most of the manuscript material mentions this. Two unused dances for this scene survive. The first is described on the manuscript as 'First Mambo'. It is 42 bars long and is marked *Moderato*. Ostensibly, this 'First Mambo' bears no relationship to the familiar Mambo from the Dance at the Gym. After a four-bar introduction, Bernstein introduces an uneasy, obsessive ostinato mainly in quavers (E–F–B–B, E–F–B– | C, D–B), notable for its prominent F–B tritones. These notes are also present in the right-hand chords that interject at the ends of phrases. The language is quite dissonant and unsettled throughout the number. At the end of this manuscript there is a note: 'to Sentimental Mambo'. This is clearly

---

[7] Zadan 1974, p. 25.

not the Mambo from the Dance at the Gym since that is anything but sentimental. Is it possible that Bernstein was referring to the Cha-Cha? Or perhaps it is a reference to a dance that has disappeared, or to one that was never written.

Another manuscript indicates not only that Bernstein changed his mind, but that there was also a direct musical link between this 'First Mambo' and the Mambo that was eventually used. Headed 'Version B (mambo)', this two-page manuscript combines ideas from both (Ex. 3.3a). This leads directly to the return of the ostinato figure of the 'First Mambo', at which point Bernstein has written 'Maria enters' (Ex. 3.3b).

A note at the end of this manuscript suggests two possible continuations and provides a clue as to how the 'First Mambo' would have fitted into the overall scheme of the Dance at the Gym: 'Segue "First Mambo" … then into "Fast Mambo" for competition', and 'Alternate version B: extend 2nd ending [i.e. the 'First Mambo' ostinato] with drums, dim. for Maria's entrance and cut directly to "Fast Mambo", sub. ff'. Neither of these solutions was adopted, as the 'First Mambo' was dropped entirely.

Example 3.3a 'Version B (mambo)', autograph manuscript, showing Bernstein combining elements of the 'First Mambo' and the Mambo

Example 3.3b   'Version B (mambo)', autograph manuscript, showing Maria's first entry

The Huapango, 24 bars long, is marked 'Fast and light' and is based on a spiky little chromatic theme in quavers (B–C sharp–D sharp–E, D natural–C natural–B–A, G–A–B–C) that appears nowhere else in the score (Ex. 3.4). The manuscript is part of a substantial bundle of sketches with the title 'Crystal Cave Fragments' that also contains much of the music that was eventually used for the Dance at the Gym.

Example 3.4   Huapango, opening

'Like Everybody Else' (Act I, Scene 6)

'Like Everybody Else', sometimes referred to as 'Kids Ain't' or 'Kid Stuff', is a sharp, witty trio in which Anybodys sings about how she wishes she were a boy too ('I swear and I smoke and I inhale. / Why can't I be male / Like everybody else?'). The number was written in Washington during tryouts, but it was never heard in the show (nor was it orchestrated at the time[8]). As Sondheim recalls,

> we *were* busy in Washington for a while because Jerry had a strong feeling that there was a sag in the middle of the first act, so we wrote a number for the three young kids – Anybodys, A-Rab, and Baby John. It was called 'Kids Ain't' and was a terrific trio that we all loved.

---

[8]   Sid Ramin, personal communication.

Why, then, was this edgy and entertaining song never used? Sondheim provides the answer: 'Arthur gave a most eloquent speech about how he loved it also but that we shouldn't use it, because it would be a crowd-pleaser.'[9] Laurents confirms this:

> Another song, 'Kid stuff' [i.e. 'Like Everybody Else'], which might have been … successful with the audience, was written in Washington immediately after we opened there. Steve and Lenny played it for Jerry, me and the producers, we all agreed it was terrific and it was. Then, regretfully, I pointed out it would tip the show over into musical comedy … the song was out before it went in.[10]

According to Sondheim, Robbins wanted a number for Lee Becker,[11] the original Anybodys. After Laurents explained why he thought the song was inappropriate at this point in the show, Bernstein and Sondheim agreed to its removal and so, on a majority vote, it was cut.

Revisions and Additions

There was never a lot of surplus music in the show, but several numbers were subjected to major revision. These alterations had an impact ranging from the very first bars (just how should *West Side Story* begin?) to the very last (the final, unsettling F sharp was an afterthought – it does not appear in any of the manuscript sources or in the first edition of the piano-vocal score). The following is a summary of those numbers with the most significant changes.

Act I, Scene 1: The Original Opening

At least three numbers composed for the opening scene were tried out and rejected for various reasons. 'Mix!' and 'This Turf Is Ours!' were for later in the scene and were both cut (see above), but the most extensive number to be rewritten was the original 'Opening', later called 'Prologue' in its refashioned, purely instrumental form. A complete manuscript fair copy of the original version exists in Stephen Sondheim's handwriting,[12] as does a complete sketch by Bernstein; the number was evidently replaced quite late on, as copies of a piano-vocal score of the vocal Opening were reproduced for use in rehearsals.[13] The musical components of this original opening number were later reworked as the Prologue and the Jet Song,

---

[9]   Zadan 1974, p. 25.

[10] Laurents 2000, p. 351.

[11] Also known as Lee Theodore and Lee Becker Theodore. She died in 1987 at the age of 54.

[12] A photocopy is in LBC.

[13] Copy in the Sid Ramin Papers at Columbia University.

with some change in the order. Briefly, the original vocal number was structured as follows: in the Opening and the Prologue the music is similar at the start, beginning with the same syncopated chords, the main difference being that originally the falling tune was sung by Baby John ('How long does it take to reach the moon-a-rooney?'), joined by Mouthpiece, Snowboy, Action and Diesel.[14] Then, following three bars of the syncopated chords, the next music, sung by all the gang, is the tune that was later used in the middle of the Jet Song (bar 100 onwards), with lyrics that already look forward to the dance, still referred to here as the 'Crystal Cave' ('And when those chicks dig us at the Crystal Cave they're gonna give, gonna give like they never gave'). The syncopated chords and the falling tune return as Riff enters 'almost whispering', and there is a short passage where the gang talk together, before Riff leads the other Jets in the fast music later used from bar 140 of the Prologue onwards. Eventually the excitement subsides and the opening chords and falling tune return, leading to a new section for Riff: 'My Greatest Day' is an early version of the main part of the Jet Song. After this, the syncopated chords return, and the number ends with Riff whistling the first five notes of the falling tune, and a final bar that is identical to that of the Prologue.

The original Broadway cast recording starts the Prologue with the rising 'shofar call' (see Chapter 4), as does Bernstein's manuscript piano score, and this is clearly the music described by Irwin Kostal as the 'opening three-note motif, fanfarish in style' that Bernstein had played during rehearsals. Moreover, this three-note motif is also to be found in the professionally copied piano-vocal score of the Prologue that was printed for rehearsals, a copy of which in the Sid Ramin collection (with Jerome Robbins's signature in the upper right corner) has an annotation in red ink: a bracket around the opening bars (the fanfare) and a note written above, 'optional curtain music' (Ex. 3.5).

Example 3.5 Prologue, opening, as it appears in Bernstein's autograph

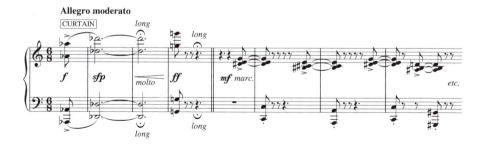

---

[14] Block 1997, p. 253 includes a music example from this passage.

However, the Ramin full score and all the printed scores of *West Side Story* (apart from the *Symphonic Dances*) begin without this musical call to action, starting straight in at the uneasy syncopated chords. There was clearly some indecision about this, as the earlier vocal version of the Opening also begins straight in at the chords.

Act I, Scene 2: 'Something's Coming'

The last song to be added to *West Side Story* was 'Something's Coming'. It was written on 7 August 1957, 12 days before the Washington opening. Bernstein described the song in a letter to his wife Felicia:

> I missed you terribly yesterday – we wrote a new song for Tony that's a killer, & it just wasn't the same not playing it first for you. It's really going to save his character – a driving 2/4 in the great tradition (but of course fucked up by me with 3/4s and what not) – but it gives Tony balls – so that he doesn't emerge as just a euphoric dreamer.[15]

Stephen Sondheim made a small musical contribution to this song:

> We wrote that during rehearsals, because Larry Kert, playing the lead, needed a number to give him some strength at the beginning of the show. ... We thought we could launch it by having him sing a song early on, a specific kind of song called a 'two-four', a very driving kind of showbiz song. Larry and Judy Garland were the champs at that kind of song – as in 'The Trolley Song'. I thought we ought to write a two-four for him. Lenny Bernstein wrote the verse part and said how do you make this into a two-four? He knew what it was, but it's a showbiz term more than a musical term. So I started to ad lib with the thumb line (that is to say, the cello line, an inner voice). That's what I contributed, the two-four part of that.[16]

Sondheim's instincts played an important part in determining the kind of song this was to be, but, as he makes clear, the music is almost entirely Bernstein's own (and the surviving manuscripts are in Bernstein's hand). This number also caused problems for the orchestrators. According to Sid Ramin: 'Every show seems to have one number that needs constant rewriting and re-orchestrating. That distinction went to "Something's Coming".'[17]

---

[15]   Letter dated 8 August 1957, LBC.

[16]   Stephen Sondheim in conversation with Jeremy Sams, National Theatre, London, 1 June 1993.

[17]   Ramin 2001.

Act 1, Scene 4: Dance at the Gym

One manuscript of the Mambo is entitled 'Fast Mambo (Merengue)' and gives the dance more or less as it appears in the final version. Another manuscript, part of the 'Crystal Cave Fragments' already mentioned, contains the rest of the music for this scene, along with the cut Huapango. There is also an eight-bar sketch for the Mambo where it is called 'Atom Bomb Mambo'. These bars are the equivalent of bars 130–36 of the Dance at the Gym in the final version,[18] but here the last four bars are set to two possible sets of sketched lyrics: 'Mushroom! Va va voom! Fall out! Router bout [?]', or 'Warhead. What you said? Neutron. Man you're gone!' The titles of two dances eventually included in the Dance at the Gym are slightly different in the manuscript sources: the Blues has a title page describing it as 'Brotherhood Hall: Blues', while the Jump is entitled '(Competitive?) Jump (Crystal Cave)' and begins with a four-bar introduction (borrowed from the bass line in bars 228–31 of the 'Prologue') that was subsequently cut. See also **Cut Numbers**, above.

Act I, Scene 5: Balcony Scene and 'America'

The Balcony Scene seems to have been as problematic as the opening. At one time or another, at least three different songs – all of them, incidentally, surviving in the show – were intended for the scene. The first was 'Somewhere'. A surviving page of typescript in LBC is headed 'Balcony Scene ("Heaven")', the lyrics – by Bernstein himself – beginning with Tony singing 'Where is darkness gone? / Where is all darkness gone? / What new earth are we living on? / Can it be / Heaven?' The tune for this song was recast with new lyrics as 'Somewhere' and moved to the Act II ballet, but elements of it appear in many places elsewhere in the work – including the final version of the Balcony Scene, where it is to be heard in the underscoring near the end, and the closing bars (see Chapter 4).

Another song – probably intended to follow 'Somewhere' rather than to replace it – was a strong candidate, even during rehearsals. This was 'One', in other words 'One Hand, One Heart'. A fair copy of the piano-vocal score is headed 'Act I Sc. 4. Duet: One … (Balcony Scene)'. On the title page, the last two words have been crossed out and '(Wedding)' added in their place. The lyrics in this manuscript are clearly intended for the Balcony Scene.

The gentle triple-time melody of 'One' has a complex history. Among the manuscripts for Bernstein's *Candide* there is a love duet (for Candide and Cunegonde) composed for Act II, scene 3, but ultimately cut. Intriguingly – given its eventual destination – this was to have been followed by a 'Marriage Ceremony', which was also cut. In the *Candide* 'Marriage Ceremony', scored for chorus, with lines spoken by Candide and Cunegonde, the 'One Hand, One Heart' theme serves as the main idea – first in unison, then in four-part harmony – for a rather learned number that

---

[18]   2000 VS, p. 44.

Bernstein describes on the manuscript as a 'Chorale Prelude on the theme of the Love Duet'.

In *Candide* the 'Love Duet' theme is written in steady dotted minims, and after its relocation in *West Side Story* it was to stay like that until very late in rehearsals – after the cast had moved to Washington. Even the copied orchestral score of 'One Hand, One Heart' has the dotted-minim version, with the revision added in coloured pencil.[19] It was Sondheim who urged Bernstein to make the change to three crotchets in the first and third bars, in order to accommodate some more intelligent lyrics:

> I remember that the tune of 'One Hand, One Heart,' which Bernstein originally wrote for *Candide*, had only a dotted half note to each bar. I realized I couldn't set any two-syllable words to the song, it had to be all one-syllable words. I was stifled, and down in Washington, after my endless pleas, Lenny put in two little quarter notes so that I could put 'make of our' as in 'Make of our hearts one heart.' Not a great deal, but at least a little better.[20]

While it appears that a reprise of 'One Hand, One Heart' in the Marriage Scene (Act I, scene 7) may always been envisaged, there was a problem with it in the Balcony Scene. Arthur Laurents, for one, felt that it didn't capture the mood of a rapturous first encounter: 'I objected to "One Hand, One Heart" for the Balcony Scene as being too pristine for hot, passionate young lovers. Lenny and Steve liked it because it was pristine until Oscar [Hammerstein] came to a rehearsal and disagreed with them.'[21]

The solution required some new material. 'Tonight', a song that was already an important musical element of the Quintet, was a far more fervent expression of young love for Tony and Maria, and the duet version, reverse-engineered from the Quintet, was written during rehearsals in July 1957 (a manuscript containing revisions – but still not the final version – is dated 4 July 1957). It was subjected to considerable further change in the weeks leading up to the opening. The first lines are a case in point. One of the later manuscripts (headed 'Balcony Scene – Newissimo') gives them to Tony, who sings: 'What are you? Tell me everything you are, Maria.' Another manuscript – headed 'Under the Balcony (underscoring to precede Balcony Scene') – is presumably later still, as the lines are given to Maria and are as in the final version ('Only you, you're the only thing I'll see forever').

The end of Act I, scene 5 always included 'America', but the music for this had a long history. In the summer of 1941 Bernstein spent a few weeks in Florida, where he worked on the Clarinet Sonata and on a ballet – unperformed and unpublished – called *Conch Town*, for which a piano four-hand score survives. This score provided the material for the main 'America' theme (Ex. 3.6a), and the music of the

---

[19]   Copy in the Sid Ramin Papers, Columbia University Library.

[20]   Zadan 1974, p. 23.

[21]   See Laurents 2000, p. 351, although Sondheim has suggested that it was 'Tonight' that Hammerstein failed to find sufficiently soaring (see Banfield 1993, p. 34).

Example 3.6a   *Conch Town* (1941), the tune later used for 'America'

Example 3.6b   *Conch Town* (1941), the tune later used for 'Puerto Rico, you lovely island'

Example 3.6c   *Conch Town* (1941), the music later used for the Taunting Scene

introduction ('Puerto Rico, you lovely island'; Ex. 3.6b), as well as the ideas derived
from both themes that are used for the Taunting in Act II (Ex. 3.6c). Bernstein said
of this number: 'I had conceived an idea for a ballet when I was in Key West in
1941. I was crazy about Cuban music. The ballet was to be called *Conch Town*.
It never got finished. It was always lying around and part of it got used in *West
Side*.'[22] Before reaching its final destination in *West Side Story*, the 'Puerto Rico'
tune made another appearance as a 'Lute Song' – one of several numbers dropped
from *Candide*.

---

[22]   Gussow 1990. Part of *Conch Town* was also used as 'Variation III: Danzón' in
Bernstein's ballet *Fancy Free*. As for how Bernstein got to know Cuban music, his daughter
Jamie has said that 'in 1941 he was down in Key West composing and the Cuban radio station
came drifting over his radio. And when he heard the Cuban music, he was sold for life!'
(Jamie Bernstein interview with Michael Tilson Thomas, PBS *Great Performance* broadcast,
29 October 2008).

The manuscript fair copy of the piano-vocal score of 'America' is close to its final form, although Asunción, one of the three principal singers in the manuscript of this number, was a character who had disappeared from the cast list by the time the 'Winter 1956' script was in circulation. A final chorus ('Sooner or later, America / Makes us a State in America. / When we're a State in America, / Then we migrate to America!') originally follows on from Anita's 'Everyone there will have moved here!' in the manuscript (and in some early scripts), but this was cut, to be replaced by the closing instrumental music.

Act I, Scene 6: 'Cool'

The autograph fair copy of the song does not include the fugue, and the song opens with two bars that were subsequently cut. The fugue is written on a separate manuscript (the title page calls it 'Cool (Dance)', and the first page of music is headed 'Continue from "Cool"'). Additional music for the fugue, presumably written at Robbins's request, is to be found on three pages of inserts (labelled 'A', 'B' and 'C').

Act I, Scene 7

See the discussion of 'One Hand, One Heart' in Act I, scene 5, above.

Act I, Scene 8: Quintet

The number described in the 2000 edition of the piano-vocal score as 'Tonight – Ensemble' and in earlier sources[23] as 'Tonight (Quintet and Chorus)', for Maria, Tony, Anita, Riff, Bernardo, the Sharks and the Jets, is usually referred to as the Quintet. In Bernstein's manuscripts, and in the early scripts, that's just what it was – to be sung by five soloists without any chorus, though a note in one of Bernstein's manuscript song lists ('Quintet – Gangs too?') suggests that the idea of adding the gangs was one he had in mind. Changes in the Quintet are otherwise fairly minimal, apart from the cutting of an additional verse for Anita, before she sings 'Anita's gonna get her kicks tonight': 'Anita's gonna have her day / Tonight. / Bernardo's gonna have his way / Tonight. / He tosses me a tumble / Most nights; / But when he's had a rumble / He turns on his brights.'

A very early two-page sketch for this number, headed 'Romeo', includes three of the main ideas ('The Jets are gonna have their day', 'Tonight' and 'We're gonna rock it tonight'), each written out separately; of these, only one has a sketch for a possible lyric: 'Tonight, tonight, / And every other night / Of my life'. A fourth idea on this sketch was not used in the Quintet, but it is reminiscent of the Scherzo from the Ballet Sequence in Act II. A second sketch for the Quintet shows Bernstein fitting

---

[23] For example in the song lists for the Washington, Philadelphia and New York programmes in 1957 (copies in the author's collection).

the three themes of the earlier sketch, along with Anita's music, into the complex contrapuntal texture.

Act I, Scene 9

As has already been noted, 'Mix!' was moved to this scene, but eventually it was cut, to be replaced by the instrumental 'Rumble', described on the title page of the manuscript as 'New Rumble'. An additional section (23 bars), presumably written when more music was called for, is headed 'Rumble: insert before siren'. It is likely that the number was composed to an outline of the action written out by Robbins, a close match to the final form of the scene:[24]

1. Entrance of groups
2. Dialogue
3. a. Drums lead to
   b. explosion of fight between Bernardo & Riff
   c. The killings
4. The Free for All
5. Whistle. *Exit* of kids
   MARIA

Act II, Scene 1: Ballet Sequence

A great deal of manuscript material survives for the ballet, and it shows evidence of extensive rewriting. One of the autographs of the first part of the Ballet Sequence (beginning with Tony's 'And I'll take you away, take you far, far away out of here') includes a continuation of the same music that subsequently vanished, sung by Maria ('Somewhere there must be a place where we feel we are free'), then by the two of them together. This led in turn to a version of 'Somewhere' that has more than a hint of *verismo* opera. Tony and Maria sing the tune in soaring *fortissimo* octaves (the lyrics beginning 'Love will show the way. / Our love will show the way'), while the accompaniment still uses the driving syncopated rhythms of the earlier 'And I'll take you away' music. The final version of this scene, with 'Somewhere' sung by a nameless offstage voice, creates an entirely different effect.

The plan of this complicated number was something that gave Robbins and Bernstein a lot of trouble. Several options were outlined by Bernstein on a page of notes (Figure 3.1). Some of Bernstein's descriptions of the sections in the ballet are different from those in the published scores. 'Kaleidoscope' was in fact the music for No. 13a ('Ballet Sequence'), the section that now begins 'And I'll take you away'. In one early manuscript, headed 'Duet into Kaleidoscope', this is purely instrumental apart from an interjection from Maria ('Oh Tony, Tony, Tony') that

---

[24] LBC.

was cut. The passage is notated in 3/4 rather than 3/2. This led directly into the 'Green Scene', the present No. 13b, now called 'Transition to Scherzo'. The 'New Tentative Music' mentioned on Bernstein's plan exists in one of the sketches (headed 'New Tentative?') and is an early version of the 'Nightmare' music for No. 13e ('Procession and Nightmare').

Figure 3.1   Bernstein's notes on the Ballet Sequence

SIMPLER

T & M remain where they are.

– dancers attack doors & fences

– T & M sing Somewhere. R & B appear at
end of song, leading to Procession, etc., return
to Kaleidoscope & T & M.

– use tentative [music] & scherzo.

– Better: T & M not leading procession = c.f.
end of show.

MORE COMPLEX

T & M participate in Ballet.

– dancers accumulate then Somewhere.

– no Scherzo

SIMPLEST OF ALL

VERSE – KALEIDOSCOPE – SOMEWHERE – PROCESSION – KALEIDOSCOPE – VERSE – SOMEWHERE REPRISE.

Objection to the return of Kaleid.: Makes whole effort seem to have been in vain. All the build-up of harmony culminates in a sense of failure. Only point left to be made is subtle one of no magic – love is real & earnest. Not a very inspiring point to end on. If T & M are *in ballet*, could he take her off to bed *from* the green scene itself?

I – Underscore from *killer*. Perhaps underscore only from *I swear I will.* (Movie-ish? Dialogue goes toward *tenderness*.)

A. Tony sings equivalent of last speech

1. ♫ ♫ ♫ | ♪. ♫ ♩ |

2. ♩ ♪ | ♩ ♪ | ♩ ♪ | ♩ ♪ | ♩ ♪ | ♩. –

3. Should mean: desperate urge to freedom.

B. Transition < of doors & fences.

1. T & M run

2. Others run

C. Green Scene. (♪ ♩...) Pure music to scherzo, or to Somewhere, or as pure music here.

1. T & M sing Somewhere (Dancers accumulate through song).

a) are they out of breath?

b) Is lyric about somewhere, or *here*, since song is sung in new set.

2. Somewhere instrumental. T & M *dance* pas de deux.

3. New tentative music. People join them, leading to Scherzo.

D. Climax
1. If sung Somewhere – Riff & Bernardo on end of song, leading to procession (to instr. Somewhere)
2. If instr. Somewhere – R & B on end of Scherzo. Procession to short reprise of Somewhere (instr.)

E. Return of doors & fences transition. Tony repeats opening verse. Short reprise end of Somewhere – new lyric meaning: Rest, trust in me, I'll take you there. Off to bed.

Robbins, too, drafted several different plans for the Ballet Sequence, and it is probable that the exact form of this complex scene was decided upon only at the last moment. Telling evidence for this is to be found in the Ramin full score, in which there is a longish section that was orchestrated before being dropped: a ten-page insert headed 'New Intro to Ballet Sequence'; this includes a passage in 6/8 where Tony sings 'We'll find it, a place for us / It's got to be there / It's got to be somewhere' on a theme based on part of the Rumble that is in turn derived from the Prologue.[25]

One final note on the 'Somewhere' theme itself. A very early sketch of the tune in LBC has lyrics jotted on it, including couplets that begin 'Rain was rain to me', 'Stand right there for me' (both deleted), 'Stand apart from me' and 'Just as I to you'. Another, much fuller sketch (including some music that was never used) is entitled 'Somewhere (Whatsisname)', below which 'Balcony' has been written and crossed out. This provides evidence of Bernstein's initial intention to use the tune in the Balcony Scene; as for 'Whatsisname', Bernstein explained its origins to Mel Gussow: '"Somewhere" was a tune I had around and had never finished. I loved it. I remember Marc Blitzstein loved it very much and wrote a lyric to it just for fun. It was called "There goes What's his name".'[26]

Act II, Scene 2: 'Gee, Officer Krupke'

According to Arthur Laurents, 'Gee, Officer Krupke' was added during rehearsals in New York. Laurents suggested an idea for a new number and, as he told Craig Zadan, met with resistance:

> Nobody wanted 'Officer Krupke'. … They all said that it was a cheap musical comedy number. But I tried to be a little intellectual and talked Shakespeare's clowns and I felt it was really necessary, and then there wasn't that much dissension. We originally did the number with the idea that it would be performed early in the

---

[25]   The Rumble passage is from bar 24 onwards, 2000 VS, pp. 131–2.

[26]   Gussow 1990.

show but because of the scenic scheme it couldn't. And in the end, I think it was perfect just where it was.[27]

Bernstein apparently already had a tune to hand: according to Humphrey Burton, it had been written for the Venice scene in *Candide*, the final line of Latouche's original lyric being 'Where does it get you in the end?'[28] At least one of the collaborators thought the song was in completely the wrong act. When Sondheim saw the 'Krupke' scene during the Washington tryouts, it jarred:

> One of my objections to 'Krupke' was always that I felt that it was out of place in the second act, that where it should occur was in the first act, and that 'Cool' should occur where 'Krupke' was. Because here were a group of kids who are running from a double murder, and for them to stop and do this comic number about social situations seemed to me to be out of place. And I kept nudging and bugging Jerry and Arthur and Lenny, 'Couldn't we please reverse the two?' And we didn't.

Laurents insisted that there was a good reason to keep it where it was: 'I thought that the tension in the second act needed relief.'[29] He won the day, though in the film version the place of the two songs was reversed.

Act II, Scene 3, into Scene 4: 'A Boy Like That'

The title page of the fair copy of the Anita–Maria duet is headed 'A Boy Like That / Once In Your Life / (Maria, Anita, later reprise by Tony)' and there are 174 bars of music, compared with 122 bars in the final version. Set in C minor (the published score is a tone lower, in B flat minor), the differences are apparent on the first page: after Anita sings 'A boy like that, who'd kill your brother', Maria interjects with 'I know', and she continues to punctuate the end of each phrase of Anita's song, until 'Stick to your own kind', after which Maria adds 'I love him so!' (Ex. 3.7).

The section beginning 'A boy who kills cannot love' is unchanged, but after that there are numerous alterations to both the music and the lyrics. The transition into 'Once In Your Life' (later changed to 'I Have a Love') is quite different. The 'Once In Your Life' music ends with Maria soaring to a top B, *fortissimo*, and Anita then sings a reprise of some twenty bars of the opening 'A Boy Like That' music, now starting with the lyrics 'You better run, go run, Maria'. (For the four bars beginning 'This is a time not for love' – the equivalent of the earlier 'A boy who kills cannot love' – Bernstein has written a different accompaniment, with the bass line rising in chromatic quavers.) This is followed by a reprise of 'Once In Your Life' sung by Tony; the stage direction at the top of the manuscript of this page states: 'Through

---

[27] Zadan 1974, p. 21.
[28] Burton 1994, p. 269.
[29] NPR 2007.

Example 3.7 'A Boy Like That', early version, with Maria's interjections

the scrim, singing to Doc in the Drugstore'. As the song ends, he soars to a long top C (though Bernstein also writes an *ossia* that ends the song a tone lower, Tony singing a B flat). The stage direction makes it clear that Tony's reprise was to cover the scene change to the drugstore for Act II, scene 4. In the final version the song is followed by three pages of dialogue in which Schrank interrogates Maria, before the scene changes. The lyrical ardour of the two lovers in the earlier manuscript version has a soaring, operatic quality, but the revised version is harser in tone and has a far tighter dramatic focus.

Two later manuscripts give different endings of the duet. Once Tony's music was cut, and Anita's reprise that came before it, Bernstein ended the number with long, held octave Bs (this passage is in B major, rather than the G major of the final version) for Maria and Anita, with a *fortissimo* close. The other manuscript has a similar ending, but with Maria singing alone, again with a loud finish. A single page is headed 'New end of Boy Like That' and gives the conclusion of the song as in the published score, other than the key (on this inserted page it is in A major).

Act II, Scene 4: Taunting

The music for Anita's taunting (2000 VS, p. 208, bar 5 onwards) is derived from the 'Puerto Rico' introduction to 'America', and this highly charged rhythmic variant stretches back as far as the two tunes of 'America' itself: like them, it is to be found in the 1941 ballet *Conch Town*. As we have seen above, this was an abandoned work that was to prove a fruitful source for *West Side Story*. A later, undated sketch includes both the 'Puerto Rico' theme and the 'Taunting' version on a leaf that also has sketches for 'It Must Be So' (*Candide*) and 'Build My House' from *Peter Pan*.

Act II, Scene 6: Finale

As Bernstein himself admitted, he made several attempts to set Maria's final speech (originally written by Laurents as a dummy lyric), but these came to nothing and no musical sketches appear to survive.

The last bars of the whole work were subject to later alteration. Originally there were four bars of C major chords (including in the Ramin full score), but one of these was cut. The first time that the final C major chord was destabilized by an ambiguous low F sharp played on the second beat (as in the preceding bars) was in the *Symphonic Dances from West Side Story*. This note is also to be heard in the 1984 recording of the complete work conducted by Bernstein, and is in the definitive editions of the full score (1994) and piano-vocal score (2000). It is not, however, in any of the manuscript sources, nor in the Ramin full score, nor in the first edition of the piano-vocal score. Sid Ramin is surely right when he suggests that 'after Lenny found all those tritones, I think he felt he had to add it right at the end'.[30]

---

[30]   Sid Ramin, interview with the present author, 25 September 2007.

The manuscripts for *West Side Story* are an absorbing record of the creative process, and of the kinds of changes that were made in collaboration with the rest of the team, and in response to their criticisms. The earlier versions of 'Somewhere' and 'A Boy Like That' are just the sort of numbers that Bernstein must have been thinking of when he revealed something of his bruised creative self in a heartfelt letter to Felicia, written on 28 July 1957. Bernstein was on a plane to Miami, where he had reluctantly agreed to attend the annual convention of Columbia Records. But there was an urgent need for him to be back in New York:

> Home tomorrow, in time (I hope, barring airport Miamisms), for a RUN-THRU of Act One. Imagine – already! Where does the time all go to? In a minute it will be August & off to Washington – and people will be looking at *West Side Story* in public, & hearing my poor little mashed-up score. All the things I love most in it are slowly being dropped – too operatic, too this & that. They're all so scared & a commercial success means so much to them. To me too, I suppose, but I still insist it can be achieved with pride.

Chapter 4
The Score

This chapter falls into two parts. The first considers general issues that apply to the whole show: the question of genre, features of the musical language, the use of the orchestra, and the process of orchestrating a Broadway show; the second is an examination of the musical numbers in *West Side Story*.

The Question of Genre

West Side Story was billed as 'a new musical' on the programmes and publicity for the early performances. In the first entry of his invented 'West Side Log', Bernstein gave what were ostensibly his initial thoughts: 'making a musical that tells a tragic story in musical comedy terms, using only musical comedy techniques, never falling into the "operatic" trap. Can it succeed? It hasn't yet in our country.'[1] Whether Bernstein was right about the novelty of telling a tragic story in terms of musical comedy is open to question: when Robbins, Laurents and Bernstein first considered the project in 1949, tragedy had certainly been a feature of Broadway in the recent past, including two outstanding examples – Rodgers and Hammerstein's *Carousel* (1945) and Kurt Weill's *Street Scene* (1947). *Carousel* was described as 'A Musical Play', though Lewis Nichols noted in his review that the score was 'more nearly operatic than Broadway',[2] without any suggestion that this was a problem. While the first edition of the vocal score of *Street Scene* described the work as 'An American Opera',[3] the original Broadway *Playbill* called it 'A Dramatic Musical'. Brooks Atkinson, reviewing *Street Scene* in the *New York Times* (10 January 1947), declared that it was 'a musical play of magnificence and glory', and one that 'finds the song of humanity under the argot of the New York streets'. Moreover, the portrayal of humanity in Weill's show (and the Elmer Rice play on which it is closely based) includes poverty, abuse and murder, as *West Side Story* was to do, and the action of both takes place in the city within a time-span of 24 hours.

Was the 'opera trap' perhaps a problem first identified by Jerome Robbins and Arthur Laurents that was later taken up with zeal by Bernstein as an issue? This certainly seems possible, given that the composer himself was to fall into the trap on a number of occasions during the writing of *West Side Story* (while for other

---

[1]   Bernstein 1957, entry for 6 January 1949.
[2]   Nichols 1945.
[3]   *Street Scene: An American Opera*, New York: Chappell & Co. Inc., 1948.

composers, such as Weill and Rodgers, it seems not to have been a trap at all). Bernstein returned to the subject in a log entry for March 1956: 'Chief problem: to tread the fine line between opera and Broadway, between realism and poetry, ballet and "just dancing", abstract and representational.' That autumn, in October 1956, just under a year before *West Side Story* opened, Bernstein presented a programme on 'American Musical Comedy' for the *Omnibus* series of television documentaries.[4] As Humphrey Burton put it, 'With *Candide* going into rehearsal and *West Side Story* virtually finished, he was well placed to discuss the subject.'[5] Much of Bernstein's discussion can be related directly to the question of what he and his collaborators were setting out to achieve in *West Side Story*. Near the start of the telecast, Bernstein identifies something he sees as a difficulty:

> The more a show gets away from pure diversion, the more it tries to engage the interest and emotion of the audience, the closer it slides toward opera. And the more a show uses music to further its plot, the closer it moves towards the same pole. Now just how does a plot get furthered by the use of music? There are a number of ways – ballet, underscoring, choral devices etc.

One of the shows he singles out for approval is Gershwin's *Of Thee I Sing*:

> A marvelous story, serious and funny in a way no show had ever been before; glorious songs perfectly integrated into the scheme; a highly American subject; natural American speech; sharp brilliant lyrics; an all-over unity of style embodying wide variety … it's musically elaborate: it has counterpoint, it uses underscoring … it has borrowed freely from operetta in *technique*; but its soul is the soul of musical comedy.

Bernstein then turned to the role of dancing in Broadway shows:

> Ever since 1936, when Rodgers and Hart came up with *On Your Toes*, dancing has come into its own as a plot-furthering medium. In the show, Rodgers and Hart devised a scenario for a ballet called 'Slaughter on Tenth Avenue' which not only has its own ballet plot, but also participates climactically in the plot of the whole show. … This ballet, choreographed by George Balanchine, broke ground for the building of a whole tradition of plot-dancing … the whole look and sound of musical comedy has been radically changed.

Finally in this documentary Bernstein looked to the future, drawing a slightly strained parallel with Mozart's development of the *Singspiel* in *The Magic Flute*:

---

[4]   The complete script is printed in Bernstein 1959, pp. 152–79.

[5]   Burton 1994, p. 264.

We are in the same position; all we need is for our Mozart to come along. If and when he does, we surely won't get any *Magic Flute*; what we'll get will be a new form, and perhaps 'opera' will be the wrong word for it. There must be a more exciting word for such an exciting event. And this event can happen any second. It's almost as though it is our moment in history, as if there is a historical necessity that gives us such a wealth of creative talent at this precise time.

It is unlikely that Bernstein had anyone other than himself in mind when making these prophecies – but finding that 'new form' was to be a struggle for him, and it involved some painful musical sacrifices along the way. At the end of July 1957, just before rehearsals for *West Side Story* moved to Washington, and with the start of tryouts less than three weeks away, Bernstein was frustrated by just the 'operatic' question that had dogged his thoughts from the start. On 26 July 1957, he was having to come to terms with music being cut from the show, confiding to his wife Felicia, who was in Chile: 'The show – ah, yes. I am depressed with it. All the aspects of the score I like best – the "big", poetic parts – get criticized as "operatic" – & there's a concerted move to chuck them.'[6] Two days later he wrote in a similar vein to Felicia about his 'poor little mashed-up score', and that 'all the things I love most in it are slowly being dropped – too operatic, too this and that'.[7] An examination of the manuscript material makes it possible to speculate on what some of these casualties may have been – perhaps the *verismo* version of 'Somewhere' with Tony and Maria, or the original 'A Boy Like That' with Tony's reprise of 'Once In Your Life'. By his own admission, Bernstein needed encouraging out of the opera trap at times, to avoid just the problem he had identified in the *Omnibus* programme, the 'slide toward opera'. Laurents, Robbins and Sondheim were clearly crucial in avoiding such slides in *West Side Story*, but not in the way Bernstein suggests. Sondheim described the revision of the songs as follows:

> Lenny's endless complaint that his score was getting eviscerated because it was too 'operatic' – none of us (Arthur, Jerry and me) said that, so who made him change things? The record company? Hal and Bobby? Never. The songs were changed for the reasons songs should be changed: they were too clumsy, too long-winded, too monotonous, not theatrical, whatever.[8]

But as well as the much-discussed 'opera trap', was there also a parallel risk of a 'ballet trap'? Burton Bernstein (Leonard's brother) wrote to Felicia in early August 1957 (an undated letter), just before the company moved to Washington, and gave her a witty description of a run-through without sets and costumes, played to an audience of theatre insiders in New York:

---

[6] LBC.

[7] LBC.

[8] E-mail from Stephen Sondheim to the present author, 28 September 2009.

Firstnik, *West Side Story* is going to be a large hit and lives up to our highest
expectations. ... The run-through I saw was before an ideal audience of theatre
folk, so one shouldn't really gauge it by audience reaction – but still, it was quite
exciting. The strange thing (something I've never experienced before) is that B.
Lennuhhtt[9] comes off as second best: the show actually is a monster ballet (a jot
repetitious in spots) where no one is actually directed but choreographed instead.
It's too much of a good thing, if you know what I mean (you know what I mean?).
There's so much balletics going on on stage that the music is shunted into second
place by the sheer physical force of arms, legs and torsos. But on the whole (and
you know how I hate to say this about a run-through from past experience) the
show is in frighteningly good condition and looks like a sure thing. I hope that
by the time I see it with sets and costumes and everything in Washington next
week, Jerry will have been convinced that there's too much ballet for the show's
own good – or am I being naïve? Anyway, there's very little to fix, outside of
Lennuhhtt's nose ... So come home already.

It is not hard to see why Burton Bernstein wondered about this 'monster ballet',
given just how important dancing is to every aspect of *West Side Story*. The primacy
of dance – especially as a plot-furthering device – is hardly surprising since it was
Robbins who had conceived the whole project in the first place. But its dramatic
centrality also inspired some of the finest music in the score, from the Prologue,
through the Dance at the Gym, to the 'Cool' Fugue and Rumble in Act I; then in Act
II, the Ballet Sequence (conceptually harking back to the 'dream ballets' in shows
such as *Oklahoma!* and *Carousel*), to the numbing brutality of Anita's Taunting in
the drugstore, and the wordless, final procession.

Is *West Side Story* the 'new form' looked for by Bernstein in his *Omnibus*
broadcast? Privately, he certainly hoped it was. He wrote to Felicia on 8 August
1957: 'It's murder, but I'm excited. It may be something extraordinary'; and on 13
August: 'I tell you this show may yet be worth all the agony. As you can see, I'm
excited as hell – oh so different from *Candide*.'

In the 1985 Dramatists Guild Landmark Symposium, the four collaborators
were asked to sum up whether they believed *West Side Story* represented a turning
point for the Broadway musical. Sondheim surely gets to the heart of the matter by
identifying the show's innovation not so much in terms of the story it told, but in the
way this was done:

Essentially, it's a blend of all the elements – music, book, lyrics, dance. More than
subject matter, its innovation has to do with theatrical style. We were influenced
by the movies – there was a fluidity to the staging which had a cinematic quality
... No show has ever been staged – I'm talking about the larger sense, not just
Jerry's work – or conceived this way as a fluid piece which called on the poetic

---

[9]   A family pet-name for Bernstein.

imagination of the audience. This is something that's taken for granted now. Prior to *West Side Story*, shows had been staged fairly stodgily … It's not exactly the first time that convention had been broken down – it was broken down a little in *South Pacific* and *Allegro*. But *West Side Story* has been the major influence.[10]

Bernstein's assessment concentrated more on the creative courage of the whole project:

> I agree with what Steve has said, its influence went far beyond the subject matter. It has a kind of … bravery in which we all fortified one another, to the point where we could all try our utmost; not trying to break rules, not trying to go further – because you get nowhere trying to go further – but having the bravery to follow your instincts and follow one another's instincts in order to produce something new, something that has never been envisioned before. It's not so much what it's about, it's how bravely it's done.[11]

Robbins was unwilling to 'theorize about how or if the show changed future musicals', but claimed that for him

> what was important about *West Side Story* was in our *aspiration*. I wanted to find out at that time how far we, as 'long-haired artists,' could go in bringing our crafts and talents to a musical. Why did we have to do it separately and elsewhere? Why did Lenny have to write an opera, Arthur a play, me a ballet? Why couldn't we, in aspiration, try to bring our deepest talent together to the commercial theatre in this work? That was the true *gesture* of the show.

Laurents summarized the collective aim of the whole team: 'We all had real respect for each other and, without doing it overtly, challenged each other to do our best. That's all we thought about – doing our best.'[12]

All of this was held together by a strong book, which is also one of the shortest for any Broadway show. In an interview with Michael Kantor, Sondheim declared:

> The book of *West Side Story* is a miracle. It's when you realize how much gets done in terms of story-telling and action, and how little there is in the way of lines. … And yet, it's packed with action. There's not a scene in which something … at least one really important event happens, and you know, writing an event is not just a matter of stage direction. … When you look at the way Tony and Maria meet, they meet and fall in love in eight lines, and he convinces you, you believe it … It's

10 Guernsey 1985, pp. 53–4.
11 Guernsey 1985, p. 54.
12 Guernsey 1985, p. 54.

partly because there's that music playing underneath, the Cha-Cha, and the music is wonderful for conveying just that, much better than if it were sung.[13]

'I didn't do all this on purpose': Elements of the Musical Language

Bernstein himself often stressed the importance of the interval of the tritone (augmented fourth) in the score, and its use of sharpened fourths in general. A much later manuscript page of motifs used in *West Side Story* (LBC) includes quotations of nine fragments in the composer's hand. The interval of an augmented fourth in the melody, or a sharpened fourth present in the melodic line or in the harmony, can be found in every one of these examples. Ultimately, Bernstein came to regard the tritone as a crucial unifying feature of the musical language of *West Side Story*, as did a number of later commentators.[14] Certainly, there are numerous instances peppering the work, though not all of it.

If the tritone came to represent irresolvable conflict in musical terms, mirroring the culture of warring gangs in the story, this could be offered as a further reason for the abandonment of 'Mix!' as the music for the rumble at the end of Act I (see Chapter 3): in terms of its musical language, 'Mix!' was something of a stylistic misfit – conflict without tritones – whereas the replacement Rumble is bristling with them, as is the Prologue. Even the show's one comedy number, 'Gee, Officer Krupke', makes colouristic and humorous use of the same interval – but here the Jets are poking fun at the hapless Krupke, rather than fighting turf wars. Elsewhere in the score, however, explicit tritones are absent, although sharpened fourths are to be found in much of the harmony. Striking examples occur in the Balcony Scene and in Maria's 'I Have a Love' (and, by extension, the return of the same music in the work's orchestral epilogue).

But this apparent motivic or intervallic consistency was never a planned decision on Bernstein's part and it seems simply to have evolved as one of the work's defining musical characteristics. The relatively haphazard way in which most Broadway scores are composed – and *West Side Story* was no exception – suggests that any over-arching motivic plan would be unlikely. And so it proves: the testimony of Irwin Kostal, one of the show's orchestrators, clarifies the composer's own 'discovery' of the preponderance of tritones in the score:

> One afternoon when our rehearsal came to an unusually long halt, Sid [Ramin] and I were sitting with Lenny reviewing all the music in *West Side Story*, and Lenny was sitting there in a reflective sort of mood, and he quietly began to analyze his melodies and harmonies and expressed some surprise at things he was noticing, things he had

---

[13]   Stephen Sondheim, in an unused segment from his interview with Michael Kantor for the 2004 documentary series *Broadway: The American Musical* (transcript kindly supplied by Mark Eden Horowitz, Library of Congress).

[14]   Swain 2002 (pp. 221–64) and Block 1997 (pp. 245–73) are two outstanding examples.

not consciously thought of before. He reviewed the music from a compositional standpoint. He pointed out how his opening three-note motif, fanfarish in style, seemed to recur in every song ... The song 'Cool' begins with these three notes, and they are reiterated in one way or another forwards and backwards for the first four measures. The song 'Maria' begins with these three notes, then repeats them quicker and becomes the familiar song we all know. The song 'Who knows' ['Something's Coming'] once again begins with three notes. ... Much of the incidental music also is built on these same three notes. Lenny explained all this to us and to himself. He said he had never noticed all these similarities. Only in retrospect was he finding out how his mind had been working.[15]

Sid Ramin confirmed Kostal's reminiscences, and added that Bernstein was excited to find this unifying element in the music and subsequently took delight in hunting for more examples.[16] Bernstein, too, made it clear that the motivic coherence of the score was more or less a happy accident – one that he claimed started with the opening phrase of 'Maria'. He told Mel Gussow:

it had those notes. I think that was the kernel of the piece, in the sense that the three notes of 'Maria' pervade the whole piece – inverted, done backward. I didn't do all this on purpose. It seemed to come out in 'Cool' and as the gang whistle. The same three notes.[17]

In fact, while tritones are a pervasive feature of the score, Stephen Sondheim recalls that he was the person who drew Bernstein's attention to this:

It was actually I who pointed out to Lenny that there were a number of tritones in the songs. I even suggested that he include some in the songs where they didn't exist, such as 'I Feel Pretty.' Lenny later claimed that the score was built around the tritone, which is nonsense since half the score was taken from other shows and ballets.[18]

Sondheim is right to emphasize that tritones are only part of the story, and one reason for that certainly lies in the self-borrowings from earlier works.

The rising or falling perfect fourth at the start of melodies is another feature of several songs in *West Side Story*. This was already an established Bernstein trait,[19]

---

[15] Kostal, unpublished memoirs.

[16] Sid Ramin, interview with the present author, 25 September 2008.

[17] Gussow 1990.

[18] Stephen Sondheim, e-mail to the present author, 13 November 2008.

[19] Numerous earlier examples can be found in all of Bernstein's previous Broadway shows, for instance in 'New York, New York' from *On the Town*; in 'Christopher Street', 'What a Waste', 'Pass the Football' and the 'Conga' from *Wonderful Town*; and in 'The Best of All Possible Worlds', 'Oh Happy We' and 'Make Our Garden Grow' from *Candide*.

but never more so than here: 'Tonight', 'America', all the elements in the Quintet, and some of the Taunting Scene are obvious examples, but the most potent use of this interval is when perfect fourths and tritones are combined, as in the rising motif that dominates much of the Prologue and the Rumble.

Bernstein's former assistant Jack Gottlieb has explored another possible source of inspiration for this three-note rallying cry. In *Funny, It Doesn't Sound Jewish*, Gottlieb examined specific influences from synagogue music and Yiddish songs on Broadway composers, and he devoted a chapter to Bernstein. Gottlieb demonstrates the similarity between a traditional shofar call and the three-note 'shofar' figure in *West Side Story* (Ex. 4.1).[20] In Jewish scripture, the shofar – an instrument usually made from a ram's horn – is blown to announce holidays, to accompany processions, and, more tellingly, as a musical proclamation of hostilities, a signal for battle to begin. The most famous example is Joshua and his army at Jericho (Joshua 6: 2–5):

> The Lord said to Joshua, 'I have handed Jericho over to you, including its king and his warriors. You are to encircle the city with all your soldiers and march around it once. Do this for six days. Seven priests are to carry seven shofars in front of the ark. On the seventh day you are to march around the city seven times, and the priests will blow the shofars. Then they are to blow a long blast on the shofar. On hearing the sound, all the people are to shout as loudly as they can; and the wall of the city will fall down flat. Then the people are to go up into the city, each one straight from where he stands.'[21]

Example 4.1 A traditional shofar call and the 'shofar' figure in *West Side Story*

Gottlieb also describes ambiguities between major and minor thirds as being characteristic of synagogue music, and of early Yiddish secular song.[22] In various forms, either in melodic lines or in harmonies, this is another stylistic marker in *West Side Story*, from the first chords of the Prologue, where major and minor are heard together in clusters. In terms of parallels with origins in Jewish traditional music, the

---

[20]   Gottlieb 2004, p. 179.

[21]   Adapted from the translation in *The Complete Jewish Bible*. Other versions translate shofar as 'horn', 'ram's horn' or 'trumpet'.

[22]   Gottlieb 2004, p. 180.

most striking examples occur in the melody of 'Maria' at 'And suddenly that name will never sound the same to me' (bars 11–14), and later at 'Say it loud and there's music playing, say it soft and it's almost like praying' (bars 21–5). Elsewhere this ambiguity can be heard in 'Tonight' (the melodic and harmonic shift from 'Nothing else but you, ever' to 'And there's nothing for me but Maria', in bars 34–8); in the chords at the climax of the Mambo (from bar 158 onwards, rocking between triads of C major and E flat major); in the combination of melody and harmony at 'Just play it cool, boy' in 'Cool' (bars 34–6); in parts of the Rumble (for instance in bar 27, and also in the crushing chords in bars 41–7, derived from the opening of the Prologue); and in 'Forget that boy and find another' in 'A Boy Like That' (bars 5–6).

There are other parallels with synagogue music: the shape of the benediction quoted by Gottlieb in another chapter of his book[23] finds a clear echo in 'Maria', when her name is repeated over and over during the introduction (bars 3–4 and 7–8); another is the instrumental underscoring (bar 43 onwards) in 'One Hand, One Heart', similar to the 'Call to the Torah' quoted by Gottlieb.[24]

But while the synagogue influences may have come from music that had been part of Bernstein's memories since childhood, the ethnic sounds and rhythms he needed in *West Side Story* had to come from elsewhere. For this he drew on another enthusiasm: the rhythms of South and Central America. As we have seen in Chapter 3, he had included several ideas evoking Latin American dance in his unperformed ballet *Conch Town*, composed in 1941 when he was in his early twenties, and this was subsequently plundered for *West Side Story*. Two years earlier, Bernstein made two arrangements of Copland's *El Salón México*, for solo piano and for two pianos (published by Boosey & Hawkes in 1941 and 1943). In *West Side Story*, named Latin American dances include the Cuban mambo and cha-cha, the Puerto Rican seis (the 'Puerto Rico' introduction to 'America' is marked 'Moderato. Tempo di "Seis"') and the Mexican – or rather, stretching a point for the purposes of *West Side Story*, the Gulf of Mexican – huapango ('America'). The 'Taunting' music – recycled from *Conch Town* – has an angry rhythmic drive, the quavers irregularly grouped in threes and twos, which have clear Latin roots.

Despite these influences – as well as those of Stravinsky, and musical allusions that may have their roots in Beethoven (the slow movement of the 'Emperor' Concerto in the contours of the melody at the start of 'Somewhere') and Wagner (the 'Redemption' motif from the *Ring* echoed in 'I Have a Love' and in the closing bars of the epilogue) – Bernstein's score does not sound derivative: this is music which, besides being fresh and vibrant, has the stamp of a composer whose voice is not only instantly identifiable but also obstinately memorable. Though there are borrowings from various earlier works, most of the score is stylistically coherent; in places where it is perhaps less so ('America', 'I Feel Pretty'), the dramatic situation justifies the use of a particular song.

---

[23] Gottlieb 2004, p. 215, ex. 12.22a.

[24] Gottlieb 2004, p. 173, ex. 9.27a.

The Role of the Orchestra

The purely instrumental music in *West Side Story* is one of the score's most original features. Bernstein began the process of greatly expanding the orchestral contribution to a Broadway show in *On the Town* (1944),[25] but in *West Side Story* the orchestra takes on a pivotal role, becoming an integral part of the drama. Though an overture was added for the National Tour that followed the initial Broadway run,[26] this is seldom used (it is a typical medley overture beginning with the Quintet, followed by 'Somewhere', and ending with the Mambo).[27]

Plunging straight into the action makes for a far more arresting opening, but the question of how best to do this was not resolved until rehearsals were under way, when the sung Opening was replaced by the orchestral Prologue. This has no singing, but represents that drama entirely through instrumental music and dance. The role of music as one of the plot-developing elements of the work is at once apparent from the jagged dissonance in the Prologue, and setting the street scene with purely instrumental resources lends it starkness and brutality while also emphasizing the primacy of dance on the stage.

Act I includes several other extended stretches of orchestral writing, the longest of which is the Dance at the Gym culminating in the volcanic Mambo. The rhythmic aggression and explosive energy of its music brilliantly matches the combative, competitive choreography devised by Robbins (Jets) and his assistant Peter Gennaro (Sharks) for this scene. 'America', too, contains extended dance episodes, but the remaining orchestral passages in Act I are more unusual. The most powerful is the 'Cool' Fugue. The idea of fugal writing in a Broadway show is unorthodox (Frank Loesser's earlier 'Fugue for Tinhorns' in *Guys and Dolls* is contrapuntal but not really fugal); but so, too, is the sheer extent of this passage, comprising 102 bars of complex instrumental writing, in the middle of a song that is itself only 173 bars long. The Fugue amounts to well over half the number and was possibly the most complex instrumental music heard on Broadway to date.

The final orchestral passage in Act I is the Rumble. This threatening, brittle and highly charged music closes the act. The only vocal contributions are a few isolated shouts as the rival gang members engage in open warfare, and violent, senseless death becomes an inevitability. It is the orchestra that takes a central role in developing and articulating this climactic moment in the drama.

---

[25]   The orchestration for *On the Town* is credited to Leonard Bernstein, Hershy Kay, Don Walker, Elliott Jacoby and Ted Royal.

[26]   Sid Ramin, interview with the present author, 25 September 2008. The copy of the full score in the Sid Ramin Papers includes the 'Temporary Overture', assembled for the National Tour and using duplicated copies of the existing pages of the Quintet, 'Somewhere' and the Mambo. At some point the 'Temporary Overture' became more permanent, but it is difficult to make a case for using it in a production.

[27]   2000 VS includes the Overture as an appendix on pp. 212–19.

Act II opens with 'I Feel Pretty', but embedded in this is an old-fashioned Entr'acte: the first 138 bars of the number are for orchestra alone. Straight after 'I Feel Pretty' comes the Ballet Sequence, a complex structure which – almost perversely – includes a good deal of singing just when it is least expected. It begins (No. 13) with some unusually urgent, sinister underscoring which leads into the start of the ballet proper (No. 13a), with Tony's 'And I'll take you away, take you far, far away'. No. 13b, Transition to Scherzo, is purely instrumental, a recollection of the meeting music from the Dance at the Gym in Act I. No. 13c is the Scherzo, which leads into the second, and much longer, song embedded in the *West Side Story* ballet sequence, 'Somewhere'.

In Act I the orchestra had provided the musical and dramatic context in which murder could take place on the stage. In Act II it serves as a scandalized witness to rape in the Taunting Scene. Beginning with a pre-recorded version of the Mambo as underscoring (it comes from a juke-box), when the live orchestra enters, it does so with music of such uncompromising brutality that words become wholly unnecessary: even without the traumatic stage action, the message is stark and sordid as the Jets attempt to rape Anita, and only Doc's interruption – 'Stop it!' – brings them to their senses.

After the death of Tony (who expires during a desolate partial reprise of 'Somewhere') and Maria's last speech, it is left to the orchestra to bring *West Side Story* to a close. A solemn procession lines up to carry out Tony's body, Maria watches, and then follows the cortège. We are left with no words, but the mingling of three motifs: 'I Have a Love', 'Somewhere' and 'Maria'.

Sid Ramin and Irwin Kostal: Orchestrating the Show

Despite the immensely important role that instrumental music plays in *West Side Story*, the actual orchestration was started late in the show's development – as was the norm for Broadway musicals. With the notable exceptions of Victor Herbert and Kurt Weill, Broadway composers have not usually done their own orchestrations,[28] but instead they have entrusted the task to specialists. In the case of *West Side Story*, Bernstein was closely involved in the process, but two other musicians did the vast majority of the work. The 1994 full orchestral score credits 'orchestration by Leonard Bernstein with Sid Ramin and Irwin Kostal', but as the composer explained in 1985, this gives a misleading impression:

> Sid Ramin and Irwin Kostal assisted me. Actually they did more than assist, they executed the orchestration. After the others went home at two-thirty in the morning, we had pre-orchestration sessions in which I would indicate exactly what

---

[28] George Gershwin did orchestrate *Porgy and Bess*, a work he described as an 'American Folk Opera', but not his Broadway musicals.

I wanted, note by note, in a shorthand that is intelligible only to orchestrators. They would come back with the score a couple of days later and have a final post-orchestration session at the same time as a pre-session on the next number coming up. So they really executed it in a way without which I couldn't have gotten the score finished.[29]

The size of the proposed orchestra had already been the cause of some bickering between Bernstein and the producers while Cheryl Crawford was still involved in the show, and the number of players changed during the summer of 1956 – more than a year before the opening, with much of the music still to be written. In a letter to Roger L. Stevens dated 10 July 1956,[30] Crawford gave her view of the contract, 'which I thought you should see before the lawyers look it over'. About the orchestra she wrote:

I think to guarantee 30 musicians before knowing the theatre and the cast is foolhardy on our part. The cost of 30 plus conductor plus assistant and contractor, but without any doubles, is over $5,000. As you know, the amount of sharing a theatre will do on this is conditioned by what names you have in a cast and I honestly don't know of any stars right for this show. Besides, in a medium size house this can be a heavy burden. Even *My Fair Lady* in that big barn has only 30. The Merman show[31] is to have 26, the Judy Holliday show 28.[32]

On 13 July, Robert H. Montgomery (Stevens's lawyer) wrote to his client summarizing the contract between the producers and the creators of *West Side Story*. He, too, mentioned the orchestra: 'There is to be a minimum of 30 musicians. (Note that Miss Crawford strenuously objects to this).' It seems that Crawford got her way on this, as a memorandum of 20 September 1956 from Montgomery to Stevens gives a revised figure: 'The orchestra is to consist of not less than 26 and not more than 30 – the exact number to be agreed upon between Bernstein and you six weeks prior to the first day of rehearsals.'[33]

Some undated notes, jotted down on tiny slips of paper and probably dating from 1957, show Bernstein thinking in terms of 28 players: five reeds, seven brass, two percussion, piano, guitar and strings. However, the details of reed doublings and of the string distribution change. Two of the three lists also propose a Reed I part that is just for flute doubling piccolo (Fig. 4.1). The most unusual choice – consistent in all three of Bernstein's orchestral plans, and a distinctive feature of the final orchestration

---

[29]   Guernsey 1985, p. 51.

[30]   Roger L. Stevens Collection, Library of Congress.

[31]   Presumably a reference to *Happy Hunting*, which opened at the Majestic Theatre on 6 December 1956.

[32]   *Bells Are Ringing*, which opened at the Shubert Theatre on 29 November 1956.

[33]   Roger L. Stevens Collection, Library of Congress.

– is the Reed V part, written for a bassoon with no doubling. This was no accident, and the reason for it is charming: it was intended for a particular player, Sanford Sharoff. He had been a classmate of Bernstein's at the Curtis Institute, and the two remained friends. Sharoff was in the first-night pit band of *Candide* in 1956, as well as in *West Side Story*.[34] Ramin and Kostal did him proud, and Ramin remembers that they found writing this bassoon part an enjoyable challenge.[35] Another highly unusual Broadway sonority was that of three bass clarinets, made possible by some judicious distribution of instruments among the reed parts.

Figure 4.1   Bernstein's notes on orchestration

Fl. picc – alto S. (+Cl?)		Fl. picc		WW		
Cl – E♭		Bn		Fl Picc		
Cl–Bcl–Ten S.		Cl–Bcl–E♭ Cl		Cl–E♭		
Cl–Bcl–Bass S.		Cl–Sax–(Fl)		Cl–Bcl–Ten. Sax		
Bn	5	Cl–Sax–(Ob)		Cl–Bcl–Bass Sax		
				Bn only?		
3 Tpt (1 screamer)		5 WW				
2 Hns		7 Br		3 Tpts		
2 Tbns	7	2 Perc		2 Tbns		
		2 Pno & Guitar		2 Hns?		
7 Vlns		12 Str.				
4 Vc		—		5 + 7		= 12
1 Cb	12	28				
				Piano, Guitar; 2 perc.		4
Piano, Guitar, 2 perc.	4	9 Vln 7 Vln (7 Vln 4 Vc)				
	—	(no Vlas) 2 Vlas		Str		12
	28	2 Vc 2 Vc		7 Vlns		
		1 Cb 1 Cb		2 Vla		
				2 Vc		
				1 Cb		

Bernstein drew up a list of personnel headed 'Orch possibilities'[36] in which he names specific players. These included some of Broadway's finest musicians, among them Herb Sorkin as one of the concertmasters (leaders), Frederick Vogelgesang as assistant concertmaster and Joe Lewis as pianist. Vogelgesang (another graduate of the Curtis Institute) was a gifted violinist, pianist and horn player, and he was also credited as assistant conductor for the production.[37] Joe (Joseph) Lewis later

---

[34]   Sharoff died in 2006, at the age of 87. An obituary was published in the Journal of the Local 802 of the American Federation of Musicians: *Allegro*, 106 (5) (May 2006), online at www.local802afm.org/publication_entry.cfm?xEntry=89974603.

[35]   Sid Ramin, interview with the present author, 25 September 2008.

[36]   LBC.

[37]   One of Frederick Vogelgesang's most extraordinary achievements is a recording of the Brahms Horn Trio op. 40 made in 1964, in which he plays all three of the parts. His later

became musical director for the 1960 revival, but for the original run he was the show's pianist. Lewis was responsible for asking one aspiring Broadway musician to substitute for him when he went on vacation – thus giving John Kander his first work on Broadway.[38]

The definitive orchestration, as executed by Ramin and Kostal and given in the 1994 full score, is similar to that in Bernstein's early plans, but there are several more doublings to the reeds (apart from Reed V), the percussion section has been expanded to a total of five players (one of them playing just timpani), and the piano and guitar parts have extra doublings:

Reed I: piccolo, flute, alto saxophone, clarinet in B flat, bass clarinet

Reed II: clarinet in E flat, clarinet in B flat, bass clarinet

Reed III: piccolo, flute, oboe, English horn, tenor saxophone, baritone saxophone, clarinet in B flat, bass clarinet

Reed IV: piccolo, flute, soprano saxophone, bass saxophone, clarinet in B flat, bass clarinet

Reed V: bassoon

2 horns in F

3 trumpets in B flat (2nd doubling trumpet in D)

2 trombones

Broadway credits as assistant conductor included *Redhead, Greenwillow, 110 in the Shade, Ben Franklin In Paris* and *The Rothschilds*.

[38] Kander (b. 1927) recalled how this came about in an interview with Mike Wood for the William Inge Theatre Festival at Independence, Kansas: '*West Side Story* had just opened [in Philadelphia], and somehow or another I ended up at the opening night party at a place called the Variety Club in the old Bellevue Stratford Hotel. ... There was a bar in the center, I remember, and, in my memory, like eight or nine deep trying to get to the bar, and I was ... not very aggressive, and I would sort of raise my hand, and couldn't get a drink. And this little, short, bald man was in front of me ... and he said, "What do you want? When I order my drink, I'll get yours." He got me a beer, and we talked for a while afterwards. His name was Joe Lewis, and he was the pianist with *West Side Story*. And that was really all there was to it. We kept up ... and then once I got a call from him saying he was going on his vacation, "Would I like to sub for him in the pit?" which is usual. ... So I subbed for him for about three weeks in the pit of *West Side Story*, and Ruth Mitchell, who was the stage manager at that time, was having to put a lot of new people into the cast. She always needed a pianist, and that was my job for that period, and we got used to each other. ... I'm really convinced that if I'd had the guts to get my own drink at the Variety Club bar, I would never have had a career of any sort. It was just a series of accidents that came from that' (www.ingecenter. org/interviews/johnkandertext.htm).

Timpani

Percussion (four players: traps, vibraphone, 4 pitched drums, guiro, xylophone, 3 bongos, 3 cowbells, conga, timbales, snare drum, police whistle, gourd, 2 suspended cymbals, castanets, maracas, finger cymbals, tambourines, small maracas, glockenspiel, woodblock, claves, triangle, temple blocks, chimes, tam-tam, ratchet, slide whistle)

Piano / celesta
Electric guitar / Spanish guitar / mandolin

Violin I–VII
Cello I–IV
Contrabass

Sid Ramin was born in Boston, Massachusetts, in January 1919,[39] a few months after Bernstein, and the two had been childhood friends in Boston. As schoolboys they had explored new music together: Ramin recalls Bernstein buying the music for Gershwin's *Rhapsody in Blue*, then sitting at the piano and sightreading it – complete with an instant transposition of one passage that Bernstein thought worked better in a different key, an early indication of his prodigious talents. Bernstein's datebook first mentions a meeting to discuss *West Side Story* with Sid Ramin on 20 June 1957. Ramin agreed to take on the project provided he could do so in collaboration with Irving Kostal.[40] 'Sid and Irv' (Ramin and Kostal) met Bernstein on 26 June, and the datebooks show that he saw them again on 18, 22 and 24 July, and on 2 August, and they were also present at many of the rehearsals. Following the orchestral rehearsal on 14 August, Bernstein wrote to his wife the next day: 'Orchestra reading all day yesterday – a thrill. We have surprisingly good men, who can really play this terribly difficult stuff (except one or two of them) – & the orchestrations have turned out brilliant.' Bernstein and Ramin met again on 23 August, presumably to make revisions following the show's opening on 19 August.

It was after the first meeting between Bernstein and Ramin, on 20 June 1957, that Ramin called Kostal to ask if he would be interested in working on the show with him. The idea that they collaborate was Ramin's, and Kostal recalls the end of the discussion: '"How do you feel about it?" Sid asked. "Let's do it," was my immediate response.'[41] At the time, Kostal was assisting Don Walker with the orchestrations for Meredith Willson's *The Music Man* ('Marian the Librarian' and 'Trouble In River City' were among the songs Kostal arranged). But the prospect of *West Side Story* was enough to lure him away from *The Music Man* – the show, incidentally, that won

---

[39] Ramin's birthdate is 22 January 1919. His year of birth is often given wrongly as 1924.

[40] Sid Ramin, interview with the present author, 25 September 2008.

[41] Kostal, unpublished memoirs.

the 1958 Tony Award for Best Musical, beating *West Side Story*. Ramin had been producing weekly orchestrations for *The Milton Berle Show* and joined RCA as a staff arranger in about 1956; in 1953, he had worked as assistant to Don Walker on the orchestrations for Bernstein's *Wonderful Town*. Sharing the work on *West Side Story* meant that it could be done at great speed. It needed to be: Ramin recalls that they had to get the job done 'in three weeks'.[42]

The first meeting of Bernstein and both orchestrators was on 26 June 1957 *chez* Bernstein, in the Osborne Apartments, across the street from Carnegie Hall. Plans were quickly put in place:

> Lenny agreed to have Sid and I do the orchestrations with the proviso that Lenny himself would orchestrate along with the two of us ... One of the first things Lenny, Sid and I did was visit the Winter Garden Theatre on Broadway to study the acoustics and also to hear the orchestra we might have to use.[43] ... When Lenny heard the house orchestra at the Winter Garden Theatre, he groaned in despair. In particular he could not stand the two cellists in the orchestra. ... Then he asked us if we could hear the violists. We said no. At our next meeting, Lenny asked us how we felt about eliminating the violas from the orchestra. Sid and I had many times used all kinds of different instrumentations, and we readily agreed to a two-part string section, celli and violins ... between us we decided to have two very good cellists play the difficult parts, and use the two mediocre players only on the loud parts, the tuttis, and, of course, the more simple parts.

Ramin, too, remembered how the three of them went about working on the orchestration for the show:

> During the preparation of West Side Story we had what Lenny called 'pre-orchestration' meetings. Although he was a master orchestrator in the true classical tradition, the modus operandi in Broadway theatre was to utilize musical arrangers. The arduous demands of the theatre did not allow composers the necessary time to orchestrate and arrange their own music. Irwin Kostal ... and I would meet with Lenny and examine every measure of the score in detail, discussing all orchestral possibilities. Although the sketches were very complete, he encouraged and

---

[42]   Sid Ramin, interview with the present author, 25 September 2008.

[43]   It is not clear what they might have heard the orchestra play. The production at the Winter Garden immediately before *West Side Story* was *Ziegfeld Follies of 1957*, which, incidentally, included Carol Lawrence in the cast. However, this closed on 15 June 1957, before Bernstein, Ramin and Kostal met for the first time. The New York rehearsals for *West Side Story*, before the show moved to Washington for the tryouts, took place not at the Winter Garden Theatre but at the Broadway Theatre on West 53rd Street. From Kostal's account, it seems likely that they heard the Winter Garden orchestra at a specially arranged audition in its own theatre.

welcomed all suggestions, especially the more popular musical embellishments that may not have occurred to him as a classicist. Irwin and I would return with our scores a few days later for a 'post-orchestration' meeting. Red pencil in hand, Lenny would delete or add to our scores. When we had, in moments of inspiration, contributed ideas that had not been discussed, he would either say 'Bravo!' or 'Now, why did you do that?' Irwin and I would sometimes question Lenny about the ranges and limits of certain instruments that he suggested we use. As Broadway arrangers and orchestrators we were instinctively cautious about the ability of theatre musicians to play what Lenny wanted. He would invariably say, 'Of course they can play that!' And he was right: they always did.

Orchestrating for the theatre is exhilarating but, at the same time, exhausting and, on occasion, confusing. *West Side Story* was orchestrated in a total of three weeks. Every show seems to have one number that needs constant rewriting and re-orchestrating. That distinction went to 'Something's Coming'. It was common for shows to have out-of-town runs in cities such as Philadelphia, Toronto and New Haven: in this case we were in Washington, D.C. Jerome Robbins, the director and choreographer, didn't particularly like the orchestration. Stephen Sondheim, the lyricist, was not thrilled, either. We kept rewriting and reworking for several days and finally, in desperation, we went back to the original version. Suddenly, everyone approved.[44]

The art of Broadway orchestration usually requires an element of arrangement: creating a more varied texture in the accompaniment than the piano original might suggest. Such seems to have been the case with 'Tonight': 'in a preliminary meeting', Kostal recalls,

Lenny asked us what we were going to do with the song 'Tonight'. I suggested, based upon Lenny's own use of a repetitive rhythm pattern at the beginning of the song, we make it a 'beguine.' He was beside himself. A direct quote: 'I do not compose beguines' … but when I sat at the piano and played a sort of variation of a beguine accompaniment, he finally agreed but insisted we disguise it.

In the last-minute addition, 'Something's Coming', the harmonization of 'Around the corner, or whistling down the river' was apparently inspired by a suggestion made by the orchestrators: the addition of moving inner parts, in this case in the cellos, doubled at the octave by violins.[45] Kostal described Bernstein's reaction: 'He thought it over, and then sat down at the piano and improvised a two-part descending harmonic line that was typically Bernsteinesque and added a new dimension to the song.'

Bernstein certainly took a very active part in the work that Ramin and Kostal produced. Kostal recalled that, in the orchestral score, 'sometimes the writing is

---

[44]   Ramin 2001.

[45]   1994 FS, pp. 74–5.

Lenny's, sometimes Sid's and sometimes mine. Even though Sid and I did the orchestrations, there can be no doubt that we only fulfilled Lenny's instruction.' Ramin confirmed that Bernstein was closely involved in the whole process: 'Lenny was a real stickler for detail', and he added that the orchestration of every number was reviewed and revised with great care.[46] Kostal commented that 'only time prevented him from scoring everything himself'. The complete score (reproduced from Ramin and Kostal's manuscript) in the Sid Ramin Papers bears witness to Bernstein's revisions, and Ramin remembered with amusement that, 'When Lenny ran out of red pencil, he'd change to a green one, or blue, or whatever he had.'[47]

Once the orchestrations started to be heard in rehearsals, Ramin and Kostal also had Robbins to deal with. Apparently he had an aversion to the flute, as they discovered during one rehearsal.

> He objected to a musical section played by our five reeds with the flute playing the top notes. Lenny turned to Sid and I and said quietly, 'Fix it, give him what he wants, put the oboe on the top notes.' We did this within the hour, and the next time this passage was played, Jerry said 'That's better.' Lenny turned to Sid and I and said, 'It sounds the same to me, what about you guys?' Sid and I both agreed it made no difference whatsoever. … But this was the kind of detail we had to cope with.[48]

The Musical Numbers

Act I

1.   Prologue – Instrumental
2.   Jet Song – Riff and Jets
2a.   Jet Song Chase. Change of Scene – Instrumental
3.   Something's Coming – Tony
3a.   Something's Coming Chase. Change of Scene – Instrumental
4.   The Dance at the Gym: Blues – Instrumental
4a.   Promenade – Instrumental
4b.   Mambo – Instrumental
4c.   Cha-Cha – Instrumental
4d.   Meeting Scene – Underscore
4e.   Jump – Underscore
5.   Maria – Tony
6.   Balcony Scene [Tonight] – Maria and Tony
7.   America – Anita, Rosalia and Girls

---

46   Sid Ramin, interview with the present author, 25 September 2008.
47   Sid Ramin, interview with the present author, 25 September 2008.
48   Kostal, unpublished memoirs.

7a.	America to Drugstore. Change of Scene – Instrumental
8.	Cool – Riff and Jets
8a.	Cool Chase. Continuation of Scene – Instrumental
8b.	Under Dialogue *and* Change of Scene – Underscore and Instrumental
9.	Under Dialogue – Instrumental
9a.	One Hand, One Heart (Marriage Scene) – Tony and Maria
10.	Tonight. Ensemble – Maria, Tony, Anita, Riff, Bernardo, Sharks and Jets
11.	The Rumble – Instrumental

Act II

12.	I Feel Pretty – Maria, Francisca, Rosalia, Consuelo
13.	Under Dialogue. Underscore, Tony
13a.	Ballet Sequence – Tony and Maria
13b.	[Ballet Sequence continued] Transition to Scherzo – Instrumental
13c.	[Ballet Sequence continued] Scherzo – Instrumental
13d.	[Ballet Sequence continued] Somewhere – A Girl
13e.	[Ballet Sequence continued] Procession and Nightmare – Entire Company, Instrumental, Maria and Tony
14.	Gee, Officer Krupke – Jets
14a.	Change of Scene – Instrumental
15.	A Boy Like That *and* I Have a Love. Duet – Maria and Anita
15a.	Change of Scene – Instrumental
16.	Taunting Scene – Underscore and Instrumental
17.	Finale – Maria and Tony [and Entire Company]

Act I

1. Prologue

The vexed question of how the show should open has already been discussed in Chapter 3. In the published score, it begins with unsettling, syncopated chords, characterized by simultaneous major and minor thirds, and made more threatening by uneasy silences, punctuated by finger clicks (added as an afterthought;[49] Ex. 4.2). This sets up the first thematic idea, which emerges after 11 bars. Initially heard on alto saxophone and vibraphone, the contours of this melody are unmistakable: a rising octave, a falling triad, then a further jump down a tritone: E–E–C sharp–A–D sharp (Ex. 4.3). This initial motif is joined by another syncopated motif – derived from the opening chords – in parallel thirds (Ex. 4.4).

---

[49] Bernstein's manuscripts of the Prologue and the rehearsal score have silent bars.

Example 4.2 Prologue, opening

Example 4.3 Prologue, bars 12–13

Example 4.4 Prologue, bars 21–7

The two combine to produce an increasingly energized soundscape, mirrored by Robbins's staging: Jets and Sharks flitting on and off the stage, waiting for the thrill of violence to erupt. Bernardo and the Sharks enter (bar 134), to the most forceful version yet of the 'shofar' motif. A Shark trips up a Jet, and from here the 'shofar' motif is used as the springboard for a more animated section (bar 140) with bustling piano and traps supporting the tune on reeds, soon reinforced by brass. At its climax, the Prologue positively exults in violence, the whole orchestra playing the descending part of the first theme (bar 182), following this with a yet more jubilant variant (bar 198), an inversion of the same idea (Exx. 4.5 and 4.6).

Example 4.5 Prologue, bars 182–5

Example 4.6 Prologue, bars 198–201

Virtually every phrase of this number has explicit tritones in the melody, or, immediately following the blast on Krupke's whistle, in chords that include sharpened fourths (bars 262–5). The 'Prologue' ends with a telescoped reprise of the opening (bars 269–79).

2. Jet Song

Originally the musical material for this song was embedded in the vocal version of the Opening, which is substantially longer than its instrumental replacement. But while the rehearsal score of the Opening includes the Jet Song music within it, not all the elements come in the same order, and the lyrics are different. Still, the two numbers as they now stand have such close links that the Jet Song functions as the vocal consequence of the instrumental Prologue. As a self-standing number, it begins with 'Prologue' music under dialogue; at bar 24, the opening chords, transposed down a tone into B flat major, are speeded up to provide a more animated syncopated accompaniment over a four-note repeating pattern: B flat–G, B flat–F sharp, in 6/8. This rhythmic engine has a strong feeling of two-in-a-bar, but this is disrupted by Riff's tune, punched out in crotchets, three per bar, full of breathless momentum and pushing towards bar 44, where the Prologue theme returns to the words 'You're never alone, You're never disconnected!' Much of the rest of the song is based on material already heard in the Prologue. The optional cut music (from bar 93 to bar 128) – the passage beginning 'Oh, when the Jets fall in at the cornball dance' – was placed earlier on in the vocal Opening, and it provides part of the musical source material for the Blues in the Dance at the Gym.

3. 'Something's Coming'
The last song to be added to the show, 'Something's Coming' was put in to give Tony a stronger dramatic profile from the outset. By the time Bernstein composed this number the prevalence of tritones in the score had presumably become apparent, since this song is full of them. Along with sharpened fourths, the other characteristic of the melody is flattened sevenths, both of which are to be found in the Jet Song, as is the ambiguity of duple and triple time in the outer sections of both songs, and the fast tempo. This makes good dramatic sense: after all, Tony is a member of the same gang. But while 'Something's Coming' has features that mark out the earlier music for the Jets, the song has a more optimistic and less aggressive outlook than the two preceding numbers – there is a certain bright-eyed hope about it that sets Tony's music aside from the negativity and gang mentality of Riff and the Jets. As for the melody itself, it almost seems like a breathless pre-echo of 'Maria'. The music for 'Who knows? / There's something due any day; / I will know right away. / Soon as it shows' at the start of 'Something's Coming' has several points in common with the 'Maria' tune, not only in its use of the tritone, but the repeated rising idea, G sharp–A–B. Indeed, if the D is placed an octave lower, the rising figure precisely matches the contour of the 'Maria' opening. When the start of this song is recalled in the first bar of the Dance at the Gym, its dreamy transformation sounds even closer to the 'Maria' melody, which is yet to emerge (Exs. 4.7a and b).

Example 4.7a   'Something's Coming', bars 7–17

Example 4.7b   'Maria', bars 9–11

4. The Dance at the Gym
    Blues
    Promenade
    Mambo
    Cha-Cha
    Meeting Scene
    Jump

This is an extended sequence of dances, two of them Latin American in origin, and its importance lies not only in the considerable spectacle provided, but also in sharpening the focus of the rivalry between Jets and Sharks – through competitive, if not downright combative, dancing – as a means of advancing the plot through music and dance.

The stage directions immediately preceding this scene describe a remarkable transformation as Maria

> begins to whirl in the dress as the shop slides off and a flood of gaily colored streamers pours down. As Maria begins to turn and turn, going offstage, Shark girls, dressed for the dance, whirl on, followed by Jet girls, by boys from both gangs. The streamers fly up again for the next scene.[50]

The combination of Oliver Smith's sets and Jean Rosenthal's lighting design here worked together to produce a moment of extraordinary visual magic, accompanied by music that begins with an echo of 'Who knows?' from 'Something's Coming', which in turn looks forward to 'Maria' (see Exx. 4.7a and b, above).

After this brief transformation, the first dance is a brassy Blues, the main tune of which (bars 8–12, and so on) is derived from a part of the Jet Song that is sometimes cut: 'Oh, when the Jets fall in at the cornball dance, / We'll be the sweetest dressin' gang in pants',[51] interrupted by the opening chords of the Prologue. In this dance the Jets have the hall to themselves, and the music is full of their musical fingerprints until the end of the dance, when Bernardo, Maria, Anita and Chino enter. This time the syncopated Prologue chords are disjointed, the silences tense and uncomfortable.

---

50   1958 LIB, p. 27.
51   1994 FS, pp. 43–6, starting at bar 100.

Jets, Sharks and their womenfolk are now set for a confrontation at the gym. Glad Hand, the well-meaning master of ceremonies, encourages the dancers to mix, and the stilted little 'Promenade' (marked 'Tempo di Paso Doble') gives them time to find their places – the gangs ignoring Glad Hand's doomed attempt at social engineering by reaching for the partners they wanted in the first place – in time for the explosive Mambo. After the big loping Blues and rhythmically prim Promenade, the eruptive impact of the Mambo is all the more thrilling. Launched by a fusillade of Latin percussion (bongos, timbales, cowbells and traps), this is a violently confrontational and competitive dance which leaves the Jets marginalized. The main Mambo theme begins in bar 72 with a two-bar phrase ending with pairs of descending notes, and the next two bars are a varied repeat of this. If the first three numbers introduced us, musically speaking, to the world of the Jets, here are the Sharks: the Mambo theme is a cousin – at least in terms of its melodic outline and especially the ends of phrases – to 'A Boy Like That'. As Tony enters towards the end of the Mambo, Bernstein introduces some rugged fragments of what is to become the 'Maria' motif (at first in trombones), and energy levels subside as the music leads directly into the Cha-Cha, a delicate dance arrangement that gives a more developed foretaste of the as-yet-unheard 'Maria' tune. This becomes still more apparent in the ensuing Meeting Scene (where the underscoring includes all the essential components of 'Maria'). As the focus returns to the others at the dance, a reprise of the 'Tempo di Paso Doble' gives way to the Jump, spiky, dry and unsettled before it peters out under dialogue.

5. 'Maria'

This song begins with one of the very few moments of recitative-like music in the show, sung over a stepwise-descending bass in crotchets which is to return in the Balcony Scene. Bernstein's setting of the text here captures the obsessive pleasure of new young love through the repetition of Maria's name, the last phrase of which seems to generate the first phrase of the main theme of the song. The 'Maria' tune has already been extensively trailed in the latter part of the Dance at the Gym – present in the Mambo, the Cha-Cha and the Meeting Scene. This might be thought to undermine its impact here, but the reverse is the case: at last the tune can blossom in its lyrical glory. The melody is full of sharpened fourths and tritone intervals, but instead of suggesting conflict and violence, as they have up to now, these have become an expression of yearning, an ardent outpouring of a love between members of conflicting groups. The tune itself has other potent features too. The major/minor ambivalence in 'And suddenly that name / Will never be the same to me' (A natural on 'suddenly', A flat on 'never'), and the use of triplets – the repeated 'Maria' during the introduction, and throughout much of the song itself – to propel the sense of rapture across the barlines.

Once the song was composed, the first person to play it to Jerome Robbins was Stephen Sondheim. It was an occasion that taught the younger man a useful lesson in how to stage a number of this kind:

Leonard Bernstein was away on a concert tour, and I had to play the first numbers to Jerry. I played him 'Maria, I've just met a girl named Maria and suddenly that name will never be the same to me – pause', and he said, 'What do you want him to do during that pause?'. I said, 'Well he just stands there.' He said, 'You try and stage that. Give me something to do – stage it for me.' And I've taken that advice to heart ever since.[52]

6. Balcony Scene

The instrumental underscoring that opens the scene is derived entirely from 'Maria', and the descending crotchets from the start of the 'Maria' recitative (now in minims) accompany the first singing to be heard in the scene: Maria's 'Only you, you're the only thing I'll see forever'. But after two bars Bernstein animates this with a new, gently propulsive syncopated idea that is to become one of the song's principal motive forces, giving this duet a much livelier sense of youthful rapture than Tony's preceding solo. The 'Tonight' tune is very ingeniously constructed, although it moves in regular eight-bar phrases. Starting with an aspirational rising fourth, the melody is notable for its unexpected changes of direction and the seductive mobility of the harmonies. The first eight bars are in B flat major, each phrase-ending drawn to the supertonic (C), which is also a strong presence in the harmony, oscillating for the first four bars between chords of B flat major coloured by the addition of C, and C major with the added D – all this over a B flat in the bass. The C in the melody in turn changes from being the supertonic to becoming the leading note for the next eight bars ('Tonight, tonight, there's only you tonight'), which shift into D flat before moving towards F major. Again, the F that ends this phrase becomes the leading note for the start of the next ('Today, all day I had the feeling a miracle would happen'), which begins on a second-inversion chord of G flat major. This eight-bar phrase ends on a chord of C major; the melody note here, also a C, this time becomes a supertonic approach to the return to B flat major ('For here you are'). Incidentally, Bernstein's earlier sketches for this tune always had the modulation up a minor third at the ninth bar, though what is probably the earliest sketch (at a time when 'Tonight' was intended as only one of the component parts of the Quintet) fizzles out on the third note of the 11th bar. As was noted in Chapter 3, the 'Tonight' duet was a late replacement, but the result is an inspiration; on its first appearance in this nocturnal tryst, the melody is filled with all the elation of young love, but when it reappears in the Quintet, it seems to take on a darker and more frenetic quality, lending it a new but no less euphoric meaning.

The end of the duet has several reminiscences of one of the songs that was initially considered for the Balcony Scene, but that was moved to the Act II ballet. During Tony's miniature soliloquy on the 'Tonight' tune (starting at bar 121), and in the ensuing dialogue, the bass clarinet, bassoon and flute play music from 'Somewhere'.

---

[52] Sondheim, in response to an audience question at the National Theatre, London, 5 March 1990.

The most memorable moment in this beautiful passage of underscoring is the modulation into C flat major (bars 127–36; Ex. 4.8), where the two ideas – the bassoon playing 'Somewhere' and the strings playing 'Tonight' – come together in a magical combination, at just the moment when Maria reappears on the balcony.

Example 4.8 Balcony Scene, bars 127–36

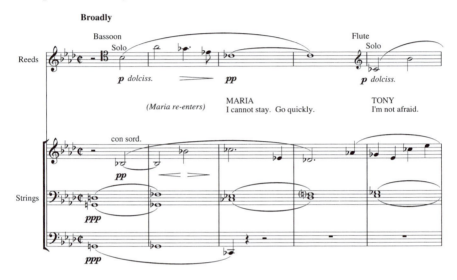

Again, it is the 'Somewhere' theme that provides the material for the last four bars of the number (bars 151–4). In one earlier manuscript ('Balcony Scene – Newissimo'[53]) there is even more of the 'Somewhere' tune: four bars of it before the first vocal entry (here Tony singing 'What are you? Tell me everything you are', later changed to Maria's 'Only you, you're the only thing I'll see forever').

7. *'America'*

This is a song and dance number for the Puerto Rican girls that tackles some serious issues with a light touch. At the time, though, it was the song that stirred up some controversy – albeit rather a storm in a teacup. Sondheim and Bernstein recalled it in the Dramatists Guild Symposium:

> Sondheim: I got a letter complaining about the one line 'Island of tropic diseases', outraged on behalf of Puerto Rico, claiming that we were making fun of Puerto Rico and being sarcastic about it. But I didn't change it.
>
> Bernstein: Opening night in Washington we had a telephone message from *La Prensa*[54] saying that they'd heard about this song and we would be picketed when we came to New York unless we omitted or changed the song ... telling us everybody knows Puerto Rico is free of disease. And it wasn't just that line they objected to. ... They didn't hear 'Nobody knows in America / Puerto Rico's in America' – it's a little hard to hear at that tempo. We met that threat by doing nothing about it, not changing a syllable, and we were not picketed.[55]

Latin American rhythms had long fascinated Bernstein, from his first publication – a solo piano transcription of Copland's *El Salón México* – and his early ballet *Conch Town*, both dating from 1941. 'America' itself is marked 'Tempo di Huapango (fast)'. As has been noted above, this was a kind of Mexican dance-song marked by cross-rhythms – exemplified in the 1941 orchestral *Huapango* by José Pablo Moncayo (a composer Bernstein met at Tanglewood in 1942, the year after composing *Conch Town*). When the 'America' theme first appeared in *Conch Town* it had no separate

---

[53]   LBC.

[54]   The oldest Spanish-language newspaper in New York, founded in 1913. In 1963 it amalgamated with *El Diario* to become *El Diario La Prensa*. Even the *New York Times* took up this story, with an article by Howard A. Rusk, MD: 'The facts don't rhyme: an analysis of irony in lyrics linking Puerto Rico's breezes to tropic diseases' (29 September 1957): 'Today', Dr Rusk informed readers, 'Puerto Rico has no significant disease problems related to its tropical climate', going on to cite copious statistics, and concluding that 'Mr. Sondheim's lyrics will probably remain unchanged and Puerto Rico's morbidity and mortality rates will continue to decline. In the meantime, *West Side Story* is a dramatic and effective production and Puerto Rico is a healthy island.'

[55]   Guernsey 1985, p. 53.

tempo marking, but Bernstein was presumably aiming to add local colour at this point in *West Side Story* – and here, too, it is a real dance-song – even though he may have got the country wrong, since the huapango is usually thought to be from Mexico rather than from Puerto Rico.

The main verse–chorus sections of 'America' are a judicious mixture of satire and celebration. The musical energy derives from the cross-rhythms, whose origins lie in the dance-song form on which the number is based. Coming after the contrast of Puerto Rico as a 'lovely island', then an 'ugly island', the main section drives forward with good humour to its riotous conclusion; it is not one of the most musically demanding numbers in the show, but since the spectacle is coloured by some amusing and ironic social commentary, it certainly works at this point.

8. 'Cool'

This song is one of the clearest instances in the score of the use of tritones in a melody ('Boy, boy, crazy boy') and of major–minor combinations (the chords under 'Get cool, boy!'). The structure of the number as it eventually developed is highly unusual, since more than half of the song is not only instrumental but also fugal. The start of the fugue is based on a subject that (eventually) uses all 12 notes of the chromatic scale. Its first four notes have more than a hint of Beethoven's *Grosse Fuge* about them, moving up a semitone, then a seventh (in Beethoven a diminished seventh; in Bernstein a minor seventh),[56] and down a semitone (Beethoven: G–G sharp–F natural–E; Bernstein: C–D flat–C flat–B flat).[57] Maybe it is stretching a point to suggest that Bernstein's subsequent development of this fugue might also owe a debt to Beethoven's model, notably the jagged dotted rhythms of the countersubject. However fanciful this may be, Bernstein creates here a stunningly exciting jazz fugue the like of which had never been heard on Broadway before. Now-familiar motifs from earlier in the score are used to propel the music, especially the 'shofar' call, and – only at the climax – the 'Cool' tune itself, given a gloriously flamboyant big-band treatment, marked 'Tutti sock' on Bernstein's manuscript (Ex. 4.9), an indication that sadly didn't make it into any of the published scores.[58]

A reprise of the song follows (this time sung by all the Jets), then fragments of the dotted counter-melody from the fugue return and gradually disintegrate, ending with a nihilistic descent in octaves, B–F sharp–C, using the song's opening interval in reverse to bring the number to a close.

---

[56]   The second, third and fourth notes of the fugue are also the first three notes of 'Somewhere', as noted by Block (1997, p. 265).

[57]   A parallel already noted by Banfield (1993, p. 37).

[58]   'Sock' as Bernstein uses it here was a jazz and swing term referring to a final chorus. Evan Hunter's *Second Ending* (1956), a gritty novel contemporary with *West Side Story*, uses it in a way that could almost be describing Bernstein's music here: Hunter writes that the band 'rode into the sock chorus like a storm cloud of marauders'.

Example 4.9 'Cool', bars 123–8, from Bernstein's autograph manuscript, marked 'Tutti sock'

9 and 9a. 'One Hand, One Heart' (Marriage Scene)
The number begins with a passage under dialogue that is a reprise of the Cha-Cha from the Dance at the Gym. When the song itself begins (bar 35), the introduction starts with eight bars of 'Somewhere' music, just as the original Balcony Scene version had done – but at that time it was almost certainly intended to follow 'Somewhere', whereas here it becomes another pre-echo of a song we have yet to hear. When 'One Hand, One Heart' was moved to the Marriage Scene from the Balcony Scene during rehearsals, very little needed to be changed. Bernstein and Sondheim needed to write new dialogue for Maria and Tony over the underscoring in bars 43–66, replacing the earlier balcony dialogue, and there is evidence for just such a change on the manuscript dated 4 July 1957. At that point, the melody was still in dotted minims, one note per bar. Only after this did Bernstein rewrite the vocal line, at Sondheim's urging,[59] to begin with three crotchets and a dotted minim. Once Maria and Tony start to sing, each phrase of their rather hymn-like tune grows from the third degree of the scale, widening the interval to the second note of the phrase each time: B flat–C flat, B flat–D flat, then B flat–E flat. The falling fifths on 'One hand, one heart' (bars 95–8 and, a tone higher, bars 133–6) are certainly better suited to the quiet intimacy of this scene than to the blissful first encounter for which the song was originally intended.

Arthur Laurents has told an amusing anecdote about this song, which he seems to have found a little dull:

---

59   See Banfield 1993, p. 35.

Out of town, whenever the first slow notes of 'One Hand' were played, three doors in the auditorium opened and three of the collaborators walked out for the 'cigarette song.' Poor Lenny, heaviest smoker of all, stayed inside, gasping for a cigarette but moved. Music makes some composers weep. Especially their own.[60]

10. *'Tonight' (Ensemble)*

This number follows on immediately from 'One Hand, One Heart' – a brutal interruption of Tony and Maria's reverie. At the time of the first performance this was noted as a number with clear operatic roots, drawing, as Richard Coe observed in the *Washington Post*, on 'the patterns of grand opera' to produce 'an astonishingly intricate quintet'.[61] By the time of the New York premiere it was no longer a quintet in the strict sense, as Riff and Bernardo were joined by their fellow gang members for much of the number.[62] A stand-alone scene – always conceived as such – this ensemble begins with raucous chords over an ostinato bass line: E–F sharp–G sharp, in *marcato* crotchets, a pounding pattern, seemingly contemptuous of the barlines, which is played 14 times, then ten times, and which punctuates the whole number. The start is coloured by suggestions of whole-tone harmonies (raucous chords of E and C shrieking over the ostinato bass) that also return – in conjunction with the ostinato – as a kind of instrumental line of demarcation between the sections of the number. Jets and Sharks express hatred and derision about their rivals – but not directly to them – in a melody that seems to spit with aggression, beginning with a descending fourth, until they unite in their thrill at the prospect of the fight that is to come, and all sing 'We're gonna rock it tonight, / We're gonna jazz it up and have us a ball!', the first time in the number where the harmony stabilizes, and this time the melody begins with a rising fourth. Anita sings a slinky variant of the gangs' opening music (over the same ostinato), and her last two notes also serve as the first two notes of Tony's 'Tonight' (Ex. 4.10). As mentioned above, this was the first number in which Bernstein used the 'Tonight' tune: the Balcony Scene duet version was derived from its appearance here. In the Quintet, the 'Tonight' melody emerges from a very different starting point – specifically from the rising fourths ('Tonight!') that end the belligerent verse sung by Jets and Sharks, and Anita's variant of it, oozing sultriness and the prospect of gratification.

This original placing of the 'Tonight' melody was thus part of a complex, developing musical texture. At the end of Tony's verse, the opening music returns as Riff and Tony sort out fight tactics. Maria then takes up the 'Tonight' theme, rising above the fray – animated by the antagonistic quavers from the opening combined with the rising three-note assignation idea (two semiquavers and a longer note, on

---

[60]   Laurents 2000, p. 351.

[61]   Coe 1957a.

[62]   A note in 2000 VS states that 'if the scene is staged with more than the designated five people, the members of the gangs may sing with their respective leaders (except in bars 103–125)'.

Example 4.10 'Tonight' Ensemble, bars 64–74

the word 'Tonight') derived from the end of each phrase of the gang music. All this is sung by Riff, Tony and Anita ('sexily'). Gradually the others on the stage join in with music of increasing density and blood-lust. Rhythmic variety is added by treating the gang music in augmentation (Sharks in bars 130–32), and introducing a new idea in descending minims ('They began it', starting with the Sharks in bar 134) as Tony joins Maria in octaves on the 'Tonight' theme. At bar 142 ('Agitato') the Quintet moves towards an inexorable conclusion. At first the two gangs surge forward with their initial quaver idea, first in thirds, then in unison ('We're gonna rock it tonight'), just as the two lovers reach the joyous final phrase of the 'Tonight' theme. A raging, tumultuous C major conclusion thus cements the triumph of both love and hatred at the end of this extraordinary and dazzlingly original number. There is a headlong momentum in this ensemble that seems to recall Verdi, but it is operatic urgency rather than operatic excess that has provided the point of departure here: there is no sense whatsoever of Bernstein falling into an 'opera trap'; instead he has created a Broadway reinterpretation of a model that was the ideal fit for this critical moment in the drama.

Frank Rich has proposed an interesting alternative view of the ensemble that looks not to opera but to film, with its rapid intercutting and juxtaposition of disparate ideas, drawn together to create a climactic whole:

> Bernstein's bringing all his themes together – it's such highly charged drama. It's the fulcrum of the show, dramatically, when everything has become like a train rushing forward, in a tragedy. And you have this sense of cinematic cross-cutting, done without cinema; done by the art of the theatre. That is pretty hard to beat.[63]

11. The Rumble

Marked 'Tempo di Prologue', this is both dramatically and musically the inevitable, deadly outcome of the opening scene, even though it was not the first music planned to be here (see Chapter 3). Making extensive use of the 'shofar call' tritones and numerous derivatives of it, often heard as little fragmentary shards, the climax comes with the most numbing restatement of the 'shofar' idea, as Bernardo kills Riff. The killing of Bernardo by Tony a mere ten bars later intensifies the sense of a murderous frenzy, all sense of control lost. Act I closes in the same way as it began, with a purely instrumental number, and while that symmetry is certainly elegant, the music is anything but: it portrays brutality with an immediacy that is shocking. In terms of sheer boldness, the score is as innovative here as the drama: Bernstein's music is at its most relentlessly uncompromising. The corpses of Bernardo and Riff are all that is left on the stage at the end, as a slow curtain is accompanied by the chimes of a distant clock which serve as a tolling memorial bell, and by the death rattle of a high E flat xylophone tremolo in the orchestra.

---

[63]   NPR 2007.

Act II

12. 'I Feel Pretty'

This fast waltz-song begins with an extended instrumental version (in E flat major) that functions as the show's Entr'acte before the voices enter. After the carnage at the end of Act I, it can seem wildly out of place, a problem identified by Arthur Laurents: '"I Feel Pretty" was prototypical Hammerstein, and a puzzle. Hardly what a Puerto Rican girl would sing, out of the style of the show, but the audience loved it. They still do, and it still doesn't belong.'[64] Sondheim, too, has made no secret of the misgivings he has, not least about his own lyrics. He is harshly self-critical. It was apparently Sheldon Harnick who first suggested that in this song the lyrics were too clever, too sophisticated. Sondheim recalled:

> I had this uneducated Puerto Rican girl singing, 'It's alarming how charming I feel.' You *know* she would not have been unwelcome in Noël Coward's living room. Sheldon was very gentle but I immediately went back and wrote a simplified version of the lyric which nobody connected with the show would accept. So there it is to this day embarrassing me every time it's sung.[65]

Given that two of the collaborators have expressed such reservations about the song, it is something of a surprise to find that it is always such a hit on stage. Is it no more than a crowd-pleaser? From a practical point of view it serves a dual purpose: as an entr'acte and as a rare moment of light relief. One of the few other lighter songs that had been considered – albeit one with a much sharper edge ('Like Everybody Else') – had never made it into in Act I (see Chapter 3), so aside from the delicious sarcasm of 'America', this is the only hint of humour in the score until the high jinks of 'Gee, Officer Krupke'. However, the situation of Maria daydreaming about being in love while her friends mock her has an engaging absurdity about it – and it is a song that could work only at this moment in the show: while the audience has witnessed what has happened, Maria does not yet know about the tragedy at the end of Act I. It is surely this tension that makes the number dramatically effective, Maria's blissful ignorance preceding her discovery of the shocking truth a few moments later.

13. Ballet Sequence

Under Dialogue
Ballet Sequence
Transition to Scherzo
Scherzo
Somewhere
Procession and Nightmare

---

[64] Laurents 2000, p. 351.
[65] Zadan 1974, p. 23.

There was nothing new about a second-act ballet in a Broadway musical, but Robbins and Bernstein took quite a novel approach for the *West Side Story* ballet. Though this is a dream sequence, like the *Carousel* ballet, it covers a surprisingly wide emotional range: the desperate need for Tony and Maria to escape; an idealized world in which gang violence is banished; a self-contained song ('Somewhere') expressing the hope that such a place may one day become a reality; a solemn procession; memories of the recent past recalled in the Nightmare; and, to end, a partial reprise of 'Somewhere'. This final form of the ballet was only arrived at after numerous revisions and – as has been noted in Chapter 3 – at least one of these was even made after the orchestration had been completed and the full score reproduced. According to Carol Lawrence, Robbins originally planned to use two dancers to represent Tony and Maria:

> Jerry Robbins had chosen dancers from Ballet Theatre to play the parts of Tony and Maria in the Ballet; but I asked him if Larry Kert and I could at least learn the steps and try to play our own roles. He finally agreed and we worked like demons to please him. We did get to dance and it was one of my favorite times on any stage.[66]

The Ballet Sequence begins with agitated underscoring after Maria has beaten her fists on Tony's chest, calling him 'Killer killer killer killer killer'. As Tony tries to explain to Maria what he has done, the music is a dark and urgent syncopated recollection of the 'Maria' motif. This persists in the orchestra as Tony begins to sing ('And I'll take you away'), joined by Maria in octaves on 'Somewhere there must be a place we can feel we're free'. After this, the orchestra continues with more insistent rhythmic patterns, all based on the 'Maria' motif and its variant in the Cha-Cha. At the start of the next section, headed 'Transition to Scherzo' in the published scores, it is again the 'Maria' motif that dominates the musical argument, but here in a slower, sweeter context. The last four bars of this Transition speed up, using rhythmic ideas that are to dominate the coming Scherzo, one of Bernstein's most elegant and rhythmically alluring musical ideas, a more complex – and less settled – equivalent of the kind of music heard in the Cha-Cha in Act I. Towards the end of this section, the 'Maria' motif becomes much more insistent (from bar 112 onwards), heard over the top of the rhythmic tag that first appeared at bar 72. Twice as slowly, that same tag brings the section to a close, followed by a horn playing a B on a pause, giving the note for the start of 'Somewhere'. Sung by 'A Girl', this marks the moment at which the show is at its most distant from the grim realities of life, and closest, perhaps, to the tradition of 'dream' ballets that are found in a work like *Carousel*, with the obvious difference that here it is sung. But by giving the song to a nameless voice, the idealized dream-world is removed from the characters in the drama – an inspired stroke that emerged during the process of revising and refashioning the ballet. The musical antecedents of this song are

---

[66] Carol Lawrence, personal communication.

relatively unimportant, I think, however striking the parallels with Beethoven (especially) may be: Bernstein had the melody in mind long before *West Side Story*, but its use here, and the references to it elsewhere in the score, are memorable in their own right. The melody has a bewitching unpredictability about it, despite the ostensibly straightforward phrase structure (in eight-bar groups). The two-note 'Somewhere' motif first appears in a descending form in the eighth bar (bar 130 of the Ballet Sequence), and a melody that initially leads downwards at the end of every phrase then takes on a more aspirational turn when the 'Somewhere' motif is inverted ('Some day!, somewhere', bars 139–40), to powerful expressive effect. What follows – the 'Procession and Nightmare' – begins with an instrumental recollection of the song, with the 'Somewhere' motif heard at the same time as the tune of 'I Have a Love'. In the seventh bar of this section (bar 167 of the Ballet Sequence), the tune of 'There's a place for us' is heard in the orchestra, and two bars later the company starts to sing the opening of the melody as a kind of round. This fizzles out – a last fragment finished by the orchestra after a general pause – the music then becoming increasingly agitated and violence erupting as the syncopated rhythms of the opening of the whole Ballet Sequence return in their most violent guise. At the height of this 'Nightmare' section, the music of the Rumble is recalled; it subsides uneasily on a sustained oboe note leading to a shortened reprise of 'Somewhere', sung by Tony, then by both the young lovers.

14. 'Gee, Officer Krupke'

At this point in Act II, the Jets turn briefly from thoughts of gang violence to their own collective dysfunction. Sondheim, for one, has expressed doubts about whether a song of this kind really belongs at this point in the show (see Chapter 3). In terms of the overall trajectory of the drama, it is hard to disagree with him. But a good production certainly vindicates Laurents's instincts for a moment of relief, not least because the number is so skilfully written and also provides an all-male counterpoise to the all-female Shark girls' 'America' in Act I: both are engagingly cynical observations on social issues that are fundamentally serious. 'Krupke' is great musical slapstick – burlesque theatre gags in the score (even the tempo marking is 'Fast, vaudeville style'), including the only instance in the show of comedy tritones (the first two notes of each verse), and lyrics that are brilliantly sharp and funny (none more so than Baby John's lines as the female social worker: 'Eek! Officer Krupke, you've done it again. / This boy don't need a job, he needs a year in the pen. / It ain't just a question of misunderstood; / Deep down inside him, he's no good!'). Besides the zany humour, another feature of this song is that the Jets are seen to be mercilessly sending up one of their potential allies: the cop who throughout the show is more or less on their side rather than that of the Puerto Ricans (who are viewed with the deepest suspicion by both the forces of law and order in the cast, Schrank and Krupke). Moreover, performed by a gang whose leader has recently been murdered, the song portrays the Jets as quite a callous group of youths. The point is never laboured, of course, but in this song the Jets seem indifferent to human tragedy, finding it easier to mock someone else (and each other). This may well add to the song's effectiveness, and it certainly lessens the potentially jarring effect of 'Gee, Officer Krupke''s position in the show.

15. 'A Boy Like That' and 'I Have a Love' (Duet)

After the extensive revisions briefly described in Chapter 3, this duet became one of the strongest songs in the show. The brusque, savage two-bar introduction sets up the first part of the number with its grinding major and minor seconds, jagged accents, disruptive rhythms and irregular barring. This is at the darkest end of the musical spectrum – the orchestration includes the inky sounds of three bass clarinets – with Anita giving full vent to her feelings: in the score she is marked to sing 'bitterly', but there is rage too, her music relentlessly repeating phrases dominated by major and minor seconds, the same intervals that are heard sounding simultaneously in the orchestra (Ex. 4.11).

Example 4.11   'A Boy Like That', bars 36–9

Maria's first interjection ('Oh no, Anita, no!') is a striking change – in terms of register, and in terms of the shape of her first phrase, in crotchets rather than Anita's spitting quavers – but she then takes up a phrase already sung by Anita ('A boy who kills cannot love') with new lyrics ('It isn't true, not for me') and more luminous orchestration. At the end of this phrase, instead of coming to an abrupt conclusion as Anita's had done ('Very smart, Maria, very smart!'), her line blossoms into a more lyrical theme ('But my heart knows they're wrong'), heard in combination with a reprise of Anita's opening music. Only then does Maria attempt to take control of the situation, telling Anita she 'should know better': now the lyrical theme that had been an almost desperate counterpoint to Anita emerges fully fledged as 'I have a love'. Bernstein's tune begins with small oscillations stepwise over a gently syncopated accompaniment, but then the melody opens out with rising minor sevenths ('I love him; I'm his'), and later the intervals widen still further to major ninths ('But hold him, hold him forever'), each time falling a note (first a semitone, then a tone) at the end of the phrase – an achingly eloquent expression of Maria's love. Finally, Anita capitulates, and in a moment of tenderness the two sing a partial reprise of the melody, mostly in thirds, although doubts certainly linger in the orchestral part: the voices finish on a long G, but they are cut off by the plunging phrase that had originally set the line 'Right or wrong, what else could I do', now heard *fortissimo*, and leading to an uncertain close as Anita tells Maria that Chino has a gun and has started a manhunt for Tony.

16. Taunting Scene

Heard after a pre-recorded reprise of the Mambo from the Dance at the Gym (to be heard as if coming from a juke-box), the music for this shocking and sordid scene was mainly drawn from *Conch Town*, but its driving force and its lack of harmonic and rhythmic stability make it an apposite accompaniment to the chilling stage action, in which Anita is taunted and then assaulted – all but gang-raped – by the Jets at Doc's drugstore. (According to the directions in the libretto, Anita 'is encircled and driven by the whole pack. At the peak, she is shoved so that she falls in a corner. Baby John is lifted up high and dropped on her.') Heard in the context of *West Side Story* rather than the original ballet, this seems like a grotesque reworking of 'America' (both the 'Puerto Rico' introduction, and the main song): music that had been used earlier for caustic jokes about Puerto Rico has now become a cruel perversion of the same material, to express the horrifying reality of life for a Puerto Rican woman as a despised immigrant. Though not included on the original cast album, this instrumental number is – thanks to its dramatic situation – one of the most disturbing moments in the whole score: a painful, disillusioned counterpart to the instrumental Rumble in Act I.

17. Finale

Tony is fatally wounded, but still hopes to escape with Maria. She holds him close and starts to sing part of 'Somewhere' ('Hold my hand and we're halfway there'), without any instrumental accompaniment. She is briefly joined by Tony in this stark, pathetic reprise, but he dies, and she falters; the third bar of her 'Somehow, someday!' is finished, after the shortest of pauses, by the orchestra, which then plays the tenderest *pianissimo* recollection of the 'Somewhere' theme as Maria rests Tony on the ground and brushes his lips with her fingers. The company has gathered on the stage, and Maria turns on Sharks and Jets alike in her blistering speech. Finally, disgust and resentment spent, she turns and holds out her hand to Chino, then to Action – Shark and Jet – and says her last private words of love to Tony, words first used in the Balcony Scene: 'Te adoro, Anton.' The final moments of *West Side Story* are a powerful, ritualized symbol of warring factions shocked into a moment of unity and some sort of dignity. The Procession music based on 'I Have a Love' is heard over tolling bass notes, a final recollection of 'Somewhere', and, as Maria follows the cortège proudly off the stage, the musical ends with a combination of notes that recalls the very start of the show – in descending order: G–E–C–F sharp, coming to unquiet rest here with three quiet chords of C major, rendered desolate by the F sharps that undermine them.

Chapter 5

Reception

The Show's Backers

The private individuals who finance a Broadway show are essential to its success. By May 1957, the new production team of Bobby Griffith and Hal Prince was in place, and they set about raising the necessary funding from 'angels'. Though Cheryl Crawford had abandoned the project, her original co-producer, Roger L. Stevens, remained associated with the production. Stevens was a remarkable Broadway figure: a property developer by profession and someone who relished the big gesture – none bigger than in 1951, when he led a syndicate to buy the Empire State Building.[1] Stevens gave enthusiastic support to *West Side Story*, and this extended to organizing the opening-night party in New York. His continued involvement resulted in rather a convoluted formula for the original production credits: 'Robert E. Griffith and Harold S. Prince (by arrangement with Roger L. Stevens)'.

The Roger L. Stevens Collection in the Library of Congress includes extensive documentation of the arrangements for the financial backing of *West Side Story* which reveals that he gave the production a helping hand by enlisting the support of several of his associates in real estate, as well as making a substantial investment of his own in the show. Griffith and Prince set up a limited partnership called the West Side Story Company, and each of the backers became limited partners in this company. The original partnership agreement, dated 28 June 1957, lists 173 backers, along with the sums they invested. They include the violinist Mischa Elman ($1,250), the composer Isadore Freed ($1,500), the publisher and composer Albert Sirmay ($500),[2] the playwright Richard Bissell ($750), the actor Stephen Douglass ($600),[3]

---

[1] According to the obituary in the *New York Times* (Pace 1998), Stevens bought the Empire State Building for 'a bit more than $50 million, then a titanic sum; he more than doubled his investment when he sold his interest in the building three years later'.

[2] Albert Sirmay [Albert Szirmai] (1880–1967) was a Hungarian operetta composer who moved to New York in 1926 and took a job with Chappell & Co., becoming music editor for the likes of Gershwin, Porter and Kern. He is credited as the editor of the piano-vocal scores of Rodgers and Hammerstein's musicals: *Allegro*, *Carousel*, *Flower Drum Song*, *The King and I*, *Me and Juliet*, *Oklahoma!*, *Pipe Dream*, *The Sound of Music* and *South Pacific*. He was also editor of the piano-vocal score of Weill's *Lady in the Dark*.

[3] Douglass was the star of two earlier Prince and Griffith successes, *Damn Yankees* and *The Pajama Game*.

the actress Thelma Ritter ($1,000),[4] Alfred R. Glancy Jr ($6,000) and Ben Tobin ($12,000) – two friends and former business associates of Roger Stevens in Detroit – and Herbert Sondheim ($6,000), Stephen's father. Other noteworthy names include the racehorse magnate Alfred Gwynne Vanderbilt ($1,000), the philanthropist and public health campaigner Mary Woodard Lasker ($6,000), and James C. Kellogg ($1,200) – appointed Chairman of the New York Stock Exchange in 1956 – who was an alumnus of Williams College, where Sondheim had also studied. A little later Helen Coates, Bernstein's former piano teacher and his longtime secretary, made a small investment of $300.

These backers were reasonably fortunate with *West Side Story*, as it was soon turning a modest profit. Weekly statements compiled by the company manager (Clarence Jacobson) are to be found in the Roger Stevens papers. The following examples are taken from the return for the week ending 5 April 1958, just over six months into the show's run. Gross box-office receipts for the week were $56,616.08, with net receipts of $41,462.06. The total weekly expenses amounted to $29,857.05, giving the show a profit for the week of $11,605.01, and total profits to date (since the opening on 26 September 1957) of $152,750.28. Production costs of $49,344.01 are set against this, leaving a net profit to date of $103,406.27. But this was hardly a spectacular commercial success: other shows, like *The Music Man*, were doing much better business at the time. Hal Prince recalled that there were often seats to be had, and audiences did not always respond well: 'The show did not … sell out for the year or so it ran on Broadway. It also had maybe a hundred walk-outs every single night – people totally confused by what it was, and rejecting it.'[5] But it was not long before the backers did very much better out of *West Side Story*. As Prince said, 'It went off to be a movie and the movie became a big windfall for our investors, for everybody.'[6]

The Roger Stevens papers also reveal what the running costs were for the show. In the same week (ending 5 April 1958), payroll and extra salaries made up over half the weekly outgoings, amounting to $16,838.52. Salaries included $4,253.12 to the principals and $3,546.25 to the chorus. Under permanent salaries, 'orchestra' is shown as being paid $450.00, but under extra salaries, musicians account for $3,110.59. The figure of $450 was most probably the salary for Goberman as the show's musical director, while $3,110.59 was the total paid to the orchestral players.

Each month, Prince and Griffith sent a full financial statement, certified by a firm of accountants, to each of the show's backers. Many of these statements

---

[4] Thelma Ritter (1902–1968) was joint winner of the 1957 Tony Award for Best Actress in a Musical for *New Girl In Town* (the award was shared with her co-star, Gwen Verdon), the show on which Griffith and Prince were working when they agreed to take on *West Side Story*. Best known as a film actress, she has the curious distinction of having been nominated for an Oscar six times, without ever winning one.

[5] NPR 2007.

[6] NPR 2007.

were accompanied by a cheque for a sum ranging from 5 to 10 per cent of each individual's original investment, varying according to how good business was in any given month. Roger Stevens's own investment was substantial. On 9 June 1958, Prince and Griffith wrote to the investors with 'a check representing five percent profits in *West Side Story*. Business at the Winter Garden is holding up well.' Stevens noted on this letter that he had received a cheque for $2,900, suggesting that his own investment was in excess of $50,000. In fact, it was a lot more: a letter from Prince to Stevens dated 19 February 1958 assigned Stevens 'an undivided twelve (12%) per cent interest in the West Side Story Company', for which Stevens paid an additional $90,000, payable in instalments over a four-year period, up to 1 February 1962.

In short, *West Side Story* began as a respectable success on Broadway, but its financial rewards were comparatively modest until the movie deal was done.

'*West Side Story* is Extraordinarily Exciting!': Press Reaction

National Theatre, Washington DC, 19 August 1957

The *Washington Post* first carried an advertisement for *West Side Story* on 29 July 1957, three weeks before the opening: 'World Première! Opens Monday, Aug. 19th Thru Saturday, Sept. 7th. A New Musical: West Side Story …'.

Very unusually for a musical, almost nothing changed between the start of tryouts in Washington and the move to Broadway six weeks later, so the show that critics saw in all three cities was more or less the same. Sondheim summarized the minimal alterations: 'Our total changes out of town consisted of rewriting the release for the "Jet Song," adding a few notes to "One Hand," Jerry *potchkied* with the second-act ballet and there were a few cuts in the book.'[7] The capital took to the new show with enthusiasm, led by the longtime theatre critic of the *Washington Post*, Richard L. Coe. His first review appeared the morning after the opening.

> *West Side Story* is a work of art … Watching the stage at the National we are moved, and tremendously moved, by a uniquely cohesive comment on life. It may not be our personal comment on life, but it is a vibrant memorable viewpoint …
>
> The setting is not likely to have precise translators. We have a Puerto Rican gang of New York's West of Central Park and a group that's native born. There is romance here, but it is purposely not the romance of lyric theater; this is the romance of the lonely for the lonesome, not precisely the same wavelengths but close enough to be felt.
>
> The link, I think, is the music of Leonard Bernstein, sometimes soaringly melodic, sometimes cruelly sheer fighting rhythm and dissonance. There is conflict all the way, sheer, arresting, diametric, bitterly contrasting and searingly

---

[7]   Zadan 1974, p. 25.

heartbreaking. In his music, eloquently projected in orchestra and voices, Bernstein is painting an emotional portrait …

The largely unknown cast is astonishing[ly] professional. As the principal girls Carol Lawrence and Chita Rivera are immensely appealing and from the boys there are tremendously alert performances from such as Mickey Calin, Larry Kert and Kenneth Le Roy. Three cheers for uncovering so professional newcomers as these …

All told, *West Side Story* is a music drama to relish, to think about and remember.[8]

Coe's review was followed the next day by another, from Paul Hume, the music critic of the *Post*, whose comments on the score are generally welcoming, though rather surprisingly he demonstrates a clear preference for the more obviously tuneful numbers, and he has harsh words for 'A Boy Like That'. He also comments on the high quality of the show's lyrics.

Leonard Bernstein has not written the kind of show whose music can be separated from the whole and discussed by itself. It is all too much part of the total conception of the musical worked out by Bernstein and Jerome Robbins with fine assistance on the lyrics from Stephen Sondheim …

The chief elements of the show are its dancing and music. … In unusually large doses of dancing by Robbins – whose history in this field is one of consistent success – and with a taut musical score from Bernstein … the show builds in exciting tension.

The most successful songs in the show are those with fast, driving rhythm: the song 'Gee Officer Krupke,' sung by the Jets, the American juvenile delinquents; the wonderful song and dance with the calypso bounce, 'America,' done by the Puerto Rican girls, led with terrific fire by Chita Rivera; and the pile-driving dance at the gym.

It was interesting to watch the buildup in audience applause too, which frequently stopped the show while songs you will be hearing among the new top tunes got their first big hands. One of these is the love song, 'Tonight,' that comes in the Bernstein-Robbins Balcony Scene. Another of the best songs in the show, and a very neat job of the kind of variety in length of lines that Bernstein does so well, is Maria's 'I Feel Pretty.'

There are musical spots that can easily be touched up before the show is tied up and ready for New York. The duet between Maria and Anita, 'A Boy Like That,' and 'I Have a Love,' is all mixed up and weak. It could be cut or given entirely to Maria, with Anita's lines spoken first.

The dream-fantasy choreography, danced to 'Somewhere,' is too reminiscent of *Oklahoma!* and even a touch of Menotti's *Consul,* not in the music but in its total

---

[8]   Coe 1957a.

effect in the show. It ought to be slimmed down. And the opening scenes, through Tony's song, 'Something's Coming,' are slow.

In production, the show looks a beauty. In performance the question arises, 'Is it easier to teach singers to dance, or dancers to sing?' It is obviously easier to teach dancers to sing, and the dancing is so good that it is easy to pass over the fact that the Tony and Maria have a fairly rough time with the singing any time it gets above a medium volume. Six concentrated weeks with a first class singing teacher could fix this up easily.

Larry Kert's Tony, Mickey Calin's Riff, and the Maria and Anita of Carol Lawrence and Miss Rivera are dramatically solid, and they are backed up with a cast that dances and sings with the nonchalance and the hard-packed style the show needs.

Bernstein's score is filled with the touches of a man who knows the orchestra, and who has the entire repertoire of techniques in hand. He draws from the best level most of the time. Some touching up here and there – raising the pitch of 'Tonight' for Tony, and that of 'I Feel Pretty' for Maria – with some cuts and perhaps moving the 'Officer Krupke' song earlier in the show, would point this musical in the direction of a Broadway long-run hit. It has a musical director in Max Goberman who makes the most of every brilliant moment.[9]

Two weeks later, Richard Coe returned to *West Side Story* and wrote a second review under the unambiguous headline 'Musical at National is a Triumph'.[10] Having described the show as a 'work of art' in his first review, Coe develops that theme and tackles the question of whether, by taking the subject of gang warfare, the show had somehow glamorized delinquency.

Art, among other things, finds the beauty of truth in the ugliness of ignorance. This, to me, is the triumph of *West Side Story* … here four men are taking a timeless view of one of our society's sorriest phenomena, the teen-age gangs of a great city …

Last year in *Candide* [Bernstein] was being intellectually brilliant: in its successor a deeper, emotional quality is involved. It is ridiculous to say that *West Side Story* glorifies young thugs; one might as well say that *Carmen* glorifies smuggling. What the music tells us is what, in our outrage, we can easily forget: that within all of us beat the same emotions, primitive urges, lyrical dreams, cynical experiences, questioning fears.

Coe then turns to the issue of trying to categorize *West Side Story*, a question that was bound to arise given its originality and its uncompromising subject matter; this was a new musical that seemed determined to shake up any traditional views of the genre.

---

9   Hume 1957.
10   Coe 1957b.

West Side Story is the sort of work that cries for definition because in our normal laziness we are far too tempted to pigeonhole anything as this or that. This fits into many categories, not just one.

There are valid compromises in *West Side Story*, for in our democratic day art is becoming commerce. But when the boys of the Jet Gang sing 'Gee, Officer Krupke!' they are also telling us what they think of our concern about gangs. When the Puerto Rican Anita and the Shark girls sing of 'America' they state the conflicting views of young people in new surroundings. That these are wingding commercial numbers does not mean they have no place in the whole. Where they are, they fit.

Bernstein's score also speaks to us more subtly: through rhythm – a number like 'Cool,' which has some of the hesitant beat of the young; through lyrical melody – 'Tonight,' an infinitely moving modern comment on Shakespeare's Balcony Scene; through dissonance – in 'The Rumble,' a brilliantly staged fight scene; and with skilled musicianship the patterns of grand opera – 'Tonight,' an astonishingly intricate quintet.

Having described the cast as 'largely unknown' in his first review, Coe has more to say about them in his second, deriving most of his material from the artists' biographies printed in the programme. His prediction of a star career for Chita Rivera is prescient, as is his closing paragraph, emphasizing the quality of the finished work and the genuinely collaborative nature of the venture.

They have picked young people of considerable experience. The 'Who's Who' credits reveal long training and major parts for all. Carol Lawrence, the Juliet-Maria, has done a score of leading roles. Larry Kert, Romeo-Tony, has taken over for Harry Belafonte, done movie stunt work and toured the clubs. Ken Le Roy's career goes back to before the first night of *Oklahoma!*, a span which may explain why he's so excellent as the fiery Puerto Rican leader. Mickey Calin and Lee Becker, the dying Jet and Miss Anybodys, are hardly having overnight successes.

In case anyone's in the mood for predictions, I'm betting that the arresting Chita Rivera will be a major star in the Mistinguett style for years to come. Her material is great, but she gilds it with sparkle. She's been dancing only 13 years, but then she's only 24.

However, personalities are secondary to *West Side Story*. Under Robbins' command, its creators have fused talents, ideas and emotions into a pulsating work of art.

Coe's enthusiasm was not shared by all his readers, and his reviews provoked some angry letters to the editor at the *Post*. Ernest Nash of Arlington was enraged, though it's unclear whether he had actually seen the show:

Richard Coe's overlong reprise on the *West Side Story* serves no purpose other than to emphasize the doubtful taste of the theme, regardless of what musical, lyrical or dancing artistry might be involved.

New York's hoodlum gangs are hardly the material for sloppy sentimentalization. Raising these juvenile cut-throats to the romantic level of a Shakespeare classic dealing with an era long past can only be classified either as callousness or ignorance ... It is no credit to the theater that *West Side Story* chooses to see the situation otherwise.[11]

Another correspondent, A. Bloom of Washington, took an entirely different view of the show's importance for its time, even seeing broader connections with global events and particularly the mounting tension of the Cold War:

The audiences presently viewing *West Side Story* at the National are understandably moved by the conflict between two gangs ending in so much sorrow and death. Even while both sides agree to fight their rumble clean, with fists, they bring bricks and knives because the other side might prove untrustworthy. Of course, the slightest accident provokes the tragic use of these weapons.

How many were struck by the parallel with the present international conflict? The two warring groups, the terrible weapons to be used only if the other fellow proves untrustworthy, and the tragedy that faces the world if this deadly division is not stopped.

Can we see our own giant follies clearly enough, to understand that all of us are participating in developments towards the biggest rumble ever, and are we smart enough to call a halt?[12]

Erlanger Theatre, Philadelphia, 10 September 1957

West Side Story arrived in Philadelphia trailing clouds of critical glory from its three-week run in Washington. Box-office business had evidently been brisk (the *Sunday Bulletin* on 15 September described it as 'the sell-out hit musical'), and critical reaction to the production at the Erlanger in Philadelphia was hardly any less enthusiastic than in the capital's press. Henry T. Murdock in the *Philadelphia Inquirer* (11 September) wrote that the show 'spread excitement and drama and some of the best music ever given a musical show over the stage of the Erlanger last night'.[13] Two passages in Murdock's review deserve quotation. The first is headed 'Stunning Music':

---

[11] *Washington Post* 1957a.
[12] *Washington Post* 1957b.
[13] Murdock 1957.

Leonard Bernstein's music is stunning in impact and loveliness. There are 'numbers' you will hear and hear again, but there is no feeling that the young composer ever intended any of them to be separated from the whole. Their variety is amazing. There's melody that sings plaintively and exultantly. There are wild rhythms that speak the idiom of warring teenagers. There is even what one might call sinister music.

This is followed by something relatively rare among all the reviews for *West Side Story*: a detailed comment on the lyrics. Under the subheading 'Wonderful Lyrics', Murdock writes:

Keeping pace with the composer is the work of Stephen Sondheim, Bernstein's own choice of lyricist. In his first Broadway musical (he wrote the background music for last year's *Girls of Summer*), his range is as wide as his collaborators. When Bernstein writes such love songs as 'Maria' and 'One Hand, One Heart,' Sondheim finds the lyric expression. In the rugged warfare his words are militant, and in the satiric 'Gee, Officer Krupke' he collaborates with playwright Laurents in the bitterly comic panaceas urged for juvenile delinquency. *West Side Story* is a merger of established talents and new faces destined for familiarity. The lyricist belongs in this number.

In the *Philadelphia Bulletin* (11 September), Wayne Robinson's review begins with a bold proclamation:

West Side Story, the season's first musical at the Erlanger, is going to make theater history. It will go down as a landmark for the lyric stage to stand with such prior mileposts as *Oklahoma!* and *South Pacific*. It is a rare blend of many creative talents fused solidly together to bring the old ingredients of a musical play – song and dance – together in a new way.[14]

Robinson also tackles the question of the *Romeo and Juliet* derivation, offering an interesting viewpoint:

The book is by Arthur Laurents, and let's forget all that's been said about the story being borrowed from Shakespeare, who borrowed from everybody else. *West Side Story* is no more *Romeo and Juliet* than it is *Street Scene*, and it is a lot closer to the latter in feeling than the Bard. Yes, there are parallels – the Balcony Scene with the two lovers on a fire escape; the fiery friend killed in a street battle; the false news that the child bride is dead – but this production stands firmly on its own.

---

[14]   Robinson 1957a.

In the *Sunday Bulletin* (15 September), Robinson devoted a long article to profiling the cast, including Max Goberman:

> very important to the show is the bearded gentleman who conducts the orchestra. Max Goberman, a former member of the Philadelphia Orchestra's violin section under Leopold Stokowski. Goberman was 18 at that time. He is a graduate of the Curtis Institute, a former musical director of the Ballet Theater, and held the baton for such hits as *On the Town*, *Where's Charley?* and *A Tree Grows in Brooklyn*. *West Side Story* marks Goberman's return to the stage pit after five years in retirement on his New Jersey farm in Hunterdon County. 'They sent me the Bernstein score and that was it. The cows will have to wait', he said.[15]

Winter Garden Theatre, New York City, 26 September 1957

In New York, the show's notices were more mixed. Hal Prince remembered them as 'good, not great, Walter Kerr referred to it as cold, we drew audiences, but we got no awards'.[16] One report in the *New York World-Telegram and Sun* was laughably wide of the mark:

> *West Side Story* opened in the Winter Garden last evening after all the raves that rumbled in off the road. I found it as exciting (and sordid) as a subway mugging with music. And Leonard Bernstein's undistinguished score sounded like a blue-plate special of [Gian-]Carlo Menotti warmed over. Although titled 'a new musical', there is nothing to sing from it … and pitifully few laughs. The Jerome Robbins choreography is so good it should have been called a ballet instead of a musical. And it should have been half as long. Strictly for the arty set.[17]

Frank Aston's review in the same paper took a quite different line. He described it as

> a marvel peculiar to this country. Here we breed evil in our cities, but here we also parade a Bernstein and a Robbins so that a big part of this tortured world may say, 'America must be proud of boys like those.' And theatre-going Americans may reply, 'You're darn tootin', we are.'[18]

The *Journal-American* (27 September 1957) took the unusual step of conducting a 'Theatre poll: what audience thought of play', asking some of those at the opening night to give their reactions. The theatregoers quoted seem to have been quite a discerning

---

[15]   Robinson 1957b.
[16]   NPR 2007.
[17]   *New York World-Telegram and Sun* 1957.
[18]   Quoted in Suskin 1990, pp. 693 and 695.

group. 'In my opinion, the show was a smash hit. I thought Carol Lawrence was just terrific ... I couldn't find fault with the show and the choreography was outstanding.' So said Richard Mather, while Frank Snell commented that 'the particularly unusual combination of music, sets and choreography makes it sensational ... It was one of the few shows I could watch without looking for rough spots.' Abbott Johnson was less impressed, and missed the presence of a star: 'I thought the lack of an outstanding name hurt it. It seemed to me to be an excellent show for a big name star. I also thought the first act was slow in spots.' Gene Persson also found the first act 'too long', but thought the show as a whole 'very exciting, a real dancey show'. Julia Morgan and Barbara Richly both singled out the sets for high praise ('The sets were out of this world. They really went with the show completely'; 'Not only the music and dancing struck me, but those sets were great'). Finally, Don Carrett of Long Island said: 'I want to see it again, that's how much I enjoyed it. It was a fast moving, exciting show that should be on Broadway a long, long time. The sets and choreography were outstanding and the cast was simply great.'

Most critics were favourable,[19] though some expressed reservations. Brooks Atkinson was certainly not among the doubters. Returning to the show a week after his first-night review, he wrote a second review for the *New York Times* that is longer and more reflective than his earlier notice:

> With the production of *West Side Story* the musical stage recovers the maturity it had before the collapse in taste last season. It is an organic work of art. The collaborators who put it together have fused their respective contributions into a single theatrical expression that vividly portrays the life of the streets.[20]

Atkinson saw a clear distinction between the *Romeo and Juliet* source and *West Side Story*. The former is

> a lyrical, romantic tragedy set in a mythical environment. But there is nothing mythical about the environment of *West Side Story*. It is New York Today, and the principal characters are the tense, furtive, feral members of two hostile teen-age gangs, lost in a fantasy of hatred and revenge. By comparison the Montagues and Capulets are romantic.

Atkinson goes on to find similar qualities in the work to those praised by Richard Coe in Washington: '*West Side Story* finds bits of beauty in a wasteland of discontent.' He also finds lasting quality in the show:

---

[19]   See Suskin 1990, pp. 693–8 for an anthology of excerpts from first-night reviews by Frank Aston (*New York World-Telegram and Sun*), Brooks Atkinson (*New York Times*), John Chapman (*New York Daily News*), Walter Kerr (*Herald Tribune*), John McClain (*Journal-American*) and Richard Watts Jr (*New York Post*).

[20]   Atkinson 1957b.

The fundamental distinction of *West Side Story* is the courage with which it adheres to its artistic convictions and its unwillingness to make concessions to popular taste. The authors are playing for keeps. Mr. Bernstein's score has the shrill impetuosity of its subject. Despite the loveliness of the songs that Tony and Maria sing together and the mood of reverie in a dance number sung by Reri Grist, the score as a whole, with its biting orchestration, gives an impression of nervous drive, hostility, callousness, distrust. Mr. Bernstein is not glossing over the nature of his material.

And what of the idea that the show glorifies gang warfare? Atkinson observes that the show would be 'unbearable' without Tony and Maria, but that 'the contrast between the lovers and the gangs supplies perspective that makes a moving experience out of a corrosive subject'.

John Chapman, drama critic of the *New York Daily News*, was another passionate advocate of the show, declaring that:

The American theatre took a venturesome forward step when the firm of Griffith & Prince presented *West Side Story* at the Winter Garden last evening. This is a bold new kind of musical theatre – a juke-box Manhattan opera. It is, to me, extraordinarily exciting. ... In [the music], there is the drive, the bounce, the restlessness and the sweetness of our town. It takes up the American musical idiom where it was left when George Gershwin died. It is fascinatingly tricky and melodically beguiling, and it marks the progression of an admirable composer.[21]

Walter Kerr in the *Herald Tribune* was one of several critics to single out dance as the most successful element of the evening: 'the most savage, restless, electrifying dance patterns we've been exposed to in a dozen years'. Most of his review concentrated on Robbins, and the sense is one of slightly uneasy admiration rather than any real engagement with the show. As for the music, Kerr wrote that:

Robbins has been almost sacrificially assisted in this macabre and murderous onslaught of movement by composer Leonard Bernstein. Mr. Bernstein has permitted himself a few moments of graceful, lingering melody: in a yearning 'Maria', in the hushed falling line of 'Tonight', in the wistful declaration of 'I have a love'. But for the most part he has served the needs of the onstage threshing-machine, setting the fierce beat that fuses a gymnasium dance, putting a mocking insistence behind taunts at a policeman, dramatizing the footwork rather than lifting emotions into song. When hero Larry Kert is stomping out the visionary insistence of 'Something's Coming' both music and tumultuous story are given their due. Otherwise it's the danced narrative that takes urgent precedence. Which brings us to the fact that there is another side to *West Side Story*. The show is, in

---

[21] Chapman 1957.

general, not well sung. It is rushingly acted. (The dramatic postures are rarely varied.) And it is, apart from the spine-tingling velocity of the dances, almost never emotionally affecting. Perhaps the echoes of another *Romeo and Juliet* are too firm: the people often seem to be behaving as they do because of arbitrary commands from a borrowed plot. ... Don't look for laughter or – for that matter – tears.[22]

While *West Side Story* had one of its most energetic supporters in Brooks Atkinson, the other critics on the *New York Times* who covered the show were harder to please. Howard Taubman, who had succeeded Olin Downes as the paper's music critic in 1955, was less convinced than many about the show's worth. His review began with the rather tetchy assertion that 'the semantics of Broadway, based no doubt on experience at the box office, require that ambitious musical intentions should be played down or preferably not mentioned at all. Opera is a dreaded word, and lyric theatre sounds uppity.' Describing the show as 'informed with an intense earnestness', Taubman says it 'aims to use music as a full, creative partner'. As to how well it achieves that creative partnership, he is less than effusive:

> How does music function in such a tight-knit approach? Not badly when it is used as a kinetic agent to underline swiftness of motion and violence of action. Not well when it seeks to reach into the hearts of the people in the story. Where it counts most, Leonard Bernstein's score is disappointing.
>
> The fault is not entirely Mr. Bernstein's. It lies in what seems to be ambivalence of attitude on the part of the creative team. This, in turn, is motivated profoundly by the structure and economics of the Broadway theatre. ... One cannot blame Broadway for being frightened of opera. It has the reputation of being highbrow. It often requires concentrated attention. At its best it seeks to probe into the secret places of a man's deepest emotions. But who wants that kind of thing on Broadway?

Taubman seems determined to press home the point that *West Side Story* was virtually doomed to be rather unsatisfying, since writing for Broadway necessarily required artistic compromise. To bolster his argument, Taubman quotes Bernstein's own words from his invented log, and uses them to develop an argument that, by trying to avoid being operatic, Bernstein produced a score that inevitably sold out:

> Thus you find shows like *The Most Happy Fella* and *Candide* carrying water on both shoulders. They want to be searching, and they must be popular to survive. ... *West Side Story*, despite the seriousness of its intentions, has been afflicted by the problem of how to mediate the claims of the lyric theatre with those of sound commercial procedure. You have Mr. Bernstein's word for it that there was

---

[22]   Kerr 1957. See below for Bernstein's reaction to this review at the after-show party, as reported in *Time* magazine.

a problem. Note his words dated March 1956, and published in the theatre program as one of the 'Excerpts from a West Side Log':

'Chief problem to tread the fine line between opera and Broadway, between realism and poetry, ballet and "just dancing", abstract and representational.'

The issue here cuts even deeper than the 'fine line between opera and Broadway.' It involves questions of fundamental points of view toward subject matter. Were the makers of *West Side Story*, one wonders, so attracted and committed to their parallelism with *Romeo and Juliet* that treatment became more important than theme? Were they not, despite their unquestionably high aims, compromising in their handling of a theme of such gravity that it admits of no compromise.

Mr. Bernstein remarks, in an entry in his log last August, that 'not even a whisper about a happy ending was heard.' On this point there was no compromise, but by then it did not matter.

Determined to press the point about the constraints of commercial theatre weighing too heavily on the composer, Taubman turns to two specific points in the score: 'Gee, Officer Krupke' he finds lacking edge and musical challenge; as for the Ballet Sequence, the problem he detects is a lack of melodic invention. He wishes, apparently, for a scene more reminiscent of Puccini:[23]

The ambivalence of attitude had done its work. Let us see what this means in two concrete instances that conditioned musical approach.

Take the case of the number 'Gee, Officer Krupke,' which is presumably meant to be a mordantly sarcastic description of gang life by the members themselves. The little ruffians are made to relate their experience with a good cheer that would be suitable in a comic scene of a conventional musical show.

It is conceivable that the composer could have edged this number with bitterness of comment. He could have employed the orchestra to help him out. In view of Mr. Bernstein's cleverness in writing for the orchestra, there is no reason to believe that he could not have imparted a sting to this scene. But the result might have been music not immediately accessible. The 'fine line' was neglected. Broadway won out.

Now we come to a more crucial moment, the scene in the bedroom where the boy and the girl, like Romeo and Juliet, have their brief interlude of anguished ecstasy. Here surely is the place where a composer has a right to take over. Here surely is the occasion for the music to soar.

Unfortunately, the music at this point is lackluster. One cannot be sure about the cause. Was it because the composer, who was well aware that in this production scheme dancing and acting capacities had taken precedence over vocal gifts, knew

---

[23]   It is intriguing to speculate on whether the earlier – rejected – version of the music for this scene, discussed in Chapter 3, would have been more to Taubman's liking.

that he did not have the singers? If so, why not fill the orchestra with radiance? Or was it because even in this scene, which cries out for the unabashed lyricism of opera, the suspect form could not be indulged?

It may be, of course, that Mr. Bernstein, whose multitudinous musical talents have not yet disclosed an impressive gift of melodic invention, might not have been able to rise to the occasion. But the effort should have been made. This was not the time to worry about stepping over that 'fine line' into opera.

Finally, the music critic of the *Times* found something positive to say about the score, and to give credit for the introduction of innovations that are 'uncommon' in a Broadway show. Taubman describes this as the Overture, but he must be referring to the Prologue, since the Overture (entitled 'Temporary Overture' in the Ramin full score) was added later, for the show's National Tour:

> The overture to *West Side Story* promises tension and excitement. In musical and dramatic terms it is exhilarating and foreboding. Like many other places in the score, particularly the orchestrations, prepared with assists from Sid Ramin and Irwin Kostal, the music is alive with technical skills uncommon on Broadway. Rhythms, harmonies, colors have theatrical brilliance.
>
> When *West Side Story* is explosive with movement, as it is a good deal of the time, Mr. Bernstein adds to the excitement. When it reaches down into the human predicament of these twisted, bewildered kids as gangs or individuals, the music is unhappily neutral.[24]

The charge of neutrality seems a curious one, but Taubman was not alone in finding the score unsatisfactory. John Martin, ballet critic at the *Times*, thought it had 'no tunes'. He wrote of the centrality of dance in *West Side Story*, and claimed that this was more or less its only virtue:

> Make no mistake, the dance-mindedness of *West Side Story* cannot be brushed aside as immaterial, for stripped to its bones, the show has no other asset to account for its success. It has no 'names', no tunes, few laughs, almost no girls, and … virtually nothing else to please the eye. … the production's single virtue is undeniable and irresistible – it translates its subject into action, in the literal sense of the word. Its theatrical substance is realized not in talked plot but in moving bodies.[25]

John Beaufort in the *Christian Science Monitor* was cautious. He found the show 'original, stimulating, and full of style', and praised the score as 'crisp, frequently dissonant, sometimes tender, and always exceptionally well served by the

---

[24]   Taubman 1957.

[25]   Martin 1957.

orchestrations' (a rare example of any mention of these in a newspaper review). But he concludes by saying that '*West Side Story* might be more moving if the personal tragedy of Tony and Maria had been allowed to emerge more fully. As it is, form and expression dominate content.'[26]

Time magazine felt that the dancing was much the strongest aspect of the show and that 'the salvation of the serious Broadway musical may lie in neither text nor music – which, trying to coalesce, all too often merely collide – but in dancing'. Describing *West Side Story* as a 'near success', *Time* was much more circumspect about the score and the book:

> Composer Bernstein does better with his harsh, tingling music for the dancers than with his lyrical duets for the lovers, and Arthur Laurents' libretto catches rasping, inarticulate hate better than yearning, inarticulate love. When it turns away from what is savage, *West Side Story* proves more sentimental than touching. Yet in its attempt to give a topical horror story broad human appeal, the show at worst falls at times into cliché; it does not start with it. Distinguished merit *West Side Story* lacks; but its distinguishing merit, its putting choreography foremost, may prove a milestone in musical-drama history.[27]

Time also included a description of the first-night audience, and an account of the after-show party at Sardi's:

> *West Side Story* hit Broadway after smash tryouts in Washington and Philadelphia, and boasting an advance sale estimated at $700,000. First-nighters – elegant, effusive, conscious of their roles and determined to be delighted – packed the big Winter Garden Theatre and turned the opening into the gaudiest night of the new theatrical season.
>
> Afterwards, rooters swarmed over Choreographer Robbins, who could only mutter 'Thanks, thanks' as he wandered in a happy daze backstage. The chic mob then swept on to Sardi's, finally swarmed to a full-blast party given by balding, burly Producer Roger Stevens at Park Avenue's Ambassador Hotel. There the dark-haired girls and long-sideburned boys of the cast gulped champagne, danced to music from *My Fair Lady*.
>
> Composer Bernstein strode in, his greying hair dramatically atousle, a navy-blue coat draped cape-style over his shoulders with artful carelessness. Everyone was waiting impatiently for the morning papers. Bernstein brought the news to his table: 'They're all raves except Kerr' (the *Herald Tribune*'s authoritatively trenchant Walter Kerr). Added Bernstein: 'You know, Kerr's an inverted snob. He's such an intellectual that he can't stand a musical unless it's got a chorus line.'

---

[26] Beaufort 1957.

[27] *Time* 1957.

At one point in the evening, a friend sidled up to Bernstein. 'Quite a nice little evening,' commented Oscar (*South Pacific*) Hammerstein II. Startled, Bernstein stopped talking. Hammerstein hastily added: 'No, it was really memorable.' Then the two hugged each other.

Hammerstein echoed the same thoughts in the note of thanks he sent to Roger Stevens a few days later, on 1 October:

Dear Roger,
Thank you very much for having Dorothy and me at your lovely party last week, and again congratulations on the success of *West Side Story*. I also congratulate you on your courage in making the play possible. This is truly a great way to start off a new season.
All good wishes. Sincerely,
Oscar[28]

The 1958 Tony Awards saw Meredith Willson's *The Music Man* crowned with success: it beat *West Side Story* in almost every category, including Best Musical. Of the cast, only Carol Lawrence was nominated (for Supporting or Featured Actress in a Musical), but her Maria lost out to Barbara Cook's delightful performance as the librarian, Marian Paroo, in *The Music Man*. There were only two nominations in the category for Conductor and Musical Director, but even here *West Side Story* had no luck: the Tony went to Herbert Greene (*The Music Man*), not to Max Goberman. There was some consolation. Jerome Robbins won the Tony for Choreography (the only award *West Side Story* picked up in a category where *The Music Man* was also nominated), and Oliver Smith won the Tony for Scenic Design, but that was all. More surprisingly, perhaps, *West Side Story* did no better in that year's New York Drama Critics' Circle awards either. The panel (whose membership included all the New York critics quoted above) chose to give their award to *The Music Man* too. In retrospect, this seems an extraordinary choice – that same year, the Critics' Circle award for Best Foreign Play went to John Osborne's *Look Back In Anger*, but when it came to musicals they played safe, preferring the charms of the imaginary River City, Iowa, to the mean streets of New York. As Frank Rich put it: 'I don't want to take anything away from *The Music Man*, which is a very nice show and classic in its own right, but it is ridiculous that the critics [chose] that over *West Side Story*.'[29] The show had a little more luck across the Atlantic, winning the Evening Standard Theatre Award for Best Musical in 1958.

---

[28]   Roger L. Stevens Collection, Library of Congress.
[29]   NPR 2007.

Opera House, Manchester, 14 November 1958

Advertisements in the *Manchester Guardian* during October 1958 announced the 'European premiere of America's most colourful musical sensation, *West Side Story*, with actual American cast direct from the Winter Garden Theatre, Broadway'.[30] There was excitement in the press about the American company that travelled to Britain for this production. An unnamed reporter for the *Guardian* wrote that: 'Trade union and other restrictions have made most productions of American plays and musicals in Britain at best a compromise, with the sometimes sorry spectacle of English actors and choruses struggling with American accents and mannerisms.' But, as Jerome Robbins told the *Guardian* reporter, a 'special dispensation' from British Equity allowed Robbins and his all-American cast to present *West Side Story* in Manchester and London. 'Whatever the reactions to the musical itself,' wrote the *Guardian*, 'this fact alone makes it an outstanding event in the theatrical season.'[31]

At least one influential British critic had seen the original production at the Winter Garden in 1958. Kenneth Tynan began by placing *West Side Story* in a Broadway context:

> American musicals traditionally divide into two opposed categories: folksy optimism (Rodgers and Hammerstein) versus city cynicism (Rodgers and Hart) – rural versus urban, grass roots versus asphalt jungle. The king of the jungle is *West Side Story*, which comes screaming out of the tall island's Western tenements, where Puerto Ricans carve and are carved by bands of less recent immigrants.[32]

His most eloquent prose was reserved for the music and the choreography:

> The score, by Leonard Bernstein, is as smooth and savage as a cobra; it sounds as if Puccini and Stravinsky had gone on a roller-coaster ride into the precincts of modern jazz. Jerome Robbins, the director-choreographer, projects the show as a rampaging ballet, with bodies flying through the air as if shot from guns, leaping, shrieking and somersaulting; yet he finds time for a peaceful dream sequence, full of that hankering for a golden age that runs right through American musicals, in which both gangs imagine a paradise where they can touch hands in love, without fear or loss of face.

Tynan's only reservation was that he felt Robbins had

> over-stylized a situation too fresh and bloody to respond to such treatment. The boys are too kempt; their clothes too pretty; they dope not, neither do they drink.

---

[30] *Manchester Guardian* 1958a.

[31] *Manchester Guardian* 1958b.

[32] Tynan 1958.

This makes them unreal, and gives the show an air of sociological slumming. Yet it compromises only on the brink of greatness; and that, surely, is triumph enough.

The Manchester performance was reviewed in the *Daily Mirror*. Under a photograph of Chita Rivera in rehearsal, and a screaming headline – 'Romeo and Juliet among the flick-knives' – Donald Zec wrote with unbounded enthusiasm:

> The American hit musical *West Side Story* – flick-knives and delinquency on a theme by Shakespeare – burst on Britain last night. Furiously, fabulously, sensationally, it gave the Opera House, Manchester, a European premiere it will never forget. And it will be a long time before I, too, can shake off the spell of this titanic show. ... The prologue music, brilliantly composed by Leonard Bernstein, brought the sound and fury of Manhattan right into Manchester. Over the racing, raucous music, you hear the screech of police sirens, and the coarse taunts of hoodlums. ... *West Side Story* ... is a great musical – the greatest American musical I've ever seen. It's pugnacious – yet it has poetry in it. The ballet is convulsive – but it has classic style and power.[33]

Her Majesty's Theatre, London, 12 December 1958

The show arrived in London a month later, and was reviewed by the *Manchester Guardian*. The paper's critic (writing under the initials 'J.R.') thought it

> a total work that demands comparison not with musical comedy as we have known it but with Menotti's operas or with *Porgy and Bess*. Even so it is a new kind of thing: not so grand in its music as *Porgy*, weaker in vocal resource than *The Medium*, but taken straighter out of life than either.[34]

The *Guardian* was convinced by the drama, if rather unsettled by it:

> No need now to rehearse the story. It is to be taken seriously, both as a modern version of *Romeo and Juliet* (on which it improves in one matter, the plotting of the false message of Juliet's death) and as a setting forth of delinquency and racial conflict among the young of a great city. ... But deeply sympathetic though the play is in its understanding of both groups – the Puerto Ricans, who are the last immigrants into New York, and the rival gang who are the next-to-last – one can complain of a certain despair in it. The adults, the law especially, are feeble or vile. And two lines serve for moral: 'You make this world lousy'; 'That's the way we found it, Doc.' The comic chorus 'Gee, Officer Krupke,' in which the gang makes

33   Zec 1958.
34   *Manchester Guardian* 1958c.

us laugh uproariously at the discovery that 'We're distoibed,' leaves behind it a sense of something rattling and hollow.

But it is the overall impact of the show that left the deepest impression: 'As a production, as a total work for the stage *West Side Story* is superb.' While Robbins's choreography was described as 'a joy', the music drew a more tepid response:

> Where so many talents work together to a single end, some, perhaps, must fall short of the highest excellence. Leonard Bernstein's music is nearly always dramatically right: several songs – 'I Feel Pretty,' 'A Boy Like That' – are rhythmically memorable; 'Tonight' and 'Somewhere' are songs of sentiment without sentimentality; and the bursts of jazz are pulse-driving. But it would be idle to pretend that there is here anything so fresh and inevitable as Gershwin's 'Summertime.'

Still, the evening was judged 'a triumph', and *West Side Story* 'a work of art, and a highly finished and successful one'.

Winter Garden Theatre, New York City, 27 April 1960

The Music Man was still going strong on Broadway when *West Side Story* returned to the Winter Garden in 1960, after its National Tour.[35] The opening night has a unique place in the performance history of the show, as it was the only occasion on which Bernstein himself conducted any of *West Side Story* in the theatre. It was announced that he was going to conduct the whole show, but the *New York Times* set the record straight in a brief announcement a few weeks before the opening: 'Contrary to announcement by the management, Leonard Bernstein will conduct only the overture, not his entire score, at the reopening of *West Side Story* on April 27 at the Winter Garden. After Mr. Bernstein leaves the podium, the orchestra will be led by Joseph Lewis.'[36]

The New York critics all took the opportunity to write about the show again. Brooks Atkinson, who had been full of praise in 1957, was still every bit as exhilarated this time around:

> After going over the country once lightly, *West Side Story* has come home to the Winter Garden … Everyone in the audience was in a jubilant frame of mind. After Leonard Bernstein had conducted his own overture, the cheers and the

---

[35] *The Music Man* opened on 19 December 1957 and ran until 15 April 1961 for a total of 1,375 performances. *West Side Story* had 732 performances before the show closed on 27 June 1959; the return engagement at the Winter Garden in 1960 (27 April–10 December) ran for another 249 performances.

[36] *New York Times* 1960.

applause sounded like Old Home Week at Yankee Stadium. During the rest of the evening the audience saluted the most memorable ballet numbers and songs as if they had never been performed before. ... Nearly three years after it first burst on Broadway, *West Side Story* remains a major achievement of the American musical theatre. By comparison with the flaring originality of Jerome Robbins' choreography and staging, taste may seem like a petty thing. Taste seems like the property of a gentler world.

But it is the impeccable taste of the music, the lyrics and the story that seem so astonishing in *West Side Story.* Given two lots of hoodlums somewhere on the gritty pavements of New York, how could the authors of the show endow them with so much common humanity, and raise their hopes and troubles to the level of literature?

But that is what *West Side Story* manages to do. ... Mr. Bernstein's prologue is tense, shrill and metallic, but it also reaches out for tenderness. Although the ecstasies are blunted and the rapture pinched, they are present in the score. ... Without being sentimental, Mr. Robbins and his associates are compassionate. ... No wonder the audience was full of enthusiasm. *West Side Story* is a wonderful piece of work.[37]

John Chapman in the *Daily News* echoed his enthusiasm from 1957 and reprinted some of his original rave notice, before going on to say that the show was now even better:

This bold new kind of musical theatre opened again last evening at the Winter Garden and there is no reason for changing the original review. *West Side Story* is even more exciting to me now than it was in 1957. ... The music by Leonard Bernstein seems even more brilliant and daring than it was at the first opening. ... This didn't seem like a return engagement last evening. It was like the opening of a new show, a new hit. And all of us in an unusually appreciative audience had the opportunity to pay our respects to composer Bernstein after he led the big orchestra through his stirring overture.[38]

Walter Kerr in the *Herald Tribune* was still not completely won over: 'I am going to confess now that I continue to find the curiously formalized love story less than moving.' But despite lingering scepticism he had some more positive things to say than he had three years previously:

The benzedrine rhythms composer Leonard Bernstein has so brilliantly arranged for an unfriendly dance in a gymnasium jab at the eardrums like jangling street noises on a very warm night. ... And the violent mating of knife-blades that bring

---

[37]   Atkinson 1960a.

[38]   Chapman 1960.

a first-act 'rumble' to its detonating close remains as savage and chilling an image as has ever burst in the faces of a couple of thousand spellbound customers. But these things were remembered, and to be expected. I found myself, on this second visit, admiring a good many things that happen in passing and go almost unnoticed under the showers of sparks that precede or follow them.

Kerr seemed to be genuinely persuaded by 'the sweeping melodic line of Leonard Bernstein's "Somewhere"', noting too that 'Mr. Bernstein conducted the overture last evening, with all of the bite that is in the entertainment, and a strain of tenderness that sometimes is not'.[39]

A week after the reopening, Brooks Atkinson wrote another article, specifically about Bernstein.[40] He expresses the wry hope that the composer might one day spend more time on Broadway projects, and rather less as Music Director of the New York Philharmonic, but goes on to offer a warm endorsement of the scores of both *Candide* and *West Side Story*:

Not for the first time, it occurred to this theatregoer that we could make good use of this boy if he did not have so many off-Broadway commitments. He has written three impetuous scores about New York City. ...

Strictly from the musical point of view, his score for the Lillian Hellman version of *Candide* is his finest. It is in the vein of satirical operetta, written to heighten the ironies of a literary classic. ... But Mr. Bernstein's music for plays with a New York setting is infinitely superior to the banalities that keep orchestras blaring in most music shows. His scores are individual and civilized. They express the excitement of Cosmopolis, but with a skeptical attitude towards its pretensions to grandeur. ... The gestures toward humor [in *West Side Story*] are tinged with anxiety. With the exception of 'Gee, Officer Krupke,' which is Tin Pan Alley stuff, the humor has an acrid taste, for the authors cannot treat their characters with amused detachment. The New York of the street gangs is haunted with demons.

There is some charming music in Mr. Bernstein's pages – Maria's simple and exultant 'I Feel Pretty' and the romantic 'One Hand, One Heart,' which Tony and Maria sing together; and there is an almost religious tone poem entitled 'Somewhere,' which describes the sweetness of life as it might be without rancor. But most of the music conveys the nervousness of a taut community.

Not being a sentimentalist, Mr. Bernstein does not waste emotion ... he takes this ugly segment of the city as he finds it. There is a lot of pressure behind his music. It portrays human beings of fiery passions but limited capacity to express them. Everything is ready for the explosion recorded in the frenetic hysteria of 'The Rumble'.

---

[39] Kerr 1960.

[40] Atkinson 1960b.

In the busy conductor of the Philharmonic, Broadway has lost a composer and a musician who could give our musical theatre the stature of an adult art. There is mind as well as electricity and taste in the music he has written for Broadway. Let's not speculate on how many vibrant scores the Philharmonic has deprived us of. The thought is too melancholy.

Atkinson then comments on the public that has been to *West Side Story*, and how widely reactions to the show have differed:

Although *West Side Story* was generally appreciated in the press when it opened … some of its earliest audiences were outraged. To persons whose idea of the musical was conditioned by *My Fair Lady*, the severity of *West Side Story* came almost as an affront. Boy does not get girl. Neither boy nor girl is glamorous. It always takes time for an original production to find its special audience. In the case of *West Side Story* the audience has turned out to be surprisingly numerous. In 1957 who would have thought that a harsh drama about juvenile crime on the scabrous sidewalks of New York would win the respect and admiration of so many thousands of theatregoers, not only in America but abroad? … All the authors are men of artistic independence. Abandoning the clichés of Broadway, they have composed a unique work.

Ten months later, after the return engagement at the Winter Garden had closed, the New York Philharmonic Orchestra gave the first performance of the *Symphonic Dances from West Side Story* as part of a concert in Carnegie Hall on 13 February 1961, billed as a 'Valentine' to Leonard Bernstein. This suite, reorchestrated for a full symphony orchestra by Sid Ramin and Irwin Kostal,[41] comprises instrumental music that has also been reordered so as to create a satisfying concert work, rather than following the sequence of events in the show. The movements are: Prologue, Somewhere, Scherzo, Mambo, Cha-Cha, Meeting Scene, Cool Fugue, Rumble and Finale. The *Symphonic Dances* are dedicated 'To Sid Ramin, in friendship'. They went down very well with the public at the concert, but Ross Parmenter's review in the *New York Times* was lukewarm:

From the critical point of view, the real novelty of the evening was the première of Symphonic Dances from *West Side Story*. This is a twenty-two minute piece that Sid Ramin and Irwin Kostal have orchestrated 'under the supervision of Mr. Bernstein.' It is about to be released by Columbia Records, and one can predict that the 'Mambo' movement will prove popular as something to demonstrate just what one's stereophonic high-fidelity phonograph can do to shake the house. Actually,

---

[41]   As with the complete show, the formal credit reads: 'Orchestrated with the assistance of Sid Ramin and Irwin Kostal'.

the music for the show seems considerably overblown in this version, but it made a hit with the audience. Mr. Foss certainly led it with electrical spirit.[42]

On 18 October 1961, nine months after this concert, *West Side Story* had its movie premiere at the Rivoli Theatre in New York; it was hailed in the next day's *New York Times* as 'nothing short of a cinema masterpiece'. As noted in the Introduction, this was not a view shared by all the creative team, but the present study is about *West Side Story* as a stage show, so consideration of its transformation for the big screen – and the numerous alterations that were made to the book, lyrics and score – is a chapter for a different author.

---

[42] Parmenter 1961.

Chapter 6
The Original Broadway Cast Recording

As historical documents, Broadway cast recordings preserve the performances of the original singers fresh from the stage, but as record albums they were conceived to be satisfying in purely aural terms. So, while the recording may be known to a wider audience than ever experienced a show in the theatre, what we actually hear represents a rather paradoxical kind of authenticity: the original cast performing the songs, but with a shortened or significantly altered version of the score; the original orchestrations, but usually with an enlarged orchestra; little or no dialogue, and numbers sometimes presented in a different order. This may be stating the obvious, but since it is the 1957 cast album of *West Side Story* that provides the most enduring representation of the show in its 'original' form, it is worth considering the musical alterations made to transform it into a successful cast recording. *West Side Story* is an unusually well documented example of this process, not least because Bernstein was unable to be present at the session (he had to leave for Israel the day after the opening) and Stephen Sondheim provided him with a detailed report.

The original cast recording of *West Side Story* was made by Columbia Masterworks at their 30th Street Studio on Sunday, 29 September 1957, three days after the Broadway opening.[1] The custom with Columbia's cast albums was well established by then: to record a show, usually at the end of its first or second week, in one long session on the 'rest' day for Broadway theatres, invariably a Sunday at the time. The 30th Street Studio was in a building leased by Columbia in the late 1940s and was the venue for most of its recordings until the studio closed more than 30 years later – the last recording to be made there was Glenn Gould's 1981 disc of Bach's *Goldberg Variations*. A report in *Time* described the building's unusual transformation: 'Times have changed for the brick building at 207 East 30th Street, that was once the Adams Memorial Presbyterian Church. The stained-glass windows are bricked up, the pews are gone, and in place of the organ there is a glass-fronted control room which bristles with switches, plugs and dials.'[2]

The cast for *West Side Story* was a young one, with several of the principals making their first Broadway appearances in major roles, and certainly lacking experience as recording artists. And yet the recording that resulted from the session on 29 September remains perhaps the definitive document of the show, despite the musical alterations discussed below. The enduring success of this album is due to

---

[1] Two photographs from the recording session are included in Zadan 1974, on p. 24 (Carol Lawrence) and p. 26 (Sondheim and Mickey Calin).

[2] *Time* 1953.

the assurance of Carol Lawrence's Maria, Chita Rivera's Anita, Larry Kert's Tony, Mickey Calin's Riff, Marilyn Cooper's Rosalia, Reri Grist as Consuelo and the offstage voice in the 'Somewhere' ballet, and an ensemble that had been extensively coached by Bernstein and Sondheim (as well as rehearsed beyond exhaustion by the famously exacting Jerome Robbins). Behind all this youthful talent who sing on the cast recording lay Max Goberman as the incisive conductor, and Columbia's most experienced production team: Goddard Lieberson as producer, with Howard Scott as associate producer, and Fred Plaut and Edward T. Graham as the sound engineers.

The one-day session for *West Side Story* involved recording all the music and also preparing a complete edited master tape, since production of the record began the next day.[3] This was reported in the *New York Times* on Wednesday, 2 October 1957. Under the headline 'Advertising: Getting a Hit Show on the Road, Fast', the reporter Carl Spielvogel described the process of manufacturing and promoting the new record – providing some interesting details on how the show was 'sold' to Columbia in the first place, as well as the marketing involved in its promotion:

> Few marketing programs spin into action as quickly as those of record companies … [*West Side Story*] opened last Thursday to generally good reviews.
>
> By Monday [7 October], the advertising and marketing program for the album will be in full swing, and disks will be in the hands of music stores. A great deal has been happening behind the scenes to make this possible.
>
> In July Leonard Bernstein, the composer, played the score for Goddard Lieberson, president of Columbia Records, a division of the Columbia Broadcasting System. He bought the recording rights.
>
> On Aug. 19 the show opened in Washington for the usual out-of-town tryout. The next morning's enthusiastic newspaper reviews were reproduced by Columbia's marketing people and sent to their nationwide sales organization.
>
> The same procedure was followed two weeks later in Philadelphia where another tryout was held. As Hal Cook, sales vice president of Columbia, put it: 'Our first sales job is to sell our own salesmen.'
>
> Meanwhile, Columbia's art department began working on the album cover. It is part of the advertising effort, and the covers are reproduced in advertisements.
>
> Streamers were prepared reading 'Now in stock – *West Side Story*,' for eventual display in store windows. And sales and advertising people were taken to Philadelphia to see what they would be selling.
>
> Last Sunday, three days after the show opened here, the album was recorded. The sessions lasted from 10 A.M. on Sunday to 1 A.M. Monday. The manufacturing process began on Monday at Columbia's Bridgeport, Conn., plant.

---

[3]   The LP was first issued in mono as OL 5230 and was in the shops during the week beginning 7 October 1957. The stereo version, with the number OS 2001, was issued in 1958.

Also on that day, telephone solicitation of orders from distributors began. The company does not sell direct to stores. It ships only against orders, and by yesterday it had 50,000 on hand. This represents about $200,000 at retail.

By tomorrow, the first shipment will be made – to Washington and Philadelphia, since the show opened there first. On Monday the records will be available here.

Goddard Lieberson (1911–1977) was the guiding force behind Columbia's cast albums from the late 1940s to the 1970s. He was appointed to a post at Columbia Masterworks in 1939, initially with the job of challenging RCA Victor's domination of the classical catalogue.[4] Cast recordings were also made by the Masterworks division, and Lieberson's passion for Broadway resulted in some spectacular contributions to the financial well-being of Columbia Records. From its launch, he saw the potential of the long-playing record (introduced by Columbia in 1948), with its playing time of about 50 minutes, as the ideal medium for cast recordings. This was a winning formula, with large sales for such albums as *South Pacific* and *Kismet*, but Lieberson proposed bolder initiatives too: he persuaded William Paley, president of CBS (the parent company of Columbia), to provide the financial backing for *My Fair Lady*, an investment that was to generate massive rewards: from its original financing of $360,000,[5] Columbia had earned at least $33 million from the show by the late 1970s.[6] The 1956 cast recording of *My Fair Lady* was a best-seller too: the *Billboard 200* album chart listed it for 480 weeks,[7] and sales had already exceeded a million copies by the time *West Side Story* was recorded the following year.[8] (It was the massive sales of this recording that helped subsidize some of the boldest classical ventures by Columbia Masterworks, such as the series of Stravinsky conducting Stravinsky.)

William Paley was not impressed by *West Side Story* when he first heard it. Bernstein's datebook includes an appointment on 26 February 1957: '3.00: Steve here. 5.00: William Paley coming to Studio to hear *Romeo* score.' It was evidently a dismal occasion, as Bernstein later recalled:

> I remember Steve and I, poor bastards that we were, trying by ourselves at a piano to audition the score for Columbia Records, my record company. They said no,

---

[4]   Lieberson became executive vice-president of Columbia Records in 1949 and president in 1956. For more detailed biographical information see Martin Mayer, 'Goddard Lieberson: Renaissance man behind the recording booth', *Esquire* (July 1956), reprinted in Lieberson 1957, unpaginated.

[5]   Paley 1979, p. 359.

[6]   Paley 1979, p. 360.

[7]   This remains a remarkable statistic: only Pink Floyd's *Dark Side of the Moon* and *Johnny's Greatest Hits* (a Johnny Mathis compilation album) have been in the *Billboard 200* for longer.

[8]   *My Fair Lady* was recorded on 25 March 1956. On 2 October 1957 the *New York Times* reported: 'Columbia's *My Fair Lady* album is over the 1,000,000 mark.'

there's nothing in it anybody could sing, too depressing, too many tritones, too
many words in the lyrics, too rangy – 'Ma-ri-a' – nobody could sing notes like
that, impossible. They turned it down. Later they changed their minds, but that was
an afternoon Steve and I will never forget. ... There was tremendous animosity to
the whole idea.[9]

Bernstein's datebook indicates that Paley heard the score again on 3 June, this time
performed by Carol Lawrence and Larry Kert. Evidently he remained unconvinced
that Columbia should record the show. Lieberson may have shared these doubts,
at least initially. He was present at several rehearsals but did not rush to commit to
make the cast recording. According to Peter Munves, who worked for Lieberson at
Masterworks at the time,

the story I heard was that Lieberson didn't want to sign *West Side Story*. He heard
it and he didn't like it. And [David] Oppenheim who was very close to Bernstein,
probably prevailed upon him to sign. Lieberson told me to go down and see it in
tryouts in Philadelphia. The word on the street was that it was a very interesting
show. ... I was *bowled over* by the first act![10]

However, by the time Munves saw *West Side Story* in Philadelphia, Lieberson
had already been to a performance in Washington and had written in immensely
enthusiastic terms to Bernstein. We can assume from this letter that any misgivings
Lieberson may have had while the show was in rehearsal disappeared as soon as he
saw it in the theatre, at the end of its first week of tryouts. Lieberson expresses what
is surely genuine admiration and offers some shrewd comments on the structure,
the individual performances and the production; his only frank criticism is of the
ending:

Friday, August 30 [1957]

Len:
I know you're up to your ears in unsolicited praise at this point, but I've found
myself so full of this project of yours all this week that I need to let you know what
I think of it – if only as a sort of palliative which will allow me to get back into the
heart of hackwork, which is my domain right now.

   We've glutted the language with so many all-words and non-words that by
now a term like 'fine' has little meaning. But it has meaning for me, and it's that
word which I now find myself stuck with when I think about the way your talent
has combined with your material this time.

---

9   Guernsey 1985, p. 46.
10   Marmorstein 2007, p. 271.

I mistrust my initial impression a little – I really can't believe that any one thing can be the best thing of its sort in my memory – all I know is the way I felt on Saturday afternoon was very like the experience of *Anne Frank* a couple of seasons ago[11] – I kept telling myself afterwards that there must have been something wrong with me for those three hours – something wrong that enabled the play to work on me the way it did.

I must have been something like a perfect piece of audience on Saturday because I've never known anything in musical theater to do me in the way *West Side Story* did. I'm usually a pain in the neck about those things – thinking all the while, officiously, how it ought to be better done and what I'd see thrown out. But Saturday it just threw me around and that's about the end of it.

People muttered at times about Menotti – in a good way – saying that it's the most moving thing since *The Consul* – all that lobby crap – for me Menotti's always been somewhere over the fence because I don't like his use of language and I don't think the whole thing is comfortable – I never have learned to believe it – I don't know *The Consul*, but the rest of it falls the way I've described – which is a failing in me, I guess, but nonetheless a fact. If it doesn't just happen, then it isn't right.

I haven't ever seen a production which held together the way yours does – in which the units of work produced by different people fitted so well into a whole – I don't know how it really was. I know you must have had your problems – but none of them show up as scars.

For me, it has terrific power – terrific unity – excellent individual work, though I think the women are by and large better than the men – I can't say enough for Carol Lawrence this time – I've always liked her – and Rivera is beautifully inside the work – which I didn't think she'd really be – she doesn't splash out of the production as I figured she might. This probably isn't going to make her, but it's great for the show. I think the men are at least good and will improve for sure – Kert particularly. He seemed a little nervous still – but that's like a headcold and can be got rid of.

The amazing thing to me is that everything seems to work so well – with the possible exception of the 2d Act ballet, you never get the half-vision of what was attempted against the way it comes off – I know if you tried to tell somebody why the Balcony Scene works, it'd sound wrong – yet it's the most moving single musical sequence I've seen since the park bench scene in *Carousel* – which I think is a great, great moment.

The Anita–Maria duet[12] is almost on a level with the Balcony Scene for me – just amazing.

---

[11] *The Diary of Anne Frank*, dramatized by Frances Goodrich and Albert Hackett, opened at the Cort Theatre on 5 October 1955; the original production ran for 717 performances, an unusually long run for a straight play.

[12] 'A Boy Like That'.

I hope Kert gets his first two songs into shape – because they're terrific – Maria particularly – and it isn't quite happening – or anyhow, didn't on Saturday.

There's such a fabric there – and such a flow – I wouldn't have believed that it'd be possible on this earth at the end of the first week out of town. I still find it a little tough to be sure about – and yet I know how it was.

For God's sake, change the last five minutes – you don't need to say all that crap, because everything you've been saying since 8:40 has been saying it for you. And much better than any single invention could do, I think. …

I won't go on – there's nothing duller than praise, when you've had a surfeit of it, I imagine – and you're the last person in the world I'd be caught writing fan mail to – I only had to say, you really did it, man.

Do you know that when you do a work like this you give a boost to everyone who spades around in the same field? It's kind of like knowing that those productive currents and vibrations are still in the air, if you'll only work and reach and not forget.

So, thanks for it.
Goddard[13]

This does not read like the thoughts of someone who had many doubts about recording *West Side Story*. Lieberson was pleasantly surprised to find it already so cohesive, and a glance at the musical numbers in the programme for the first night in Washington reveals a song list that is identical with that of the Broadway opening – not only the songs themselves but also the running order. Lieberson mentioned that others were likening the show to Menotti's *Consul* (a work billed as a 'Musical Drama' when it opened on Broadway in 1950). *West Side Story* was perceived by some as inhabiting the world between the Broadway musical and opera, but since the comparison is one Lieberson does not pursue, he presumably did not see *West Side Story* that way: the only other musical he mentions is *Carousel*.

In view of the changes made to the end of the show on the cast recording (see below), it is perhaps worth emphasizing Lieberson's reservations about the ending. He may already have been thinking about how to produce a musically satisfying conclusion: when he urged Bernstein to 'change the last five minutes', Lieberson was referring to the scene including Tony's death and Maria's final speech, neither of which is to be heard on the cast album. According to Bernstein's datebook, he met Lieberson on 14 September – almost certainly to discuss just the sorts of changes that were going to be made. (Appendix II provides details of the score as recorded on the cast album.)

Cast albums were made under great time pressure – in a single one-day session – so thorough preparation was essential. In his article 'The Non-Visual Theatre' Lieberson described this preliminary process, as well as what he set out to achieve

---

[13]   LBC.

in the studio. In this case he is referring to *South Pacific*, but the guiding principles remained the same for most of his later cast recordings, including *West Side Story*:

> The making of a 'show album' is not, or should not be, a mere setting down of the tunes in their proper order, but, as far as possible, a recreation in aural values of excitement, tension and dramatic progress. This is not achieved just by putting microphones in front of an orchestra and singers. To take a specific and very good example: the recording procedure of *South Pacific* started long before its New York opening. Counting rehearsals, Boston and New York performances, I saw *South Pacific* fourteen times before we went into the recording studios.
>
> I also had out-of-theatre conferences with Dick Rodgers, Oscar Hammerstein, Joshua Logan, Mary Martin and Ezio Pinza. Despite all this, the most important moments are those in the studio itself. It's there that it becomes perfectly clear what is aural and what is not. It is there that ingenuity must substitute heightened musical effects for the action and scenery of the theatre. The elusive quality of atmosphere is all-important to the recordings ... I suppose it is obvious to say that one could collect together the best possible musicians, singers and conductor and still not convey the excitement of an opening night. Yet this should be the sought-for ideal in recording a complete show. Some of this excitement can be achieved technically, which is to say by the use of microphone placement. But yet more can be done by editing of the material and careful building of climaxes, just as they are carefully built in the theatre.[14]

Stephen Sondheim emphasized two aspects of Lieberson's decision-making during the sessions.[15] First, there was his thinking on tempo: that dance and other instrumental music needed to be played significantly faster on a recording than in the theatre. Sondheim mentioned this as a general trait of Lieberson's cast albums, but with specific reference to *West Side Story* he recalled Lieberson's view that it was needed so as to approach on record the kind of excitement generated by Jerome Robbins's choreography on stage. One particularly striking example is the Mambo from the Dance at the Gym: the tempo on the 1957 cast recording is significantly faster than (for example) the film soundtrack, which had to fit with Robbins's choreography. Lieberson's quest for an aural equivalent of the exhilaration of the stage scene produced a performance from Goberman and the orchestra that is quicker than the music can be danced, but it is thrilling in solely audio terms. Second, Sondheim remembered that Lieberson deliberately aimed to capture something of the show's theatricality, and its raw energy: 'Goddard liked the *rough* moments, as they were closer to theatre.'

---

[14]   Lieberson 1957, unpaginated.

[15]   Stephen Sondheim, interview with the present author, 20 September 2006.

On 23 October 1957, Sondheim wrote to Bernstein,[16] reporting on the sessions that had taken place a few weeks earlier, while Bernstein was in Israel.[17] Sondheim's account began with his thoughts on the album as a whole, then moved on to the specific problem of the Balcony Scene:

> I was amazed at Goddard's efficiency and dispatch, as well as his efforts at maintaining quality. You will probably be displeased with the record for reasons stated below as well as dozens of others, but on the whole I think it's pretty good – at least, by show album standards. It was recorded simultaneously for stereophonic tape (to be released in November as the first show so recorded)[18] and sounds much better than the record. Some of the balancing isn't all it could be, but most of the trouble we had was due to lack of time – time on the record and time in the recording studio. As we had suspected, the amount of music was way overlong. Someone had goofed on the pre-recording timing, claiming that the Balcony Scene (starting with the singing) was 2:40, whereas it turned out to be 5:10. I don't have time to go into all the suggestions for remedying this, but the only one that worked was to cut out the best part – namely, the dialogue. Consequently, to our ears, the scene has been emasculated, going straight from the second chorus to the sung 'Goodnight's, with four hurried lines spoken over the bridge between. Thus the first 'goodnight' has to start on the fifth instead of the second, which ruins it, because the second doesn't fit in with the harmony. It's too bad, but I assure you there was no other way out – at least, none that occurred to us.

This cut in the Balcony Scene excised bars 121–44,[19] with the 'hurried lines of dialogue' that Sondheim describes spoken over bars 118–20, ending with Tony's 'I love you' (taken from the middle of the cut section, but feeling here like a slightly rushed substitute for 'Te adoro Anton – Te adoro, Maria'). As Sondheim makes clear in his letter, the decision to make this cut was not an easy one, because musical compromises were inevitable, but it was dictated by the space available on the record. Since Lieberson was never an enthusiast for spoken dialogue on cast recordings, it is

---

[16]   LBC. I am particularly grateful to Stephen Sondheim for allowing me to quote from this letter.

[17]   Bernstein had flown to Israel to conduct the inaugural celebrations of the Frederick Mann Auditorium in Tel Aviv the day after the Broadway opening. See Burton 1994, p. 281.

[18]   *West Side Story* was among the earliest Columbia cast recordings to be made in stereo. The very first was *Bells Are Ringing* in December 1956, but *West Side Story* had the distinction of being the first Columbia cast album to be released on a stereo LP, as OS 2001, in 1958. *Bells Are Ringing* was also among the first batch, released as OS 2006. The open-reel tape mentioned by Sondheim was issued as a pair of two-track tapes with the number TOB 13, put on sale in late 1957 or early 1958. That set was replaced in the early 1960s by a single four-track tape with the number Columbia OQ 345.

[19]   References are to 1994 FS. The cut music appears on pp. 165–6 of 1994 FS.

perhaps not surprising that this passage was one of the necessary casualties, but the loss of some lovely instrumental music, with the strings underscoring this touching moment, is regrettable, as is the change Sondheim noted in the first 'Goodnight' that follows.[20]

In his letter, Sondheim went on to prepare Bernstein for more possible disappointments. Most of these were the consequence of limited time in the studio, but not all; the notable exception is the matter of the tempo for the Prologue:

> You are also likely to be disturbed by the following (I tell you these not to ruin your final three weeks before you hear them, but to soften whatever shocks you may get when you're finally back at the Osborne). ... Drawbacks in the recording, cont'd: A very fast tempo for the prologue, not so much to save time as to make it more interesting. Without the accompanying action, it tended toward monotony.[21] Incidentally, we included street noises and shouts throughout the album, which works very well for the most part, though they tend to drown out the music in The Rumble. 2) Larry's[22] voice on 'Something's Coming' gets a little froggy in a few places and he sang the wrong rhythm for 'come on, deliver,' but it was by far the best of the takes, because the feeling was right. Unfortunately, it was the next to last song recorded and he was very tired, having been at the session for nine hours. His best is 'Maria,' which was the first number he recorded. 3) Frank Green[23] took Larry's part in The Rumble (shouting 'Riff, don't!') and came in about ten bars too late[24] – just before the stabbing – but the orchestra played it so well, that we didn't try another take (it was already the third). Also, they forgot to blow the police whistle at the climax. (By the way, the orchestra was increased to 37 men for the recording.[25]) 4) 'America' and 'I Feel Pretty' don't sound any better on the record

---

[20]   The Columbia recording of the film soundtrack included an altered version of the cut music as part of the extended section of underscored dialogue. In Bernstein's own 1984 recording and Schermerhorn's 2001 recording, the passage is given as published in the score.

[21]   In an interview with the present author on 20 September 2006, Sondheim described this decision – which was Lieberson's – in more positive terms: not as a 'drawback' to the recording, but as an example of Lieberson following his record producer's instincts to good effect.

[22]   Larry Kert, the original Tony.

[23]   Green played Mouthpiece in the original production.

[24]   In fact it is five bars later than marked in the score.

[25]   A valuable piece of additional information. Orchestral forces for show recordings were almost always augmented from those of the actual pit band. This was also true of many later cast recordings, as the producer Thomas Z. Shepard told the present author in an interview on 11 October 2006.

than they do on the stage.[26] 5) A trumpet player goofed badly on the change of key in the final procession.[27] Oddly enough, nobody heard it until it was too late. I was out getting five minutes' sleep during it (I also slept during 'America', since the session lasted from 10 a.m. to 1 a.m.). There will be a hundred other subtle and unsubtle goofs that will probably anger you, but the general reaction to the record so far (it came out last Friday – first order being 46,000 copies – is that good?) has been wonderful. *Variety* raved, and Douglas Watt in the *News* gave it a good notice (where he objected to anything, it was to the material, not the recording). The singers were not at their best, Lenny, but they were tired.

Finally, Sondheim mentioned two decisions taken on the spot during the sessions, the first of which was a telling intervention on Lieberson's part:

One thing you ought to like: Goddard insisted that the final chorus of 'Krupke' be played very slow with a heavy vaudeville beat.[28] Jerry[29] must have had conniptions. Another sidelight: Irv and Sid[30] put a major cadence at the end of 'I Have A Love'. I had conniptions, so it was changed back to the relative minor. I presume you didn't want it changed. I certainly didn't.

Sondheim does not refer to the changes made to the ending of *West Side Story* on the cast recording, so these must have been agreed in advance (perhaps at the meeting Bernstein and Lieberson had on 14 September). The Finale of the show (full score, p. 471ff.) begins with Maria and Tony singing a halting fragment of 'Somewhere', unaccompanied, starting with 'Hold my hand and we're halfway there'. Tony dies as Maria sings 'Someday', she 'falters and stops', and the orchestra enters for the first time in the scene, finishing the phrase for her, then playing a tender recollection of 'Somewhere' for seven bars. This music is brutally interrupted by Maria's final speech, in which bitter recrimination and the pain of loss pour out, her voice initially 'cold [and] sharp' according to the directions in the script. It is a devastating moment on stage as Maria orders the crowd to 'Stay back!'. She berates them for the ease with which they pull the trigger and foster hatred ('I can kill now because *I* hate now'), and finally turns to her lost love, saying a last farewell ('softly, privately') to

---

[26]   Sondheim has never been enthusiastic about these two numbers, partly, at least, because of self-criticism of the lyrics he wrote for them.

[27]   At bar 26 (p. 474), a quiet fluff on the first note of the bar. Sondheim does not mention that a few bars earlier (p. 473, bars 19–20), we can hear what sounds like music falling off a stand onto the floor.

[28]   1959 VS (p. 177), 2000 VS (p. 189) and 1994 FS (p. 418) all mark this 'Tempo I (but held back)'.

[29]   Jerome Robbins.

[30]   Irwin Kostal and Sid Ramin.

Tony ('Te adoro Anton'). An orchestral epilogue accompanies the procession that brings *West Side Story* to a close.

On the cast recording this scene is handled quite differently. There is no attempt to replicate in sound the stage experience of Tony's death or any of Maria's reaction; neither is even hinted at on the record. Lieberson's quest for a 'recreation in aural values' here produces something on disc that constitutes a striking departure from the original. The recording gives us a scene that offers a quiet reflection, suggesting some sort of reconciliation – almost as if it is a postscript to the show itself. Here the finale begins with two bars of rocking piano accompaniment taken from the original 'Somewhere' (1994 FS, p. 372, bars 147–8), followed by a choral arrangement of the song, which leads directly to the 14-bar epilogue. As in Bernstein's autograph manuscript, 1957 RS, 1957 FS and 1959 VS, the last chord is a quiet, unclouded C major triad.[31]

Despite the trials and tribulations so eloquently reported by Sondheim, Bernstein himself was happy with the end result. On 21 November 1957 (the day after the announcement of his appointment as Music Director of the New York Philharmonic),[32] he wrote an affectionate letter of thanks to Lieberson:

> Dear Goddard,
>
> My thanks to you are so overdue by now that your beautiful gift-plant makes it imperative that I rise from my bed of pain to thank you. You did a wonderful job on the WSS [*West Side Story*] album. It must have been a hectic session, from all I hear, with split-second decisions to be made all the time – and you did a heroic job.
>
> As to the plant – it is lovely, & we thank you + Brigitte with great warmth.
>
> As to the bed of pain, I'm going to the hospital tomorrow for some check-ups on this ridiculous back of mine, as well as some enforced sleep. S-L-E-E-P, glorious word.
>
> Love, Lenny[33]

---

[31] The music that ends the movie soundtrack reinforces this chord with a low C in the bass. See Chapter 3 for further discussion of this final bar in *West Side Story*.

[32] Burton 1994, p. 282.

[33] Yale University Music Library, Goddard Lieberson Papers. Bernstein's back pain was a problem that had first troubled him when he was working in Israel a few weeks earlier.

Appendix I
West Side Story Musical Manuscripts in the Leonard Bernstein Collection, Library of Congress, Washington DC[1]

America
A-me-ri-ca. Piano-vocal score in pencil, annotated in coloured pencil, 13pp.
America / Anita's Song (Huapango). Sketch in pencil, [5]pp.
Photocopies of lyric sketches in Sondheim's hand and typescripts, [4]pp.

Balcony Scene: see *Tonight*

Ballet Sequence
Piano score and sketches in pencil, [11]pp. Includes: Transition to Pas de Deux, p. [1]; Somewhere bridge, p. [3]; Transition to Scherzo, p. [3]; Transition to Pas de Deux, p. [5]; Pas de Deux into Procession, p. [7]; Procession, p. [9]; p. [8] includes a lyric sketch for 'I Have a Love'.
See also *Somewhere*

A Boy Like That
A Boy Like That / Once In Your Life. Piano-vocal score in pencil, annotated in coloured pencil, 20pp. Note: 'Once In Your Life' became 'I Have a Love'.
Duet: A Boy Like That continuation. Piano-vocal score in pencil, 3pp.
A Boy Like That. Piano-vocal score in pencil, numbered pp. 13–16.
Duet (A Boy Like That) insert. Piano-vocal score in pencil, [1]p. Note: 'to follow p. 11, bar 1'.
New end of Boy Like That. Piano-vocal score in pencil, [1]p.
A Boy Like That / There Stands Your Love. Anita–Maria duet. Sketches in pencil, [11]pp.
Lyric sketches in pencil, [7]pp.
Photocopies of lyric sketches in Sondheim's hand and typescripts, [25]pp.

Cool
Cool. Piano-vocal score in pencil, annotated in coloured pencil, 5pp.

---

[1]   Based on information kindly supplied by Mark Eden Horowitz, Senior Music Specialist, Music Division, Library of Congress.

Cool. Sketch in pencil, annotated in red pencil, [2]pp. + title page.

[Cool] Dr ad lib [*sic*]. Sketch in pencil, 3pp.

Cool – fourth variation. Sketch in pencil, [1]p. Inscribed: 'For Irene [Sharaff?] / In spades / Love Lenny'.

Cool (Riff and Gang). Photocopy of typed lyric sheet, [1]p.

Cool (dance). Piano score in pencil, annotated in red pencil, 10pp.

Cool – extra variation / (Insert A). Piano score in pencil, annotated in red pencil, [2]pp.

Cool Insert B / Insert C. Piano score in pencil, annotated in red pencil, [1]p.

Cool fugue. Sketch in pencil, [1]p.

Dance at the Gym

Crystal Cave Fragments: Maria Cha-Cha; Promenade; Maria Cha-Cha continuation. Piano score in pencil, [4]pp.

The Meeting Scene. Piano with dialogue score in pencil, annotated in coloured pencil, 3pp.

Jump. Piano score in pencil, [2]pp.

Brotherhood Hall: Blues. Piano score / short score in pencil, 6pp.

Crystal Cave sketches in pencil, [40]pp. Includes: [Mambo], p. [3]; [Blues] Rocky, p. [9]; Cubano, p. [13]; [Jump], p. [15]; [Mambo / Atom Bomb], p. [23]; Promenade, p. [29]; Huapango, p. [30]; Inserts: Prologue & Rumble, p. [35]. Note and lyric sketches in pencil, [2]pp.

Fast Mambo (Merengue) [Mambo]. Piano score in pencil, annotated in coloured pencil, 5pp. + inserts.

Note in pencil, [1]p., 'originally with First Mambo sketch'.

See also *First Mambo* and *Mambo*

Finale

Sketch / piano score in pencil, [1]p.

First Mambo

Piano score in pencil, 4pp.

Gee, Officer Krupke

Piano-vocal score in pencil, annotated in coloured pencil, 13pp.

[Gee, Officer] Krupke sketch. Sketch in pencil, [3]pp.

Heaven: see *Somewhere*

Huapango: see *Dance at the Gym*

I Feel Pretty

Piano-vocal score in pencil, annotated in coloured pencil, 8pp.

I Feel Pretty (final chorus). Sketch in pencil, annotated in red pencil, [2]pp.
[I Feel] Pretty. Sketch in pencil, annotated in red pencil, [5]pp.
Lyric sketches in pencil on yellow legal paper, [3]pp.
Photocopies of lyric sketches in Sondheim's hand and typescripts, [10]pp.

Jet Song
Here Come the Jets (Initiation Scene). Piano-vocal score in pencil, 20pp.
Lyric sketch in pencil, [1]p.
Lyric sheets in pencil, 5pp.
Photocopies of lyric sketches in Sondheim's hand, [6]pp.

Like Everybody Else
Like Everybody Else. Piano-vocal sketch in pencil, 4pp.
Like Everybody Else. Piano-vocal score in pencil, annotated in coloured pencil, 6pp.

Mambo
Version B (mambo). Piano score in pencil, [2]pp.
See also *Dance at the Gym* and *First Mambo*

Maria
Maria. Piano-vocal score in pencil, annotated in coloured pencil, 5pp.
Maria. Sketches in pencil, [2]pp.
Lyric sketches in pencil and coloured pencil, [3]pp.
Photocopies of lyric typescripts annotated by Sondheim, [2]pp.

Mix!
Mix! Piano-vocal score in pencil, annotated in coloured pencil, 16pp.
Mix! Piano-vocal sketch / score in pencil, [8]pp. + [1]p. 'Gang Canon'.
Lyric sketches for 'Rumble Song' in pencil, [3]pp.

One Hand, One Heart
Duet: One (New) / (Marriage Scene: Tony, Maria). Piano-vocal score in pencil, 8pp.
    Dated: '4 July '57'.
(New One) / One Hand, One Heart. Lead sheet in pencil with lyrics and notes,
    [2]pp.
'Duet: One / (One Hand, One Heart) / (Balcony Scene) [deleted] (Wedding).' Piano-
    vocal score in pencil, 7pp. Note: early version, with Bernstein lyric.
[One Hand, One Heart] Bridal shop / Finale (Ophelia's scene) / One Sketches in
    pencil, [3]pp. of music + title pages. Lyric sketches in pencil, [4]pp.
Balcony Scene ('One'). Photocopy of lyric typescript with annotations, 3pp.
Marriage Scene. Photocopy of lyric typescript, 2pp., dated 3/15/56.
Photocopy lyric sketches in Sondheim's hand, [5]pp.
See also 'Love Duet' in *Candide* manuscripts.

Opening
Opening (vocal prologue). Piano-vocal score / sketch in pencil, in both Bernstein's and Sondheim's hands, 21pp. + [4]pp. of sketches. An early version of the Prologue; includes sketch for what became 'I Have a Love'.
Lyric sketches in pencil, [6]pp.
Photocopy of lyric sketches in Sondheim's hand, [13]pp.
Photocopy of piano-vocal score in Sondheim's hand, 31pp.

Prologue
Prologue (instrumental). Piano score in pencil, annotated in coloured pencil, 11pp. + [4]pp. of inserts.
Prologue. Sketches in pencil, [4]pp.

Quintet
Quintet (Tonight). Piano-vocal score in pencil, annotated in coloured pencil, 16pp.
Quintet. Sketches in pencil, [6]pp.
Lyric sketches in pencil, [2]pp.
Photocopies of typescript and lyric sketches in Sondheim's hand, [8]pp.

Rumble
New Rumble. Short score in pencil, 7pp. + 2pp. insert.
Rumble. Sketches in pencil, [5]pp.
Notes by Jerome Robbins in pencil, [1]p.

Something's Coming
Something's Coming. Piano-vocal score in pencil, 4pp.
Something's Coming. Sketch in pencil, [2]pp.
Lyric sketches in pencil, [2]pp.

Somewhere
Somewhere (vocal). Piano-vocal score in pencil, annotated in coloured pencil, 4pp. + cover.
Somewhere (Pas de Deux). Piano score in pencil, 3pp.
Somewhere vocal procession. Short score in pencil, annotated in pencil, 4pp.
Sketch in pencil, annotated in ink, [1]p., note on verso.
Somewhere vocal (G major). Piano score in pencil, 6 bars.
Duet into Kaleidoscope. Piano score in pencil, 2pp.
Green Scene. Piano score in pencil, 2pp.
Scherzo. Piano score in pencil, 3pp.
Scherzo transition. Sketch in pencil and red pencil, [1]p.
[Scherzo]. Piano score in pencil, 3pp.
[Unidentified]. Sketch in pencil, [2]pp.
Somewhere (Whatsisname). Balcony [deleted]. Sketches in pencil, [14]pp.

Lyric sketches in pencil, [6]ff. One version of the lyric is titled 'Heaven'.

Notes in pencil, [2]pp.

Photocopies of lyric sketches and typescripts in Sondheim's hand, [7]pp.

Notes in Jerome Robbins's hand in pencil, [2]pp.

Synopsis. Carbon typescript with annotations in pencil, 3pp.

Somewhere. Sketch and lyric sketch in pencil, [1]p. Predates *West Side Story*. Lyric sketch begins: 'Rain was rain to me'.

Ballet Sequence (somewhere). Piano-vocal score / short score in pencil, 11pp. + [6]pp. of inserts and sketches.

Somewhere. Photocopy of piano-violin arrangement, annotated in pencil, [2]pp., signed and dated in red pencil: 'Somewhere for Isaac ǀ Me, Oct 69.' Photocopy of note from Helen Coates states that the arrangement was 'written for Isaac Stern and Lenny to play at the rally for mayor John Lindsay in Felt auditorium of Madison Square Garden on [11] October 1969'.

See also *Ballet Sequence* and *Finale*

Taunting Scene

Taunting Scene (continuation of Mambo). Piano score / sketch in pencil, 3pp.

Taunting Tante. Photocopies of lyric sketches in Sondheim's hand, [2]pp. + cover; inside folder marked 'Romeo sketches 1 Oct, 1955'.

Taunting Scene sketch on verso of 'It Must Be So' sketch in *Candide* manuscripts.

This Turf Is Ours!

Sketch in pencil, 1p. Opening theme described as 'Prologue variant'.

This Turf Is Ours! Piano-vocal score in pencil, annotated in coloured pencil, 7pp.

Tonight (Balcony Scene)

Tonight (Balcony Scene). Piano-vocal score in pencil, annotated in coloured pencil, 12pp.

Balcony Scene revisions. Piano-vocal score in pencil, 5pp. Dated: '4 July 57'.

New Balcony. Piano-vocal score in pencil, [2]pp.

Under the Balcony (underscoring to precede Balcony Scene). Piano score in pencil, [2]pp.

Balcony Scene – Newissimo. Piano-vocal score in pencil, 2pp.

Balcony. Sketch in pencil, [2]pp. + outer folder and title page with notes (introduction only; crossed-out title: 'Bridal Shop (Marriage)'.

Leitmotif sheet

Untitled sheet containing motifs from *West Side Story*, Fair copy in pencil, [1]p.

Appendix II
West Side Story as Recorded with the Original Broadway Cast

Note: the numbering below follows 1994 FS

No. 1, Prologue: Seven bars have been added at the start (the equivalent of bars 1–7 of the *Symphonic Dances from West Side Story*); bars 1–267 as in 1994 FS; bars 268–79 cut. *Segue* from bar 267 into:

No. 2, Jet Song: Starts at bar 24 (with upbeat); bar 44ff.: 'You're never alone', extra voices added; bars 93–129 cut (marked as optional cut in 1994 FS).

No. 2a, Jet Song Chase: Not recorded.

No. 3, Something's Coming: At bars 75–8 horn, trumpets, trombones omitted; otherwise as in 1994 FS.

No. 3a, Something's Coming Chase: Not recorded.

No. 4, The Dance at the Gym – Blues: Not recorded.

No. 4a, Promenade: Not recorded.

No. 4b, Mambo: Bars 58–65, then bars 100–206, all as in 1994 FS (bars 66–99 are cut). *Segue* into:

No. 4c, Cha-cha: Bars 207–29 as in 1994 FS, then extended by 11 additional bars (for five of these bars, see **No. 9**, upbeat to bar 30ff., 1994 FS pp. 255–6).

No. 4d, Meeting scene: Not recorded.

No. 4e, Jump: Not recorded.

No. 5, Maria: Bars 3–4 and 7–8: repeated 'Maria's sung by offstage voices (marked 'Tony' in all scores); Tony sings *ossia* at bars 36–9; otherwise as in 1994 FS.

No. 6, Balcony Scene: Begins at bar 28; bars 67–75 ('Today, all day I had the feeling …') sung by Maria, not Tony as indicated in 1994 FS (but 1959 VS indicates Maria); bars 121–44 cut. The 'To-' at end of 120 is changed to 'Good-' leading into '-night' at bar 145; cello and bass *pizzicato* low A flat added at start of last bar (as in 1959 VS).

No. 7, America: Bars 1–2 repeated; bars 3–4 repeated (as marked); bars 5–6 repeated; then as in 1994 FS.

No. 7a, America to Drugstore: Not recorded.

No. 8, Cool: No vocals in bars 153–5; otherwise as in 1994 FS.

No. 8a, Cool Chase: Not recorded.

No. 8b, Under Dialogue and Change of Scene: Not recorded.

No. 9, Under Dialogue: Not recorded.

No. 9a, One Hand, One Heart: Starts at bar 60, then as in 1994 FS apart from one cut bar (bar 146).

No. 10, Tonight [Ensemble]: Bar 6ff.: sung by all Jets, not just Riff, and all Sharks, not just Bernardo (solos indicated in scores, but these also give the option that 'the members of the gangs may sing with their respective leaders'); bar 127ff.: Anita sings an octave lower than written pitch; otherwise as in 1994 FS.

No. 11, The Rumble: Siren enters at bar 117, not bar 108 as marked; otherwise as in 1994 FS.

No. 12, I Feel Pretty: Bars 1–8 and bar 9 beat 1 in the original key; the rest of bar 9 to the first beat of bar 139 cut; then from 139 beat 2 (Maria's entrance) to the end, performed a tone lower than written.

No. 13, Under Dialogue: Not recorded.

No. 13a, Ballet Sequence: Starts at safety bar (bar 24, 1994 FS p. 350), played four times. Tony's first words 'And I'll' changed to 'I will'.

No. 13b, Transition to Scherzo: As in 1994 FS.

No. 13c, Scherzo: As in 1994 FS.

No. 13d, Somewhere: Starts at bar 123; bars 132–8: no piano; bar 136 to bar 138 beat 1: no violins; bars 147–54: no piano.

No. 13e, Procession and Nightmare: Bars 190–203 cut; then as in 1994 FS.

No. 14, Gee, Officer Krupke: As in 1994 FS.

No. 14a, Change of Scene: Not recorded.

No. 15, A Boy Like That – I Have a Love: As in 1994 FS until bar 114 when the first chord (with major seventh added) is held for one bar, then cut off.

No. 15a, Change of Scene: Not recorded.

No. 16, Taunting Scene: Not recorded.

No. 17, Finale: Bars 1–14 cut; replaced with two bars of piano from No. 13d (bars 147–8, 1994 FS p. 372), followed by a new choral arrangement of 'Somewhere', derived from bars 147–59 of No. 13d (1994 FS pp. 372–3); bar 15 to the end is as in 1994 FS apart from last low F sharp, which is not on the recording (or in 1959 VS).

Bibliography

Manuscript Sources

Leonard Bernstein Collection, Music Division, Library of Congress, Washington DC (for list of musical manuscripts, see Appendix I).
Goddard Lieberson Papers, Irving S. Gilmore Music Library, Yale University, New Haven, CT.
Sid Ramin Papers, Rare Books and Manuscripts Library, Columbia University, New York, NY.
Stephen Sondheim Papers, Wisconsin Historical Society, Madison, WI.
Roger L. Stevens Collection, Music Division, Library of Congress, Washington DC.

Books and Articles

Aston, Frank (1957), 'Theater: *West Side Story*: love and hate make beauty', *New York World-Telegram and Sun*, 27 September.
Atkinson, Brooks (1950), 'First night at the theatre: Jean Arthur and Boris Karloff in an excellent version of Barrie's *Peter Pan*', *New York Times*, 25 April.
—— (1953), 'At the theatre', *New York Times*, 26 February.
—— (1955), 'Theatre: *St. Joan* with radiance', *New York Times*, 18 November.
—— (1957a), 'Theatre: the jungles of the city: *West Side Story* is at Winter Garden', *New York Times*, 27 September.
—— (1957b), '*West Side Story*: moving music drama on callous theme', *New York Times*, 6 October.
—— (1960a), 'Theatre: musical is back', *New York Times*, 28 April.
—— (1960b), 'Man of notes: Leonard Bernstein's musical career deprives Broadway of able writer', *New York Times*, 8 May.
Banfield, Stephen (1993), *Sondheim's Broadway Musicals* (Ann Arbor: University of Michigan Press).
Beaufort, John (1957), 'Musical *West Side Story*; British *Look Back in Anger*', *Christian Science Monitor*, 5 October.
Benjamin, Philip (1957), 'Gang slang', *New York Times*, 20 October.
Berliner, Milton (1957), 'At the National: West Side (success) story', *Washington Daily News*, 20 August.
Bernstein, Leonard (1957), 'Excerpts from a West Side Log', *Playbill*, 30 September, 47–8; reprinted in Bernstein, Leonard (1982), *Findings* (New York: Simon & Schuster), pp. 144–7.

—— (1959), *The Joy of Music* (New York: Simon & Schuster).

Block, Geoffrey (1997), *Enchanted Evenings: The Broadway Musical from Show Boat to Sondheim* (New York: Oxford University Press), esp. pp. 245–73.

Burton, Humphrey (1994), *Leonard Bernstein* (London: Faber and Faber).

Burton, William Westbrook (1995), *Conversations about Bernstein* (New York: Oxford University Press), esp. pp. 169–89: 'Carol Lawrence on *West Side Story*'.

Calta, Louis (1949), 'Romeo to receive musical styling: Bard's play to undergo local renovation by Bernstein, Robbins and Laurents', *New York Times*, 28 January.

—— (1957), '*West Side Story* unfolds tonight', *New York Times*, 26 September.

Carmody, Jay (1957), 'New theater season has dazzling spirit', *Washington Evening Star*, 20 August.

Chapman, John (1957), '*West Side Story*: a splendid and super-modern musical drama', *New York Daily News*, 27 September.

—— (1960), '*West Side Story* brand new hit, *Finian's Rainbow* gleams again', *New York Daily News*, 28 April.

Cheshire, Maxine (1957), 'Composer Bernstein tells capitalites: *West Side Story* is poetry', *Washington Post*, 20 August.

Coe, Richard L. (1957a), 'On the aisle: *West Side* has that beat', *Washington Post*, 20 August.

—— (1957b), 'Musical at National is a triumph', *Washington Post*, 1 September.

Coleman, Robert (1960), '*West Side Story* retains zip', *New York Mirror*, 28 April.

Downes, Olin (1953), '*Wonderful Town*: Bernstein's musical is brilliant achievement', *New York Times*, 10 May.

Dramatists Guild Landmark Symposium. See Guernsey, Otis (ed.) (1985).

Felsenfeld, Daniel (2005), disc notes for the complete recording of Bernstein's *Peter Pan*, Koch International Classics 75962.

Fuld, James J. (2000), *The Book of World-Famous Music: Classical, Popular and Folk*, 5th edition, revised and enlarged (New York: Dover Publications), esp. p. 584.

Funke, Lewis (1955a), 'Rialto gossip', *New York Times*, 19 June.

—— (1955b), 'Gossip of the Rialto', *New York Times*, 18 September.

—— (1955c), 'News and gossip gathered on the Rialto', *New York Times*, 16 October.

—— (1956), 'News and gossip of the Rialto', *New York Times*, 22 January.

—— (1957a), 'Gossip of the Rialto', *New York Times*, 3 February.

—— (1957b), 'News and gossip of the Rialto', *New York Times*, 23 June.

Garebian, Keith (1995), *The Making of West Side Story* (Toronto: ECW Press).

Gelb, Arthur (1957), 'Director signed for Wouk's play', *New York Times*, 8 July.

Goberman, Max (1959), 'Broadway to baroque: theatre conductor shuttled between Bernstein show and Vivaldi concertos', *New York Times*, 29 November.

Gottlieb, Jack (2004), *Funny, It Doesn't Sound Jewish: How Yiddish Songs and Synagogue Melodies Influenced Tin Pan Alley, Broadway, and Hollywood*

(Albany, NY: State University of New York), esp. pp. 178–83: 'Symbols of faith in the music of Leonard Bernstein'.

Grutzner, Charles (1950), 'Bronx is deadliest of teen war areas', *New York Times*, 10 May.

Guernsey, Otis L. (ed.) (1985), *Broadway Song & Story: Playwrights / Lyricists / Composers Discuss their Hits* (New York: Dodd, Mead), pp. 40–54. Also published as: 'Landmark Symposium: *West Side Story*: Terence McNally, Moderator, Leonard Bernstein, Arthur Laurents, Jerome Robbins, Stephen Sondheim', *Dramatists Guild Quarterly*, 22 (3) (1985), 11–25.

Gussow, Mel (1990), '*West Side Story*: the beginnings of something great', *New York Times*, 21 October.

Hume, Paul (1957), 'Minor musical touch-ups can make *West Side Story* a long-run hit', *Washington Post*, 21 August.

Hussey, Walter (1985), *Patron of Art: The Revival of a Great Tradition among Modern Artists* (London: Weidenfeld & Nicolson).

Jewell, Edward Alden (1944), 'War art and later: thoughts on our present upheaval and the outlook for tomorrow', *New York Times*, 23 April.

Journal-American (1957), 'Theatre poll: what audience thought of play', 27 September.

Jowitt, Deborah (2004), *Jerome Robbins: His Life, his Theater, his Dance* (New York: Simon & Schuster).

Kasha, Al, and Joel Hirschhorn (1985), *Notes on Broadway* (Chicago: Contemporary Books).

Keller, Hans (1955), 'On the waterfront', *The Score* (June), 81–4.

Kerr, Walter (1957), '*West Side Story*', *Herald Tribune*, 27 September.

—— (1960), 'First night report: *West Side Story*', *Herald Tribune*, 28 April.

Kilgallen, Dorothy (1957), 'What's in a name? Sid finds out', *Washington Post*, 24 July.

Laird, Paul R. (2002), *Leonard Bernstein: A Guide to Research* (New York and London: Routledge).

Laurents, Arthur (2000), *Original Story By: A Memoir of Broadway and Hollywood* (New York: Alfred A. Knopf).

Lawrence, Carol (1990), *Carol Lawrence: The Backstage Story* (New York: McGraw-Hill).

Lieberson, Goddard (1957), *Essays ... Written between 1948 and 1956* ([New York:] privately printed).

Manchester Guardian (1958a), 'Manchester theatres, etc.', 22 October.

Manchester Guardian (1958b), 'Youth and fervour of American actors' (by 'our own correspondent'), 10 November.

Manchester Guardian (1958c), '*West Side Story* hits London: high expectations fulfilled' (signed 'J.R.'), 13 December.

Marmorstein, Gary (2007), *The Label: The Story of Columbia Records* (New York: Thunder's Mouth Press).

Martin, John (1944), 'Ballet by Robbins called smash hit', *New York Times*, 19 April.

—— (1957), 'Dance: Broadway: *West Side Story* as an experiment in method', *New York Times*, 27 October.

Mauceri, John (2007), 'Crossing Broadway: *West Side Story*'s landmark opening and enduring legacy', *Symphony: The Magazine of the League of American Orchestras* (September–October), 14–21.

Meyler, Bernadette A. (1999), 'Composing (for a) philosophical comedy', in Claudia Swan (ed.), *Leonard Bernstein: The Harvard Years 1935–1939* (New York: EOS Orchestra), pp. 71–8.

Murdock, Henry T. (1957), 'At the Erlanger: everything sparkles in *West Side Story*', *Philadelphia Inquirer*, 11 September.

New York Times (1957a), 'Rehearsal dates', 24 June.

New York Times (1957b), 'Broadway's new season begins to stir', 28 July [with five rehearsal photographs by Friedman-Abeles].

New York Times (1960), 'Bernstein to conduct overture', 17 March.

New York World-Telegram and Sun (1957), untitled clipping, 27 September.

Nichols, Lewis (1944), 'The play: *On the Town*', *New York Times*, 29 December.

—— (1945), 'Trip on a *Carousel*: excellent musical play is derived from Molnar's *Liliom*', *New York Times*, 29 April.

Pace, Eric (1998), 'Roger L. Stevens, real estate magnate, producer and fund-raiser, is dead at 87', *New York Times*, 4 February.

Paley, William S. (1979), *As It Happened: A Memoir* (New York: Doubleday).

Parmenter, Ross (1959), 'Goberman plays Handel Sonatas: *West Side Story* conductor makes first appearance as violinist in 20 years', *New York Times*, 23 February.

—— (1961), 'Philharmonic gives "Valentine" in concert form to Bernstein', *New York Times*, 14 February.

Peck, Seymour (1957), '*West Side Story*', *New York Times*, 8 September [with seven production photographs by Fred Fehl].

Philadelphia Inquirer Magazine (1957), 'Rough time for all in a tough musical … rehearsal', 1 September [with seven rehearsal photographs including one titled 'Dancer who got hit on head by bottle is treated by doctor in Washington theater dressing room'].

Ramin, Sid (2001), 'Leonard Bernstein (1918–1990), West Side Story', disc notes for Naxos 8.559126.

Rich, Frank (2000), 'Conversations with Sondheim', *New York Times*, 12 March.

Robinson, Wayne (1957a), 'A memorable musical', *Philadelphia Bulletin*, 11 September.

—— (1957b), 'Unknowns shine in *West Side Story*', *Sunday Bulletin*, 15 September.

Salisbury, Harrison E. (1958), 'Youth gang members tell of lives, hates and fears', *New York Times*, 25 March.

Schubart, Mark A. (1945), 'Triple-note man of the music world', *New York Times*, 28 January.

Schumach, Murray (1957), 'Talent dragnet: casting for *West Side Story* caused unusual number of headaches', *New York Times*, 22 September.

Schwartz, Richard (2000), *Cold War Culture* (New York: Facts on File).

Schwartz, Stephen (2008), 'My music', *Gramophone* (November), 146.

Shepard, Richard F. (1964), 'Recording angels: disk-makers back shows', *New York Times*, 19 July.

Spielvogel, Carl (1957), 'Advertising: getting a hit show on the road, fast', *New York Times*, 2 October.

Stearns, David Patrick (1985), '*West Side Story*: between Broadway and the opera house', disc notes for Deutsche Grammophon 415 253–2.

Suskin, Steven (1990), *Opening Night on Broadway: A Critical Quotebook of the Golden Era of the Musical Theatre, 'Oklahoma!' (1943) to 'Fiddler on the Roof' (1964)* (New York: Schirmer Books), esp. pp. 693–8.

—— (2000), *Show Tunes: The Songs, Shows, and Careers of Broadway's Major Composers*, 3rd edition, revised and expanded (New York and Oxford: Oxford University Press), esp. pp. 215–16.

Swain, Joseph P. (2002), *The Broadway Musical: A Critical and Musical Survey*, 2nd edition, revised and expanded (Lanham, MD, and Oxford: Scarecrow Press), esp. pp. 221–64.

Taubman, Howard (1957), 'A foot in each camp: Bernstein's score of *West Side Story* falters between musical and opera', *New York Times*, 13 October.

Time (1953), 'Girl in the groove', 23 February [online version at www.time.com].

Time (1957), 'New musical in Manhattan', 7 October [online version at www.time.com].

Tynan, Kenneth (1958), 'At the theatre: the Broadway package … grass roots and asphalt jungle', *The Observer*, 4 May.

Wadler, Seymour (1990), 'Bernstein at camp', letter to the editor, *New York Times*, 26 October.

Washington Post (1957a), 'Letters to the editor', 5 September.

Washington Post (1957b), 'Letters to the editor', 6 September.

Watts, Richard (1957), 'Two on the aisle: Romeo and Juliet in a gang war', *New York Post*, 27 September.

Wilson, John S. (1957a), 'Four musical shows on LP disks', *New York Times*, 17 February.

—— (1957b). 'Social themes: two Broadway musicals on LP disks deal with problem of prejudice', *New York Times*, 3 November.

Wise, Brian (2007), 'The gangs of New York', *New York Sun*, 17 September.

Zadan, Craig (1974), *Sondheim & Co.* (New York: Macmillan).

Zec, Donald (1958), 'Romeo and Juliet among the flick-knives', *Daily Mirror*, 15 November.

Zolotow, Sam (1957), 'Greer Garson set to star in *Mame*', *New York Times*, 3 June [includes casting information about *West Side Story*].

Scores and Libretto

Full orchestral score (1957 FS), blue print copy reproduced from manuscript by Ramin and Kostal, with annotations, revisions and additions by Sid Ramin, Irwin Kostal and Leonard Bernstein in coloured pencil. Sid Ramin Papers, Rare Books and Manuscripts Library, Columbia University. In five volumes, 123, 146, 127, 115 and 139pp. Includes Prologue, Jet Song, 'Something's Coming Utility', Dance Hall Sequence, Maria Cha-Cha, Meeting Scene, Meeting Scene A, 'Maria', New Balcony Scene, 'America', 'Cool', Quintet, 'One [Hand, One Heart]', Rumble, 'I Feel Pretty', Ballet Sequence, 'Gee, Officer Krupke', 'A Boy Like That', Taunting Scene, Finale, and Temporary Overture.

Rehearsal piano-vocal scores of separate numbers (1957 RS), reproduced from copyist's manuscripts. The Sid Ramin Papers at Columbia University include seven numbers: Opening (30pp., replaced by Prologue), Prologue (14pp. + 2pp. inserts), Jet Song (17pp.), 'Cool' (13pp.), 'I Feel Pretty' (10pp.), 'A Boy Like That' (13pp.) and Finale (2pp.).

West Side Story (1957 Songs): eight separate songs: 'Cool' (5pp., plate number 44277), 'I Feel Pretty' (5pp., plate number 44278), 'Maria' (7pp., plate number 44279), 'Tonight' (5pp., plate number 44282), copyright deposit copies dated 30 August 1957; 'A-me-ri-ca' (3pp., plate number 44284), 'One Hand, One Heart' (5pp., plate number 44283), copyright deposit copies dated 24 September 1957; 'Something's Coming' (10pp., plate number 44289), 'Somewhere' (5pp., plate number 44308), copyright deposit copies dated 16 October 1957; New York: G. Schirmer Inc. and Chappell & Co., Inc., 3 East 43rd Street. All these songs list eight titles, but the first printings of the four published in August 1957 give the title of 'Something's Coming' as 'Something's Coming (Could Be)'. Each has a printed price of 60 cents. The eight songs were subsequently collected into a volume of vocal selections published by Schirmer and Chappell (32pp., plate number 44736), price $2.00. 'Gee, Officer Krupke' was issued as a separate song in 1960 (7pp., plate number 44790), price 60 cents. All the separate songs and the Vocal Selections have an illustrated cover showing Carol Lawrence and Larry Kert running down a New York street, printed in black and white on a pink/beige background.

West Side Story (1958 LIB): libretto. New York: Random House, 143pp. Stated as first printing on verso of title page, price on dustwrapper is $2.95. The dustwrapper has the same cover illustration as the 1957 Songs.

West Side Story (1959 VS): piano-vocal score. New York: G. Schirmer, Inc. and Chappell & Co., Inc., 3 East 43rd Street, 200pp., plate number 44415. Published on 19 February 1959 (see Fuld 2000, p. 584); copyright deposit copy dated 24 February 1959. The title page of the copyright deposit copy mistakenly credits the lyrics to 'Stephen Sondheim and Leonard Bernstein', corrected in later printings.

West Side Story (1994 FS): full score. [New York:] Leonard Bernstein Music Publishing Company LLC, [London:] Boosey & Hawkes, 474pp., plate number HPS 1176.

West Side Story (2000 VS): piano-vocal score, revised edition. [New York:] Leonard Bernstein Music Publishing Company LLC, [London:] Boosey & Hawkes, 219pp., ISMN M 051-97020-9. Edited by Seann Alderking and Charlie Harmon. Includes the Overture as an Appendix on pp. 212–19.

West Side Story (2001 FS): full score. New York: Music Theatre International, 673pp., no plate number. Rental score, not for sale. Includes the Overture on pp. 1–37.

Selective Discography, Videography and Online Items

Cast Recordings

Original Broadway cast recording (1957). Cast includes Carol Lawrence (Maria), Chita Rivera (Anita), Larry Kert (Tony), conducted by Max Goberman. Columbia OL 5230 (mono), OS 2001 (stereo), remastered CD reissue: Sony SK 60724.

Film soundtrack recording (1961). Cast includes Natalie Wood (Maria, sung by Marni Nixon), Rita Moreno (Anita, sung by Betty Wand), Richard Beymer (Tony, sung by Jim Bryant), conducted by Johnny Green. Columbia OS 2070, remastered CD reissue with additional music: Sony SK 48211.

New York studio recording (1984). Cast includes Kiri Te Kanawa (Maria), Tatiana Troyanos (Anita), José Carreras (Tony), conducted by Leonard Bernstein. CD. Deutsche Grammophon 415 253-2.

The Making of West Side Story (1984). Documentary with rehearsal footage from the sessions of the 1984 recording, conducted by Leonard Bernstein. DVD. Deutsche Grammophon 073 4054.

Leicester Haymarket Theatre cast recording (1993). Cast includes Tinuke Olafimihan (Maria), Caroline O'Connor (Anita), Paul Manuel (Tony), conducted by John Owen Edwards. CD. TER 1197 (includes Overture).

Tennessee Repertory Theatre / Nashville Symphony cast recording (2001). Cast includes Betsi Morrison (Maria), Marianne Cooke (Anita), Mike Eldred (Tony), conducted by Kenneth Schermerhorn. CD. Naxos 8.559126. Notes by Sid Ramin.

Cut Song

'Like Everybody Else', *Lost In Boston* [vol. 1] (1994), orchestrated by Larry Moore, sung by Judy Malloy, Richard Roland and Sal Viviano. CD. Varèse Sarabande 5475; reissue: Fynsworth Alley 062191.

Other Recordings Involving the Show's Creators

The Sound of West Side Story [Cool, Cool Fugue, Maria, Mambo] (1958), conducted by Sid Ramin and Irwin Kostal. The Ramin–Kostal Orchestra. Vocals by the Honey Dreamers. RCA EPA 4184 (45 rpm, 7 inch).

Symphonic Dances from West Side Story (1961). New York Philharmonic Orchestra, conducted by Leonard Bernstein. Columbia MS 6251, CD reissue: Sony SK 63085.

Symphonic Dances from West Side Story (1963). New York Philharmonic Orchestra, conducted by Leonard Bernstein, in the Young People's Concert 'The Latin-American Spirit', broadcast 8 March 1963. DVD. Kultur Video, ISBN 0-7697-1503-6. A live performance of an abridged version of the *Symphonic Dances*, comprising the Mambo, Cha-Cha, 'Cool' and Rumble, with a loud conclusion that is otherwise unrecorded.

Symphonic Dances from West Side Story (1982). Los Angeles Philharmonic Orchestra, conducted by Leonard Bernstein. CD. Deutsche Grammophon 410 052-2.

Broadcast

'A place for us: 50 years of *West Side Story*' (NPR 2007), presented by Scott Simon, National Public Radio, 26 September 2007, including interviews with Robbins, Laurents, Bernstein, Sondheim, Grover Dale, Frank Rich, Hal Prince, Carol Lawrence, Larry Kert, Chita Rivera, John Mauceri, Bill Charlap, Harvey Evans, Rita Moreno, Marni Nixon, Freddie Gershon, Kenny Birnbaum and Clarence 'Divine Eye' Maclin. Available online at: www.npr.org/templates/story/story.php?storyId=14730899

Websites (Selective List)

Leonard Bernstein Collection, Library of Congress: http://memory.loc.gov/ammem/lbhtml/lbhome.html

West Side Story: Birth of a Classic (Library of Congress, online exhibition): www.loc.gov/exhibits/westsidestory

Official Leonard Bernstein website: www.leonardbernstein.com

Official *West Side Story* website: www.westsidestory.com

West Side Story on Stage website: www.wssonstage.com

The Stephen Sondheim Reference Guide: www.sondheimguide.com

Remembering Jerome Robbins: www.nycballet.com/company/viewing.html

A Guide to Leonard Bernstein's *Candide* by Michael H. Hutchins: www.sondheimguide.com/Candide/contents.html

Internet Broadway Database: www.ibdb.com

New York Times: www.nytimes.com

Time magazine: www.time.com

CD Track List

West Side Story: **Original Broadway Cast Recording**

Recorded at Columbia 30th Street Studio, New York City, 29 September 1957
Original LP release: OL 5230, 1957 (mono), OS 2001, 1958 (stereo)

The Jets

Riff, The Leader	Mickey Calin
Tony, His Friend	Larry Kert
Action	Eddie Roll
A-Rab	Tony Mordente
Baby John	David Winters
Snowboy	Grover Dale
Big Deal	Martin Charnin
Diesel	Hank Brunjes
Gee-Tar	Tommy Abbott
Mouthpiece	Frank Green
Tiger	Lowell Harris

Their Girls

Graziella	Wilma Curley
Velma	Carole D'Andrea
Minnie	Nanette Rosen
Clarice	Marilyn D'Honau
Pauline	Julie Oser
Anybodys	Lee Becker

The Sharks

Bernardo, The Leader	Ken Le Roy
Maria, His Sister	Carol Lawrence
Anita, His Girl	Chita Rivera
Chino, His Friend	Jamie Sanchez
Pepe	George Marcy
Indio	Noel Schwartz
Luis	Al De Sio

Anxious	Gene Gavin
Nibbles	Ronnie Lee
Juano	Jay Norman
Toro	Erne Castaldo
Moose	Jack Murray

Their Girls

Rosalia	Marilyn Cooper
Consuelo	Reri Grist
Teresita	Carmen Gutierrez
Francisca	Elizabeth Taylor
Estella	Lynn Ross
Marguerita	Liane Plane

The Adults

Doc	Art Smith
Schrank	Arch Johnson
Krupke	William Bramley
Gladhand	John Harkins
A Girl ('Somewhere')	Reri Grist

Musical Director	Max Goberman

Producer	Goddard Lieberson
Associate Producer	Howard Scott
Engineers	Fred Plaut, Edward T. Graham

1	Prologue	Orchestra
2	Jet Song	Mickey Calin, The Jets
3	Something's Coming	Larry Kert
4	The Dance at the Gym	The Jets, The Sharks
5	Maria	Larry Kert
6	Tonight	Larry Kert, Carol Lawrence
7	America	Marilyn Cooper, Chita Rivera, Shark Girls
8	Cool	Mickey Calin, The Jets
9	One Hand, One Heart	Larry Kert, Carol Lawrence
10	Tonight (Quintet and Chorus)	The Jets, The Sharks, Chita Rivera, Larry Kert, Mickey Calin, Carol Lawrence
11	The Rumble	Orchestra
12	I Feel Pretty	Carol Lawrence, Marilyn Cooper, Reri Grist, Carmen Gutierrez, Elizabeth Taylor

13	Somewhere (Ballet)	Larry Kert, Reri Grist (offstage), Carol Lawrence
14	Gee, Officer Krupke	Eddie Roll, Grover Dale, Hank Brunjes, Tony Mordente, David Winters, The Jets
15	A Boy Like That / I Have a Love	Chita Rivera, Carol Lawrence
16	Finale	Carol Lawrence, Larry Kert, Ensemble

Symphonic Dances from West Side Story

Recorded at Manhattan Center, New York City, 6 March 1961
Original LP release: MS 6521, 1961

New York Philharmonic, conducted by Leonard Bernstein

| Producer | John McClure |
| Engineer | Unknown |

17 Prologue: Allegro moderato
18 'Somewhere': Adagio
19 Scherzo: Vivace e leggiero
20 Mambo: Presto
21 Cha-Cha ('Maria'): Andantino con grazia
22 Meeting Scene: Meno mosso
23 'Cool' Fugue: Allegretto
24 Rumble: Molto allegro
25 Finale: Adagio

Index